What people are s

Self Awareness and ᴍᴇᴅɪᴛᴀᴛɪᴏɴ

Self-Awareness and Meditation: An Advanced Guide for Meditators is an in-depth, accurate guide for anyone who practices meditation, especially in the West where traditional terminology is confusing. Charles Attfield has done the hard work of presenting Eastern Meditation wisdom in a form easily understood by the West, in the tradition of his teacher and founder of Synchronicity Foundation, Master Charles Cannon.
Jim Clarke, Senior staff member at Synchronicity foundation

Charles gives valuable information and insight into spiritual experience and meditation. He had close guidance for many years under an accomplished spiritual master.
Chris Lober, Synchronicity Associate

Charles Attfield, a teacher and meditator for over 30 years, has written a must-read comprehensive guide for beginner to advanced meditators searching for Self-awareness.
Loretta Demple, Member of the Tibetan Buddhist Society, Perth

Review
There is much written on Eastern spirituality and meditation by western authors. Most of it based on study of historical texts and books. This is problematic because a true understanding of the subject requires the actual experience of it. It is here where Charles Attfield provides truly valuable information and insight, having had close training and guidance for many years under an authentic spiritual master. Furthermore, he is a skilled writer, able to explain and detail the most subtle and profound spiritual experiences, as well as the everyday aspects many on

the spiritual path will encounter. I applaud his efforts, knowing that they will find much value to the spiritual seeker.

Chris Lober, Synchronicity Associate

Self Awareness and Meditation

An Advanced Guide for Meditators

Self Awareness and Meditation

An Advanced Guide for Meditators

Charles Attfield

**MANTRA
BOOKS**

Winchester, UK
Washington, USA

JOHN HUNT PUBLISHING

First published by Mantra Books, 2023
Mantra Books is an imprint of John Hunt Publishing Ltd., No. 3 East Street, Alresford
Hampshire SO24 9EE, UK
office@jhpbooks.com
www.johnhuntpublishing.com
www.mantra-books.net

For distributor details and how to order please visit the 'Ordering' section on our website.

Text copyright: Charles Attfield 2022

ISBN: 978 1 80341 231 3
978 1 80341 232 0 (ebook)
Library of Congress Control Number: 2022936045

A CIP catalogue record for this book is available from the British Library.

Design: Matthew Greenfield

UK: Printed and bound by CPI Group (UK) Ltd, Croydon, CR0 4YY
Printed in North America by CPI GPS partners

We operate a distinctive and ethical publishing philosophy in
all areas of our business, from our global network of authors to
production and worldwide distribution.

Contents

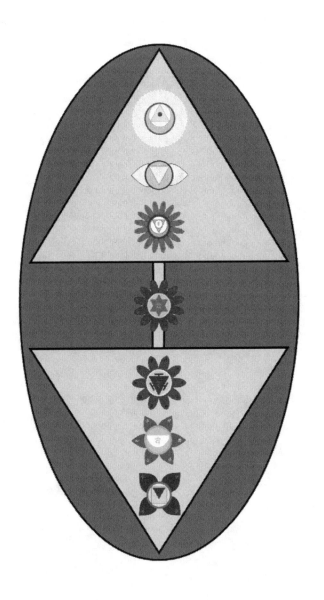

Introduction

It is said that the spiritual Master Muktananda kept the door to his library locked. Students were told that before they could gain access to the books on spirituality, they needed to gain experience first. Intellectual enlightenment will fill your head with knowledge, but without practice and experience, its help is only limited. I hope this book will be a complement to your meditation practice and encourage you to deepen it. Much of the theory in this book is combined with what you can expect as your own experience deepens. It may also explain why you are having the experiences that you do.

The best I can hope for is that this book will be read alongside your meditation practice and provide a useful reference from time to time as your awareness of Self grows. You will find differences between your experience and what is given here, but you will have a framework to better understand your own.

If this book has a purpose, it is to instill a reverence and awareness of your true essence, your Self. And yet, a book like this cannot adequately describe the Self. It cannot do anything more than point the way and assist you with knowledge and techniques to bring about this recognition of your true inner nature. It is a book about the evolution of consciousness, your consciousness, from awakening to the evolutionary cycle and the subsequent journey "home."

Perhaps the most important thing I have learned is that an egocentric perspective of the evolutionary cycle is severely flawed. In reality, the ego does nothing, as consciousness is orchestrating the show. You may think you are the doer, but that is the trick of the ego! As you progress on the path, there is a gradual shift in your awareness from the egoic doer to the trans-egoic doer. More precisely, it is a shift in awareness to the realization that there has only ever been the trans-egoic

1

Self that has ever done anything. Through meditation, you gradually return to the experience of who you really are, and your egocentric data gets replaced with a trans-egocentric awareness.

The evidence that you have of the evolution in your consciousness is your ever-increasing Self-awareness or wakefulness and the ever-increasing amplitude of your power along with the resultant palpability of your presence. All you need to do is to remain a witness to it as much as possible.

Your regular practice of meditation ultimately pays off in increased wakefulness and bliss. Invest in wakefulness as your most important life path. Accept where your feet are, accept that everything is exactly as it is, and don't buy into the illusion that it should be other than it is. You couldn't be more on schedule if you tried. If you negate yourself and believe you are not good enough, remember, you have all self-worth simply by virtue of your existence.

The book begins with a look at the evolution of humanity to the present day, remembering that this is the background through which we, as individuals, begin our own journey in a search for the Self. This moves on to a psychological perspective on why we are the way we are, including paradigms that acknowledge the soul or Self. Some techniques for self-analysis are included under the heading of psycho-analytical meditation.

We then look at the subtle energy system within, including an in-depth analysis of the Kundalini and the chakras and the effect of the spiritual transformation which follows arousal of the Kundalini.

Three chapters follow on the mechanics of consciousness, meditation pointers, and understanding dreams. These are based on many years of personal mentoring with a spiritual Master, Master Charles Cannon, founder of Synchronicity Foundation for Modern Spirituality. The chapter on dreams also includes the understanding of B.S. Goel, who also became

Self-realized.

I refer to the seven creative energies of the universe, the Seven Rays, so that you will gain an appreciation of the importance of these in psycho-spiritual understanding. This includes the awakenings and expansions of consciousness which play an important role in your evolution as you move from a purely human level of awareness to ever more subtle levels of Self-awareness. This journey involves constructing a bridge, often referred to as the rainbow bridge, between the personality and the Self, so that eventually the two are fused as you become a Self-realized being.

An entire chapter is devoted to the personal experiences of two individuals on their journey to Self-realization, B.S. Goel and Muktananda.

Finally, as an extra, there is a short supplementary course which gives practical exercises to help cement much of the information given in the theory.

Chapter 1

Search for the Self

Evolution of Consciousness

To commence our journey exploring meditation and Self-awareness, I begin by looking at our evolutionary journey so far. The first humans were little more than animals. They had no verbal communication and lived in a bliss of ignorance. Even though they had fears, they didn't have the worries that a consciousness of self brings. Although primitive, they were in the earliest stages of the development of self-awareness. Then came the Neanderthals, who were ruled by instinct and the need for survival. They lived day-to-day by hunting and gathering for food. They may not have used speech as we know it, but experienced a world of images and paleo-symbols.

The "Garden of Eden" is often thought of as a blissful state of existence, a transpersonal state from which human beings are considered having "fallen" after eating from the tree of knowledge. The Neanderthals, however, were in a pre-personal state of ignorance, which ended when they became self-conscious entities and gained the worries, guilt, and fear that come with self-consciousness.

Primitive language appeared with the Cro Magnon humans. This language included some nouns and commands. It was also at this time that the first awareness of being separate individuals appeared. Aware of their mortality, they tried to extend their inevitable death into the future. So, they planned for the future, becoming more aware of the past and losing touch with the eternal present. This coincided with the beginnings of farming, in order to ensure a supply of food for the future.

Each stage of evolution goes beyond its predecessors, but still includes and integrates them into itself. For example,

4

animals evolved from plants and were a more advanced form of life. Plants were simple life but included matter in their makeup as organic matter.

As humans gained mastery over their physical bodies, they developed their emotions. Desires, as opposed to instincts, require both an awareness of self and the wish to enhance the self. So, humans searched for happiness. Thus, began the earliest search for the higher Self. This corresponded with what we now know as the Atlantean Age. Prior to this was the Lemurian Age. Now, in the current Age, the Aryan Age, most humans are developing their mental awareness. Once physical, emotional and mental are integrated, the next stage will be to bring in awareness of the soul.

Humans contain, as a potential, all the higher levels of awareness. This potential is held within the Kundalini energy lying dormant at the base of the spine. Humans have the potential to awaken this Kundalini energy so that they can rise to a superhuman or divine level of awareness. The next kingdom in nature, the fifth, will therefore evolve out of the current human awareness.

In the Vedic tradition, cosmic or primordial energy is known as the Kundalini. This is the energy underlying the created universe. Other traditions have different names for it. The Chinese refer to it as Chi, the Japanese as Ki, the Christians as the Holy Spirit, the Ancient Hebrews, the Shekinah or Burning Bush, the Romans, Caduceus, and so on. It is the active component of the Kundalini within. There is also a dormant component of the Kundalini which only becomes active in the later stages of one's evolution, as one awakens to the true inner nature of Self.[1]

The Three Stages of Human Awareness

Before we can attain Self-realization, we must master our lives as humans in a material world. In other words, before we can become Self-realized we must perfect world realization. To reach world realization requires passing through three stages of human awareness until we are adapted to, and hopefully successful at, life as human beings. Self-realization requires journeying back, re-scripting our understanding of these stages of human awareness and realizing our true original nature as Self.

When born, we come into this life as a divine spark of Self and inhabit the human "animal" form. From birth, we develop our individual egos, our sense of identity as an individual, separate from others and the world around. Over time, we are taught to behave differently to what comes naturally, so that we become acceptable citizens in the world. We are taught that certain instincts and behaviors are not acceptable. Therefore, we are made to feel guilty if we display these. So, we learn to develop behaviors that are acceptable in the world, an artificial identity Freud termed the superego. Unfortunately, it is not as easy as this because through the process of not being accepted for how we were born, we develop many complexes, neuroses, habits, and conditionings that are difficult to live with. Every time we behave in a manner not acceptable to society or others, we are made to feel guilty. Thus, each of us develops a very complex personality, and although this can work, occasionally it does not. In Self-awareness meditation, we become more accepting of our inner nature so we can observe it from a detached perspective. Then we move beyond it to the true Self that existed prior to this.

Therefore, there are three stages in the making of an adult human. At birth, a baby comes with a pure awareness, an awareness of Oneness with the universal consciousness from which it has come, untainted by experience in the world. This is the first stage of awareness, the first-stage self.

Apart from pure awareness, the baby is born with a physical body, emotions, and a rational mind. These three sheaths form the physical being, the personality of the child, also referred to as the Primary Trinity. At this level of awareness, the child relies on instinct for survival, based on its genetic code. This is the second stage of awareness, the animal self, or the second-stage self.

The child has three basic needs. There are two physical needs, a need to feel safe and a need to fulfill hunger. There is also a spiritual need, which is the need of the spiritual being within the baby to return to its source, cosmic consciousness. With physical contact, particularly with the mother, the child's spiritual need for merger with its source gets transformed into a need for contact with someone else. Later still, this becomes the need for sex. The pleasure found in sex is an unconscious reminder of the bliss attained through merging with Source or Self. Natural reactions to the world around include curiosity, love, hate, attachment and jealousy. However, these are not instincts but a result of spiritual energy attaching itself to a reaction to form an emotion. The formula here is:

Emotion = Natural Reaction + Spiritual Energy.

Desires and delusions are also born at this time, such as the child's desire to possess its mother and the delusion that its mother belongs to him/her. Thus, the child's individual consciousness becomes trapped in thoughts and images related to the world of form. Human suffering is based on this focus in the physical world and in the evolution of worldly consciousness. This is all related to the second-stage self.

From this point on, the child learns about its world through interaction with the environment around. This includes the people the child is associated with, such as Mum, Dad, brothers, sisters and society. However, society does not allow the child to live out all desires and delusions, as there are both acceptable and unacceptable behaviors. The child learns about these through the reaction of others. Positive reactions include love, appreciation, acceptance and fulfillment while negative reactions include rejection, being ignored, and punishment. As a result, the child gains certain understandings about itself, both positive and negative. Whereas positive reactions fulfill the child's spiritual and physical needs and are pleasant and free flowing, negative reactions are frustrating and block the free flow of energy, which lead to understandings of being weak, dirty, foolish, dependent, inferior, and so on. Negative reactions are painful to experience and lead to feelings of guilt and worthlessness.

The child does not like the image it has created of itself which leads to self-hate, and self-dislike. This leads to what Freud referred to as a desire to die, a desire to escape from these unpleasant feelings. Rather than a desire to die, though, it is more an instinct to return to the original spiritual state. The child cannot bear to live in a world which creates such unpleasant feelings of worthlessness. This results in a kind of transformation within the child in which a new self-image is created, which is strong, likable, important, and great. This metamorphosis is a denial of the more real second-stage self for a self which is acceptable in the world. So, these denials are defenses against the realities of the second-stage self. As a child, this is played out in fantasies, imaginations, and associations with important people. This is an ongoing process into adulthood and serves to provide security and a sense of importance, a need to be somebody of significance in the world. This newly created self is the third-stage self and is less real than the second-stage self. Consequently, in adult life, one's behavior patterns are caused by a repetition of behaviors created in childhood. Transference of created behavior patterns towards significant others is later directed towards others in adulthood.

The third-stage self is known as the ego. The strength of the ego is determined by the degree of metamorphosis that took place as a denial of the second-stage self. At the same time, the degree of metamorphosis shows the likelihood of mental health issues, such as neuroses and other psychological problems. A person with a strong ego who has created a powerful presence in the world is also likely to suffer more when any of the worldly "securities" that have been created are upset or disturbed.

As the third stage is the furthest from the real Self, eliminating the third stage and being more accepting of the second stage, and then transcending the second stage to become the first stage, can be done through self-psychoanalysis and meditation. In Self-awareness meditation, one learns disidentification from the third-stage self, acceptance of the second-stage self and recognition of the first-stage self. Although this has been referred to by B.S. Goel as a backward journey in the mind, it is more precise to refer to it as a journey within, a dismantling of the ego to reveal the Self. As one does this, one gains a mastery of the personality, which is then used as a vehicle for the soul rather than the ego. This process requires use of the mind and willpower. To begin with, this is the lower will of the ego assisted by the soul and, later, the higher will of the soul alone, and ultimately that of the Self, otherwise known as the Spirit or Monad.

It is not possible to remove animal desires and instincts, so they need to be transcended. The third-stage self is in reality a transcendence of the second-stage self or rather a culturally acceptable denial of it. Once the mind is perfected, it should be possible to remove the support which the third-stage self has provided. This goal is achieved as one becomes an integrated personality with mastery of the physical, emotional, and mental bodies. Then, the third-stage self is gradually replaced by the transpersonal self (soul).[2]

The first-stage is the real you and witness of the second and third stages. It gets lost in the third stage believing that is who it is. This separate sense of individual awareness is the ego. In meditation, one learns to return to a witness state and then observe the third-stage self and dis-identify from it.

The entire universe comprises cosmic consciousness and cosmic energy. These are two aspects of creation. So, when we are born, we contain both cosmic consciousness and cosmic energy. At that moment, cosmic energy is at the command of cosmic consciousness (Spirit) and is, therefore, spiritual energy. Cosmic energy underlies one's physical nature and life processes. It underlies desires, animal reactions, sensations, etc. In fact, spiritual energy underlies all aspects of the created individual. We have already seen that the third stage-self results from learning to become acceptable in society. Spiritual energy is associated with that, too. However, the third-stage self has taken one away from second-stage desires, so there is a resultant conflict between the two. Specifically, the third-stage self has drives, while the second-stage self has desires. It is this conflict that can lead to neuroses, complexes, and personality disorders; drives versus desires. The stronger our ego, the greater our denial of the second-stage self. If we are too identified with the second-stage self, society will condemn this and, of course, try to create a stronger third-stage self. This constant battle between the second- and third-stage selves within us, which takes place in the mind, is where we find ourselves when we come to meditate and search for the true Self within. The third-stage self was required, however, for us to become ever more trapped in the material world, to experience the densest dimension of our being, with its associated desires, wishes, and habits. This is the most illusory and least truthful aspect of who we are.

Drives at the third stage have their own energy but also utilize energy from desires at the second stage. For example, the drive to achieve may be an attempt to gain the desire for love in a hidden, but more acceptable, way. Desires are therefore still being fulfilled, but indirectly through drives.

The second-stage self is quite stable. It is natural to have animal desires. The third-stage self, however, is not natural. It has been created because of interaction with others and comprises the need to be accepted to fulfill the expectations of others. How successfully the third stage is created will

10

determine our happiness and adjustment in society. However, competing with others and their own third-stage selves is difficult. Sometimes we are successful and at other times we are not. We find ourselves in a world of competition, criticism, self-righteousness, arrogance, acceptance, non-acceptance, etc.

To return fully to stage one, a backwards journey in the mind needs to be undertaken. Meditation assists in this process. When the Kundalini is active, it purifies the body and releases energy from all the accumulated drives, patterns, and conditioning. Therefore, a regular meditation practice will help to clear and transcend these difficulties, as does the Kundalini. As the Kundalini is at the command of the Monad, you should not try to speed it up or slow it down. A regular practice of meditation makes the process less "painful" by rounding off the edges, so to speak.

The Deeper Life

Within our deeper selves, there is a knowledge of a greater purpose and an incredible potential for growth. Fortunately, this knowledge can be tapped into and, through it, we can become more integrated. Carl Jung referred to this as individuation. This integration can also include our spiritual Self. Within each of us, there are two polarities, positive and negative. These can also be referred to as male and female. In fact, the search for one's higher Self, the "Beloved," is reflected in day-to-day relationships. Once we attain Self-realization, the final merger takes place as a divine marriage within us. As we evolve, there are expansions of awareness known as initiations. True Self-realization takes place at the fourth and fifth initiations.

Soul-realization comes when the soul and personality have combined and is often referred to as enlightenment. This is completed at the third initiation. Self-realization, on the other hand, occurs when soul awareness is superseded by Spirit or Monadic awareness. This is achieved at the fourth initiation and perfected by the fifth. Details of these expansions of consciousness are given in a later chapter. So, soul and Self-realization are two different states of awareness. However, in common parlance, Self-realization is used to cover both and refers to a state of awareness that is no longer egocentric.

Occasionally, a flash of insight may penetrate our normal awareness. When this happens, we realize that there is a deeper aspect of us that is far more universal. We are only aware of this other aspect of our being on rare occasions. Sometimes, this happens when our boundaries, physical, emotional, or mental, are pierced by the power of a greater reality. Through enquiry, contemplation, and meditation, a better understanding of this part of us can be gained. Communication is often through the realm of symbolism reflected in archetypes or myths. We may also wonder what are we really searching for in life that causes such suffering when persons or objects we have become attached to are taken away?

Myths have been handed down through the centuries and carry the understanding of glimpses into another reality, one that is common to everyone. They are stories based on archetypes in the collective unconscious. Jung proposed these archetypes were composed of mythological components within the collective unconscious. These archetypes are universal but may appear in different cultures with specific variations. For example, the mother goddess may appear as the Virgin Mary, Isis or Kali. These archetypes are "living psychic forces" which make up the content of the collective unconscious or "ordering principles" structuring the psyche, and emerging as images, processes, and attitudes. They are expressed through metaphor. Jung emphasized that archetypes are not concepts, but are numinous experiences, charged with emotion.

In Greek mythology, a sculptor, Pygmalion, created a beautiful ivory statue of a maiden. So beautiful was the maiden that he fell in love with her. Venus, the goddess of love and beauty, was so moved by his love for the maiden that she gave the statue life so they could be together. Pygmalion, falling in love with a statue personifying his highest ideal of beauty, hints at the reason we fall in romantic love with others during our life. In reality, the deeper self within which we are really searching for is our own soul. It is that part of ourselves which transcends all boundaries and links us with all the loves we have ever had. The essential nature of our soul is love, and so the more we are in tune with our soul, the more we love unconditionally. With soul awareness, there is no hurt when love is not returned. The more love is given, the more it is received. We see beyond the superficial woundings, knowing our own immortality and Oneness with all.

To gain an understanding through soul awareness, woundings confront us again and again until the bigger picture from the point of view of soul awareness is attained. Consequently, the ego may suffer loss and die to its reality, but in its place comes a greater reality and a perception from which there can be no loss. The past confronts us again and again until we realize that the past no longer works. There is only now, there is only love.

Transpersonal Crisis

Transpersonal crises are times when our psychological and physical well-being is threatened, and our psyche is opened by events or circumstances that seem beyond control. At these times, we are confronted by experiences for which we are not prepared, regardless of whether we have anticipated the experience. As a result, we are challenged to face a reality that goes beyond our normal comprehension and face the "Larger Story." As so aptly put by Allen Saunders, "Life is what happens to us while we are making other plans." How much free will do we have and to what extent is there a pre-destined plan? Or, if not a pre-destined plan, then is consciousness running the show rather than the egoic self? It is at times of grief and loss that we are challenged to take a deeper look at life, and at life itself, and consider the purpose behind it all. So, no matter how many plans we make, unless we are prepared to face up to the deeper issues, then fate will force us to take a closer look at the meaning of life. These moments can be painful as we face a reality that is beyond the limited confines of our own comfort zone. At the same time, this reality seems to threaten our very existence.

Myths can make their way into human consciousness at times of transpersonal crisis. At their most extreme, these crises may occur during psychoses, particularly those referred to by Jung as transitory psychosis. These are crises of spiritual transformation which can trigger the surfacing of images, emotions, and strange physical feelings from the collective unconscious.

As we journey through life, we create "structures of meaning," with which we create a frame of reference for understanding the world based on our life experiences. When, for example, someone close dies, we are torn between the desire to keep the old structures and the need to redefine them. A painful cognitive restructuring takes place through which we attempt to adjust to the loss and gain some sense of meaning in the loss. Our own sense of self is enhanced through transcending the loss. Through an enquiry into the meaning of life and death that takes place, we emerge with greater maturity. Given the right conditions, our own intrinsic self will move in a self-actualizing direction toward health, autonomy, and soul awareness.

The song "My Heart Will Go On," written by James Horner and Will Jennings, sung by Celine Dion, portrays the lifetime of feelings we can have for a lost loved one and yet hints at a yearning for love itself and a recognition that it is within and always with us. In the film *Titanic* the song is sung at the very end where Rose, now over 100 years old still remembers the love she found and lost 84 years previous on the Titanic. So, this loss gave her a lifetime to reflect on the meaning of love.

B.S. Goel (1989, p.26) found that the suicide of a colleague sent him into a nervous breakdown and thought he was at the point of dying himself. Consequently, he was in a state of fear of death, severe depression, and immense dependence. This lasted for about 7 days and so began an incredibly difficult period of Kundalini arousal, lasting for several years, fluctuating between the thought that he was dying to states of bliss and ecstasy. Certainly, this crisis not only challenged him to a deeper life, but it also triggered the process leading to his eventual Self-realization.

In Jayakar's biography of J. Krishnamurti, a spiritual man who lived in India, the author's mother is introduced to Krishnamurti and asks him whether she would meet her husband in the next world. He died several years earlier, and she continued to mourn his loss. The mother did not get the solace she wanted. Instead, he said to her,

"You want me to tell you that you will meet your husband after death, but which husband do you want to meet? The man who married you, the man who was with you when you were young, the man who died or the man he would have been today, had he lived?" He paused and was silent for some moments. *"Which husband do you want to meet? Because surely, the man who died was not the same man who married you."*
"Why do you want to meet him? What you miss is not your husband, but the memory of your husband." "Why do you keep his memory alive? Why do you want to recreate him in your mind? Why do you try to live in sorrow and continue with the sorrow?"
(Jayakar, 1988, p.2).

When someone dies, we suffer grief. However, the grief is not because we love the person. The grief is because we have identified love with the person. When that person has gone, we feel we have lost a part of our love. It is the memory of the person that confers suffering. So, somehow, our emotions are attached to the memory of the person. We constantly live in the "past" and in the "future." If we could only live in the "now," then we would not suffer so much.

Search for the Real

It is not only at times of transpersonal crisis, or times when we seem to have reached rock bottom, that we are challenged to contemplate what life is all about. Occasionally, a different perspective on reality is obtained in those moments of enlightenment or revelation. Then the boundaries of normal consciousness are dissolved, and a far greater, more universal perspective is gained. This may only last for a fraction of a second, and yet the revelations gained can last a lifetime. This perspective can sometimes be gained at the point when thought ceases, the moment between two thoughts.

We are constantly looking for something more, something greater than this everyday world presents us, and yet we don't quite know what we are looking for. The Self within each of us is, however, complete. This is the divine aspect within and is of the quality of the whole.

The Self is not evolving as it is already whole. This Self brings an impulse towards creation. We are not complete, but have the destiny to complete ourselves, to complete our own soul. Each of us creates our own soul that will, in time, unite with Self to give a whole being. Self is mostly masculine, whereas the soul is mostly feminine. Ultimately, the soul seeks merger with the Self, but this can only occur once the soul is fully created within. This cannot occur until consciousness is complete, because until then, the soul cannot be complete. We seek in the outer world the love that is within ourselves. In relationships, we invest this part of ourselves in the other person. We will never find it in the outer world, only its image. This image can be possessed, unlike the soul, yet is also evolving. When through loss or death we lose a loved one, we have lost more than just someone to whom we were attached; it is as if we have lost a connection with our soul. When that person dies, we withdraw the emotional investment we made in him or her and are at a loss until that investment can be made again in someone else.

The soul will never give itself to the ego. It tempts the ego to seek it, which it is forever doing, but the soul seeks the Self, a union which can only be consummated in the unconscious. The Self is the immortal love within us and yet seeks an immortal love of its own, its soul. Likewise, the soul in this life forever seeks the immortal love of the Self. A person is a part of the soul in the making and thus cannot possess the soul. When our individual consciousness is complete, the soul is complete, and the magic wedding of Self and soul can take place.

The sense of duality between the ego and the soul creates a cleavage in our life. As we search more and more for our soul, there is a feeling of being trapped in a world of illusion. This is felt even more after we have glimpsed "reality" through occasional moments of illumination. "This illumination reveals the essential Oneness that exists on the inner side of life and negates the outer appearance of separateness" (Bailey, 1988, p.417). As our personality is forged through the woundings of life to become a more suitable vehicle for the soul, the soul encourages us to search for it. When the personality and soul have become integrated, then it is possible to glimpse reality at will. The soul can then fulfill the "marriage" it really seeks with the Self, the Self-realization referred to in Eastern Philosophy.

Notes

1. In this book, Self, with a capital "S," refers to the spiritual or transcendental Self, while self with a small "s" refers to the personal self.

2. The term Self is generally used to include soul and Spirit or Monad. Correctly speaking, Monad is higher than soul and is the true Self. The soul can also be referred to as the transpersonal self, and the Monad as the transcendental Self.

Chapter 2

The Psychological Perspective

To get a better understanding of how meditation reveals the Self, it helps to know how the mind works. Over time, many approaches to psychology have developed and when this knowledge is used to assist a person to "heal," it is known as psychotherapy. First, we will look at psychology and psychotherapy, then their use in meditation for self-therapy or self-psychoanalysis.

Psychology focuses on the mind and behavior along with those attributes which allow for successful adaptation to the outer world perceived with our senses. It is relatively new, having only really come into its own in the last 150 years. As time has progressed, different theories have developed to explain why people behave and think as they do, and along with this, the techniques which can assist in change have also grown. There are now several theories, with their practitioners, who believe that their particular paradigm is the most accurate and suitable for therapy. These include psychoanalysis and psychodynamic therapies, behavioral and cognitive therapies, and humanistic and existential therapies. However, most of these approaches do not incorporate an understanding of the soul and, as with the behavioral approach, for example, depend on scientific research and resultant methods to be employed in behavioral change. Obviously, any therapeutic approach that has little understanding of the soul will be questionable in its ability to help a person achieve better soul and personality integration and even less value after Kundalini arousal or spiritual emergency.

Most clients seeking counseling or therapy do so for down-to-earth problems adequately dealt with by modern therapy.

Psychologists who have included spiritual experience and well-being are Carl Jung, Abraham Maslow and Roberto Assagioli. Their ideas have been influential in the humanistic and existential therapies, termed by Abraham Maslow (1968) as the third force in psychology (psychoanalysis was the first force and behaviorism the second). Later, emerging from these therapies, and incorporating many of their ideas, has been the concept of transpersonal psychology. This includes a fundamental awareness of the soul or transpersonal self and is a truly holistic approach. Transpersonal psychology is considered the fourth force in psychology. Researchers such as Stanislav and Christina Grof have done much to make transpersonal psychology an acceptable approach within the field of psychology. Roberto Assagioli's Psychosynthesis is an example of transpersonal psychology. There is, however, much overlap between the different therapies, as each has developed from previous approaches.

Also, reference to the Kundalini does not appear until one delves into the transpersonal sphere of psychology. Experiences which are related to Kundalini arousal, such as "peak experiences" and "bliss states," appear in the humanistic-existential concept. Psychosynthesis includes many techniques for what it calls spiritual psychosynthesis. Notably, eastern studies on the mind are more spiritual than their western counterparts and usually include an understanding of the Kundalini as well as looking at the development of qualities necessary for transcendence of the mind and emotions.

Holistic techniques for integrating the lower (psychological) mind with the higher (spiritual) mind are known as psychospiritual techniques. An important requirement for this integration is use of the will. Will and desire are the higher and lower aspects of the same attribute.

The real value in psychospiritual counseling and therapy lies in facilitating a person to enter consciously into the process of self-actualization. Self-actualization refers to the synthesis and greater functioning of all aspects of one's being and facilitates soul and personality integration. In order to outline how psychospiritual counseling and therapy work within eastern and western psychological understanding, I will look at the Psychodynamic approach, the Existential/Humanistic approach, Psychosynthesis, and the theories of Dr. B.S. Goel, who later became known as Shri Siddheshwar Baba.

The Psychodynamic approach takes as its basis the ideas postulated by Freud whose theory and orientation is known as psychoanalytic theory. Freud's construction of the mind was the first attempt in western psychology to understand the mind in a deeper way and to look beyond what it seems to be on the surface.

Freud divided the mind into the ego, the sub-conscious and the unconscious. The ego represents the conscious portion of the mind that has drives and goals. These goals are those which the individual is trying to attain in a civilized society so that they can be "somebody." The unconscious is like a storehouse of past needs, desires and hungers, fears and doubts, etc. Most of these are beyond recognition of the ego and yet they control the individual's behavior to a great extent. Within the unconscious there are two types of energy, natural desires and hungers with which the individual is born, known as the id (emotional energy), and the super-ego, which is like a moral, punishing force that was formed in the early years of childhood. This super-ego was once the outside social reality of parents and siblings, etc., which tried to block the fulfillment of the child's id desires and needs, and has now become an introjected, subjective reality in the mind. Similarly, the sub-conscious lies between the ego and the unconscious. This portion of the mind acts as a kind of gateway between the unconscious and the ego, allowing unconscious material to gain access to the ego through dreams or fantasies.

Conflicts between the id and superego result in anxiety and tension. Ego defense mechanisms attempt to balance these competing demands and to protect and strengthen the ego. Multicultural and family issues will further help to shape defense mechanisms and there may be several defense mechanisms operating at any one time. Specifically, defense mechanisms include repression, denial, projection, displacement, sublimation, fixation, rationalization, regression, conversion, identification, reaction-formation, and provocative behavior. As a result, Freud's whole idea of human happiness in psychoanalysis revolves around the fact that the more the unconscious is exposed before the ego, the better the ego will control the mind and reduce those actions that produce unhappiness.

Jung, however, differentiated between the personal unconscious and the collective unconscious. Jung believed it was important to integrate the psyche[1] and gave the name "individuation" to this process. This works through acknowledging the energies emerging from the subconscious, and the complex aspects of an individual personality that need to be balanced through identifying and working with archetypes.

Dr. B.S. Goel goes one step further and divides the psyche into first-, second- and third-stage selves. The first-stage self is the soul, the second-stage self is the unconscious as seen by Freud and the third-stage self is the superego as seen by Freud. Goel believed that once the desires of the second-stage self are exposed, these can then be dissolved by totally accepting their validity. As more and more of these desires are dissolved, the soul is revealed.

Within the existential-humanistic frame of reference, there are a group of theories which include existential, person-centered, logotherapy, Gestalt and psychosynthesis. Their approaches can be seen as an attitude toward the human condition. Consequently, they focus on the nature and meaning of relationship within the world and can be quite philosophical. They focus on men and women who are empowered to act on their world and determine their own destiny.

From an existential viewpoint, anxiety may result from alienation or it may result from failure to make decisions and to act in the world. Therefore, it is necessary for individuals to look at what their relationship to the world is like. They have freedom to act within the world, known as intentionality, and although they can be forward moving, they must remain aware that the world acts on them as well.

The most fundamental concept of the Existential-Humanistic approach is that of "Being in the World." Using terminology put forward by Vontress, this can be subdivided into the following areas of influence on the individual: Eigenwelt, which represents the person and the body, Mitwelt, which represents other people in the world and Umwelt, which represents the biological and physical world. In addition, Vontress stressed the importance of the spiritual dimension (Überwelt). Vontress focused on the therapeutic relationship as an expression of intimacy, openness, and real human exchange. He believed that only in a situation of caring and authenticity can true healing and growth occur.

Rogers believed people are positive, forward moving, basically good, and ultimately self-actualizing (experiencing one's fullest humanity). Over time, his theories changed from a non-directive approach to a person-centered approach. Additionally, he emphasized the importance of empathy and positive regard.

Maslow proposed a five-level motivational hierarchy of needs, which he saw as culminating in self-actualization. Accordingly, he saw people as intrinsically good, which is a biological feature, and believed that the inner nature, or self, possesses a dynamic for growth and actualization, but which is weak and easily frustrated and prone to sickness and neurosis. Like the Psychodynamic approach, he believed that the individual, because of his fears, rejects his basic self in order to fit into society. This creates a state of being he called the psychopathology of the average. Self-actualization included increased acceptance of the self, others and nature, increased spontaneity and creativity, increased identification with the human species, a change in values and an ability for mystical/spiritual experiences.

Psychosynthesis begins with the self, or inner identity and accepts that a person is growing and successively actualizing many latent personalities. Importance is given to the meaning that the person gives to life and that of values, including ethical, esthetic, noetic, and religious values. This approach also looks at the motivations, choices, and decisions a person needs to make and the consequent responsibilities they entail. Additionally, it acknowledges the depth and seriousness of human life and the resultant anxiety and suffering that has to be faced. In particular, there is an emphasis on the future and its dynamic role in the present. Psychosynthesis, therefore, aims at a reconstruction of the personality, initially perhaps with the most involvement from the therapist, but ultimately the client's own Self with whom he can increasingly identify.

Therefore, both the Psychodynamic and Existential-Humanistic approaches can be seen to aim at helping a person gain a better personal awareness and place in the world. Both can help the person towards greater self-actualization. In the psychodynamic approach, it is more a case of uncovering past influences, the biological needs, the key people one has related with, object relations, as well as cultural determinants to see how they affect the present. Developmental history and unconscious drives are constantly being acted out in our daily life. By uncovering the past and the complex unconscious processes, we can reconstruct the personality. In the Existential-Humanistic approaches, the value of uncovering the past is accepted, but there is more focus on techniques and methods to activate a person within the here-and-now of reality.

Goel (1993) believed that psychoanalysis, and even self-psychoanalysis, can uncover the past and transcend it, revealing the first-stage self. In the Existential-Humanistic approaches of Frankl, Vontress and Assagioli, there is a more cognitive acceptance and aspiration toward a spiritual state of Being. In order to do this, Assagioli placed great emphasis on the use of the will.

Whereas Psychodynamic therapy views the person as the pawn of the unconscious forces and environmental factors, Existential-Humanistic therapy stresses that the individual can take "charge" of life, make decisions and act on the world. They both accept that in childhood, we learn from the family and the multicultural unconscious, as borne by the family unit, as the culture bearer. We can assume, therefore, that a person is acting out the family and multicultural unconsciousness.

Furthermore, the Existential-Humanistic approaches put more emphasis on who we are and what we want to be, using visualization, decision making, choices, etc. These help us accept ourselves and build the personality. We then reconstruct the psyche, enabling us to make ourselves more suitable vehicles for the expression of our inner spirituality. The goal is the same as the Psychodynamic approach, but the technique is different.

Meditation is similar to psychotherapy in that its practice leads to greater peace of mind. By understanding the mind, a psychologist or therapist can assist you in gaining greater peace and harmony. Likewise, by understanding the mind through self-psychoanalysis and meditation, you can also gain greater peace of mind and harmony. So, by expanding the realm of psychology and meditation to include the inner Self and by using appropriate psychospiritual techniques, a more expanded state of awareness is possible.

I believe that both the Psychodynamic and the Existential-Humanistic approaches are valid in understanding and integrating the mind. Through the Psychodynamic approach it is possible to perform a "backward" journey in the mind through the animal desires to the soul, whereas, in the Existential-Humanistic approach various techniques that constitute more of a "forwards" journey are employed to reconstruct the personality and increase our spiritual awareness. Perhaps the terms "backwards" and "forwards" are illusory and, in essence, we need to move "deeper" into the different levels of our being. As such, the different paths are leading to the same goal, and so a holistic approach can be very useful.

When Spiritual Emergence
Becomes Spiritual Emergency

Moving from any stage to another brings crisis as the cleavage between the old order of needs and a newer order is sensed. It is often when the crisis reaches drastic proportions, when we feel we cannot go on anymore and the personality is totally emptied, that there is a sudden inflow of healing energy from the soul. Consequently, there are many accounts of profound Kundalini awakening which show the continual fluctuation from moments of utter despair and thoughts of imminent death to moments of bliss and connectedness with the soul. For instance, just when we think we can handle no more, relief comes. This process can last for years and is very individual to the person concerned. Sometimes, it passes with little trauma, but a lot depends on how ready we are for a transformative process that will dig to the very depths of our being. Such factors that need to be considered include how many suppressed complexes there are, and how much we are living in the super-ego! Regardless of the level of crisis, the conflict will only end when the personality has completely surrendered and has become a true instrument of the soul.

Therefore, it is important for you to consciously enter the process of self-actualization and pursue any form of facilitation that helps to unfold your hidden potentials, enhance creativity and give a deeper meaning to your life. It helps if you can consciously create a suitable vehicle (personality) for your soul. Also, learn to understand the soul's messages in whatever way they may come about, whether through symbolism, dreams, meditation, synchronicity in one's day-to-day events, coincidences, feelings of expanded awareness, or intuition.

When spiritual emergence takes on a suddenness and creates a situation that is very difficult to handle, it is known as a spiritual emergency. Because of its psychosis like appearance, it was referred to by Jung as a transitory psychosis. Often, this kind of emergency is not understood by psychiatrists and is consequently looked on as a mental health disorder and diagnosed as schizophrenia. The term schizophrenia applies to a group of severe mental health disorders with related characteristics and literally translated, it means "split mind." It is a psychotic disorder, creating a split from reality showing itself in disorganized thinking, disturbed perceptions and inappropriate emotions and actions. Spiritual emergency can exhibit these symptoms at varying degrees of intensity, but rather than being a mental health disorder, it is a crisis of spiritual transformation. So, caution is needed to distinguish between a spiritual emergency and a genuine mental health disorder. Therefore, it is important to take a balanced approach and differentiate a spiritual emergency from a genuine psychosis. Just as it is possible to diagnose spiritual emergencies as psychoses, it is also possible to diagnose something that is genuinely medical as spiritual.

Whenever a person undergoes a spiritual emergency, the spiritual energy is trying to work through the person's personality. The personality needs to be transformed before it can act as an instrument of the higher consciousness. There are two main approaches that can be taken. The first is to understand the various mental formations, behavior patterns, fears, resistances, and many other phenomena, such as transference, fantasies, hallucinations, guilt, introjection, and projection. These are the keys to unlocking the door to the unconscious mind and allowing free passage for spiritual emergence. This approach is like that found in psychoanalysis. The second approach is more concerned with looking at the here and now experiences the person must work with during the spiritual emergency and then help the person work towards a preferred state of being. Thus, by allowing the spiritual emergency to follow its own self-healing path, the person should not only find him or herself healed but also spiritually more mature afterwards. This is more of an existential approach.

Kundalini Tantra

From an eastern perspective, any method or practice that helps one to achieve union with the soul is a yoga. There are many types of yoga including hatha yoga, raja yoga, jnana yoga, bhakti yoga and Kundalini yoga. In a discourse given in April 1996, Sathya Sai Baba referred to the fact that anything that helps one to achieve union with the divine is a yoga.

Kundalini yoga is part of the tantric tradition. This accepts that the mind has experiences related to the objective world requiring the use of the senses, and yet even the mind results from the will for objective experience. However, tantra also acknowledges that the mind can be expanded and that experiences do not necessarily depend on an object. In other words, the range of experience can be broadened and go beyond the framework of the senses, beyond the framework of time and space. The dynamic potential force within the body that has the capability of bringing a person to an experience of transcendence of the material world and the senses is the Kundalini.

Kundalini yoga is the practice of a way of life that acknowledges the purpose of the Kundalini and prepares a person for an eventual awakening of it. Kundalini yoga prepares the mind and body for the arousal of Kundalini, but it should not be hurried. Kundalini yoga is intended to create and develop our awareness of the Kundalini, not necessarily to awaken it. The Kundalini, however, should be allowed to rise at the appropriate time. Any attempts to raise it before can be extremely dangerous. However, there is benefit in preparing the body and mind for it so that at the right time, the process will be easier and less traumatic.

Although the Kundalini is connected to the physical, mental, and emotional bodies, it is beyond these. The Kundalini arises from the base chakra, the seat of the unconsciousness and thus it has a connection with western psychology. When it is aroused, its goal is the crown chakra, the seat of supreme consciousness, the home of Shiva. This is the home of the super-conscious or transcendental self. In between these is the brow chakra, the seat of intuitive knowledge. The brow chakra connects the crown chakra with the base chakra via the sushumna. The sushumna is a channel for the flow of consciousness after Kundalini arousal.

Notes

1. All the elements of one's mind, including conscious and unconscious. It can also include soul and spirit.

Chapter 3

Psycho-analytical Meditation

Psychotherapy is the only form of therapy there is. Since only the mind can be sick, only the mind can be healed. Only the mind is in need of healing. Supplements to *A Course in Miracles*.

The purpose of Psycho-analytical Meditation is to explore conscious and unconscious aspects of our mind and emotions in order to heal and bring about greater harmony or balance within. The more inner harmony we have, the greater our potential for Self-awareness. A lack of inner harmony can lead to dis-ease. Of course, we find disease in all the kingdoms of nature, but for us, creating greater harmony between mind, body and emotions helps to perfect our personality, making it a suitable vehicle for soul and eventual Self-awareness.

In the quote above, to say only the mind can be sick and therefore only the mind can be healed refers to a mind that is far greater than the lower human mind, far beyond our human level of comprehension. For our purpose, though, when we refer to healing, we are looking at dissolving the emotional charge attached to our thoughtforms. Any illness or disease that we have because of, or exaggerated by, the emotional charge or belief system can also be reduced or healed. We will look at this later. As co-creators, though, our own minds have an ability to work with the higher mind and effect cures where appropriate, even some physical illnesses. Healing modalities that connect with a higher power and effect change accordingly can be wonderful in their results.

In Psycho-analytical Meditation, the first thing we do is to try to understand ourselves better. This includes aspects of our personality that we are consciously aware of, as well as unconscious aspects that are not so obvious. The conscious and unconscious aspects of the mind are not totally separate, as there is a close relationship between them.

Begin by taking a closer look at yourself. What are your values and what meaning does life have for you? What motivates you? What choices and decisions do you make to live the life that is important to you? Are you influenced by the past and what role does the future play in your current outlook and decisions? These will all give you an idea of what you may want to take a closer look at in meditation.

Through a process of self-analysis, we want to achieve two things:

- remove emotions that bind and
- increase acceptance of what is.

Most of the problems we create for ourselves are because of the belief that things should be other than they are. If we could just accept that everything is appropriate and act consciously, life would be so much easier.

When you decide to make changes, how strong is your willpower to carry these out? Take a close look at your self-identity. Observe yourself really carefully. To what extent does there appear to be a pure Self-awareness independent of your normal field of consciousness or current life situation? As you do this, realize there is a duality within who you are, a personal self and a Higher Self or soul. The personal self is generally unaware of the soul, and yet the soul is really the only self there is. The personal self reflects the soul but appears to be self-existent. Also, any effort you make towards soul alignment is more than adequately matched by the soul. The more you can synthesize this apparent division, the more wholeness there will be. The soul has a will of its own towards integration and is the greatest ally you could ever have!

Exploring your unconscious mind is a lot more difficult. Contemplate and observe your thoughts, feelings and patterns of behavior, and keep a diary of your own self-analysis if it helps. Observe your interaction with others. How do you respond or react to them? Observe your reactions to movies, fiction stories and so on, and you will also get clues to your psychic formations and behavior patterns. You need to be constantly aware of "What I do, what I feel and what I think."

As your unconscious mind communicates through symbolism, one way of exploring this is through dreams. Dreams provide a commentary on your current experience, so learning how to interpret them can be very revealing. An entire chapter is devoted to dreams. There is also a technique called conscious dreaming, where it is possible to influence dream content by consciously focusing on what you would like answers to before going to sleep.

Another technique you can try is to use self-guided imagery in meditation. While in a meditative state, create a scene in your mind, full of symbolism. As you do this, see what unconscious material surfaces as a result. For example, you could imagine yourself walking through a meadow on a warm, sunny day. There is a light breeze, and the air is filled with birdsong. You are happy and carefree. Alternatively, imagine yourself climbing a mountain, higher and higher. You know that when you get to the top, there will be magnificent scenery and a sense of achievement. Note symbols, ideas, and feelings that arise in your consciousness because of this meditation. Perhaps there may also be some answers for you to a problem you have been trying to solve. Symbols experienced this way are simpler and clearer than those in dreams, but they are also very useful. This way, you are learning to communicate with your unconscious.

Self- and dis-identification are based on the principle: "We are dominated by everything with which our self becomes identified. We can dominate and control everything from which we dis-identify ourselves" (Assagioli, 1965, p.22). There is a considerable difference between saying "I am angry about that" and saying "The emotion of anger is trying to overcome me." The self needs to disassociate itself from the weakness, fear, emotion or drive. A strong identification with one part of the personality reduces your ability to identify with other parts of the personality. Affirmations are of help here, such as "I have emotions, but I am not my emotions. I have a body, but I am not my body."

When you are clear about what you want, who you want to be in the world, and what your values are, practice in using your will to pursue those objectives will help successful achievement of them. To help "see" the future you want to create for yourself, practice in the use of the imagination, including evoking visual, auditory and other senses, will also help you towards this goal. This ideal may be a role model, a philosophy, an artistic pursuit, or a cause. It is essentially a projection outward of your own center that has the effect of assisting in an inner Self-realization. It acts as a kind of link with the soul.

In the east, however, in the past, such a process was more likely to occur between guru and disciple rather than soul and lower self. Ideally, the guru was someone who had already trodden the path of soul integration. From the perspective of soul awareness, the guru could assist the disciple on their own path. The guru gave help and advice where necessary and, as a soul-realized person, the guru represented a personification of the disciple's own soul. The guru encouraged the disciple to meditate and look within to help realize his own soul. In effect, the disciple had two avenues along which to search for his soul, the inner path and the outer path given by the guru.

Meditation and self-psychoanalysis can go hand in hand. The results of self-psychoanalysis during the day can be taken into meditation for further contemplation. Meditation will bring up its own experiences, which can also be contemplated on during the day. As our wakefulness expands, time spent in meditation increases.

After years of meditation on the brow chakra (often referred to as the third eye), B.S. Goel had an experience which he referred to as the "jet experience." A pinprick of light was seen, and his consciousness shifted to that point. From then on, whenever he meditated, he became a "witness" to events and inner aspects of himself experienced in meditation. Goel noted that with regular meditation, this point of consciousness enlarged and exposed past formations in the mind before his consciousness and freedom was then obtained from them. Although Goel believed the "jet experience" would happen to other meditators, each person's experience is unique and this shift in consciousness occurs in many ways. Self-psychoanalysis is therefore a valuable addition to meditation and, in fact, we must transcend all our past object relations before our worldly consciousness can merge with soul consciousness.

Many accounts of the experiences to be had in the higher stages of meditation point to a gradual destruction of the ego and the reality it has built up around itself. This is often experienced as a kind of death which is necessary before a person becomes a soul infused personality, and when ego consciousness is replaced by soul consciousness.

As meditation progresses, past happenings arise in one's consciousness, as these patterns and formations in the mind are gradually being revealed and the area of conscious awareness is expanding. The light of consciousness influences these memories, releasing any emotional content associated with them. When these memories come to light, the process of psychoanalytical meditation is very useful to help gain freedom from them. It's not that the memories disappear, but it frees them from unpleasant, binding emotions.

When one has reached a point of awakening on the evolutionary cycle, this process is facilitated by the Kundalini. Until that time, this is undertaken by you as an aspirant to spiritual evolution. When the Kundalini is active, it is as if a higher consciousness than your own takes over and transforms you from within.

This is all part of the gradual movement of the Kundalini from the base chakra to the crown chakra. It is a purifying passage ultimately leading to liberation and enlightenment. However, the movement is not purely linear, there is often much movement backwards and forwards between the various chakras. Consciousness may keep moving back to the base chakra and then into the mind again to continue clearing. We may also feel a sensation at the Brahmarandhra or nirvana chakra at the top of the skull, as this is where important "nerves" exist. Ultimately, these are destroyed as they bind consciousness to the ego. If pierced prematurely, a classic nervous breakdown happens. When they are pierced gradually by the Kundalini, classic experiences of unification, liberation and enlightenment occur alongside the difficult ego destroying experiences.

However, long before the "jet experience," or other notable shift in consciousness occurs, an awakened Kundalini has been working tirelessly in the background to remove obstacles and prepare the person for this later shift, which signifies a significant opening of the third eye. As we align with the soul, through self-analysis and alignment techniques, we are moving in a similar direction to that offered by meditation. Once in a while, a gradual shifting of patterns and complexes is insufficient and crises are experienced, forcing us to confront issues, sometimes painfully, so that greater soul and personality integration can be achieved. This may be the loss of a loved one, an intensely difficult shift in work relations or status or some other event that can appear to shake the very foundations beneath our feet. Our entire worldview appears to be challenged. Remember, we are talking about a disintegration of the ego and the cage or structure of meaning it has built around itself. Another way of looking at this is to realize that a large amount of karma is also being cleared at these times. The more we prepare ourselves for these crises, the less painful they will be.

Eastern philosophy refers to four aspects of our worldly existence that make up the illusion of this plane of existence. These four problems need to be overcome consecutively and this can be assisted through appropriate self-therapy. Indeed, the counseling and therapy of the future will have, as its primary goal, integrating soul and personality and the dispelling of the illusions of ego reality. These are

- the world of physical forces (Maya),
- our desires and emotions (Glamor),
- our mental life and the ideas we live by (Illusion) and
- the integrated personality opposing the will of the soul.

Thoughtforms

The act of meditation and raising your awareness, lifting your consciousness to a higher point, can bring you to a peak of awareness. Occasionally, you may feel an emotion or two surface, ready to be cleared. The time has come to do this. Of course, a thought usually accompanies an emotion. A thought may trigger the emotion, or the emotion may trigger the thought. What happens is they have combined into a "thoughtform." Much of the energy in our thoughtforms is emotional energy. In short, emotional energy is spiritual energy plus desire. This emotional energy is attached to a thought or idea, thus the emotional feeling associated with many thoughts. Once the energy is released from desire, it is available for the future use of new thoughtforms associated more and more with the higher mind rather than the lower mind. With Self-awareness and meditation, we become more and more co-creators and suitable vehicles for our souls.

By shedding the light of conscious awareness on the unwanted thoughtform, it can slowly dissipate. Usually, this doesn't happen instantly, but the more you do it, it will have less hold on you. You will also have raised yourself to a higher level of overall awareness because you have now taken emotional energy and returned it to the reservoir of spiritual energy.

Thoughtforms follow the same creative principle found throughout the universe. First, there is an idea expressed through mind (of which there are many levels from divine to human) which then gathers energy to create the required form. With humanity, the mind creates a thought which gathers emotional energy, such as a desire, and results in a thoughtform.

We gradually learn to use our mental and emotional "vehicles" to attune to our souls. Through meditation we can dissipate unwanted thoughtforms releasing the attached emotional energy to its spiritual source, freeing us from these binding fears and emotions. In advanced meditation, it is possible to tune in to illumination or intuition and create higher thoughtforms benefitting both ourselves and others.

Thoughtforms remain within our own energy field or aura, but can also find their way elsewhere. Consequently, we are surrounded by thoughtforms and need to be careful that we are not trapped by these, unable to see beyond our own constructed reality. For example, think of the fanatic who is trapped by his world of thought.

These days, thoughtforms resulting from the news, social media, advertising, which is often biased, affect people on mass. Where we receive our information from will affect our own worldview and color our own thoughtform creation. On a grand scale, consider a nation polarized between one political party and another. The political party that gains the majority vote now forms the government. We see that people's opinions, and therefore their vote, have been swayed by the mass media. The party that wins is as much a reflection of the success of media bias as it is the considered opinion of thinking individuals. Similarly, on a small scale, it is local gossip through which opinions (thoughtforms) are created by a small group of individuals. Therefore, if we come in contact with a troubling thoughtform from elsewhere, we have a choice whether to go along with it, and vitalize it, or create a counter thoughtform to send it back where it came from, such as thoughts of peace, love and harmony.

Here are some important points to remember:

A powerful thoughtform can return to its sender following the principle of "as you give, so shall you receive." For example, if you give hatred, it will come back to haunt you. Thoughtforms, when strong enough, can literally act as a poison, ruining your life in many ways, such as worry, anxiety, and hatred. Obsession with your own ideas, even if right, is problematic. Nothing is permanent, so eventually these will give way to something more truthful. Rather than fanatically holding on to these ideas, be open to change or alternative, equally valid truths.

When creating positive thoughts, formulate them clearly without the attachment of desire. Then release the thought and let it go. Ideas, as opposed to thoughts, are more likely to be from the level of soul and will therefore attract spiritual energy. Try not to let personality desire influence the thought or idea, nor be concerned with the physical effects of such thoughts. We, as the creator of our thoughts, simply need to get out of the way. If we dwell on the thought, it will add an emotional content such as desire.

We are responsible for the thoughtforms we have created and, ultimately, we destroy them. Through psycho-analytical meditation, we learn to dissipate these thoughtforms so that we can move forward in our evolution. Realistically, we must move beyond these thoughtforms and their associated emotional energy before we can begin creating higher-level thoughtforms with their illumination and higher purpose.

Our task for now comprises two parts:

1. Dissolving the troubling thoughts that are holding us back, those thoughts with negative emotions attached to them.
2. Remaining detached from new ideas and thoughts sufficiently so that emotional energy is not attached to them.

So, by shedding the light of conscious awareness on the thoughtform, it can slowly dissipate. This will not happen instantly, but the more we do it, it will have less hold on us. We will have raised ourselves to a higher level of overall awareness because we have now taken emotional energy and returned it to the reservoir of spiritual energy.

By observing thoughtforms from a detached perspective, they are not vitalized and will gradually dissolve. If the thoughtform has originated from outside of ourselves, from someone else, we can then create a counter thoughtform and send it with love back where it originated.

By avoiding negative thoughts, seeing the positive as much as possible and avoiding causing harm wherever possible, will help to avoid creating adverse thoughtforms. Ideas, both our own and of others, cause no harm as long as emotion is not attached to them. Spiritual ideas can be animated by spiritual energy and can accomplish much good.

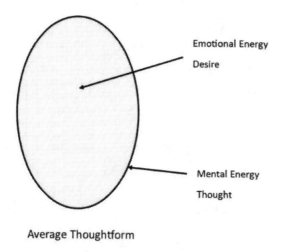

Emotional Energy
Desire

Mental Energy
Thought

Average Thoughtform

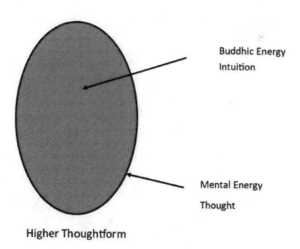

Buddhic Energy
Intuition

Mental Energy
Thought

Higher Thoughtform

Figure 1 Thoughtforms

So how do we scientifically explain the creation of thoughtforms, particularly higher-level thoughtforms?

The component parts of a thoughtform are brought into

relationship with each other by the mind of the creator:

1. It is visualized and intelligently built for a particular purpose.
2. It is vitalized by desire or higher still by illumination or intuition.
3. It has a lifespan as long as it is needed for its particular purpose and always has a connection to its source as long as the creator remains consciously aware of it.

When the meditator can meditate on the plane of the soul, it is possible to create thoughtforms of a very high level in which the soul acts as an intermediary between divine ideas and the lower mind. The meditator's task is to meditate on the intuitive wisdom of the soul, receive an idea, and clothe it in a suitable thoughtform.

When creating thoughtforms, it is necessary to intelligently apply thought, preferably gained through intuition, with an understanding of purpose and direction. And when delivering these thoughts to others to be careful in using speech, remembering that words have power, and this power will animate the thoughtform.

When creating a thoughtform:

1. Be sure to use discrimination so that thoughts are as closely aligned to truth as possible and avoid adding emotion, keeping thoughtforms as pure as possible.
2. It is through speech that we deliver our thoughtforms to others, so we need to be careful to be as pure as possible in thought and speech.

Do not allow selfish desire to be the basis of thoughts and consider the well-being of others.

Remember, we are responsible for our thoughtforms and

likewise responsible for their dissolution.

The Socratic Process

The Socratic process is a powerful method for dissolving thoughtforms. If we look at thoughtforms, we see that most are stories, stories we tell about ourselves and stories we tell about others. In effect, an event occurs and then we make up a story about it. The story is based on our understanding, our reality, and our experience. We tell stories to ourselves and to others, and these stories become thoughtforms. Usually, these stories are based on our ego interpretation of events, based on our individual history and beliefs. Stories are also used to enhance our ego or sense of individuality. Notably, one way the ego tries to assert its importance, its self-righteousness, is by finding fault in others. The more the other person is wrong, the more we believe we are right. Also, we often believe things are other than they should be!

On the involutionary cycle, we have become more and more invested in the material world, and more and more invested in who we are not. Once we have become fully invested in who we are not, awakening takes place, leading to the evolutionary cycle of return to who we truly are, our spiritual reality. So, it is from this point on that we grow in Self-awareness, a gradual growth and awareness of who we really are. It is on this path of return to Self-awareness that we can now observe our thoughtforms, dissolve unwanted thoughtforms, and replace them with a more truthful understanding of who we are with truthful, illuminated thoughtforms.

As we learn to dissolve unwanted thoughtforms and create new ones that are more truthful to who we are, we gradually go through a process of becoming more Self-aware along with an associated blissful experience of reality.

Another perspective on this, and one which leads to a more truthful experience of reality, is that we endeavor to live in the present, rather than being focused on the past or on the future. In reality, the present is all we have, and many of our destructive thoughtforms are based on thoughts of the past, or of the future. Truthful awareness, therefore, is an awareness of the present moment as it is here and now. Anything else is an illusion.

So, as we analyse our thoughts, we ask ourselves, is this true? And if this is not true, what would we be without this story? If it is not true, convert it into a positive, truthful thoughtform. This continual process of analysing thoughts and beliefs and questioning their truthfulness is known as the Socratic process or method.

Interestingly enough, Socrates, who is credited with the Socratic process, ultimately concluded that "all I know is that I know nothing." Consequently, through his relentless process of self-inquiry, he had dissolved all of his illusions about himself.

Breathwork

The Indian practice of pranayama (controlled breathing) is the "Science of Breathing" in which the vital life force is used for mental peace, psychic evolution and spiritual attainment as well as physical well-being. In the more advanced forms, it can unearth deeply buried psychic material, bringing it before our consciousness and consequent dissolution. In essence, it is a form of psychoanalysis. Pranayama has been around, tried and tested, for thousands of years.

The Science of Breathing is also the science of Laya-yoga or the science of the centers (chakras). To what extent is breathwork safe and at what point do we need to consider the other effects it may have on our system, which at present we don't always understand, e.g., the effect it has on the chakras and how pranic energy is stimulated and directed? Likewise, what affect does it have on the etheric body, which, amongst other things, acts as a safety net between our day-to-day awareness and astral energies? The astral body is also known as the emotional body.

A pranayama technique, known as Bhutashuddhi Pranayama, is given in the chapter on Advanced Techniques. This technique combines pranayama and a chakra meditation.

Chapter 4

Kundalini Awareness—Awareness of the Divine Energy Within

She lies dormant in the Muladhara Chakra in the form of a serpentine power or coiled up energy known as Kundalini Shakti. She is at the centre of the life of the universe. She is the primal force of life that underlies all existence. She vitalizes the body through Her energy. She is the energy in the sun, the fragrance in the flowers, the beauty in the landscape, the Gayatri or the Blessed Mother in the Vedas, She is the colour in the rainbow, intelligence in the mind, devotion in worship.

(Swami Sivananda Sarasvati as quoted by Swami Sivananda Radha, 1992, p.25.)

The Kundalini is a transformative energy which, for most people, lies dormant in the base chakra. She is often depicted as a snake-like serpent lying coiled, waiting for the right time to be aroused from her slumber. When the time is right, she will awaken and begin a complete transformation within the person. This will include the body, mind, and emotions.

To help us understand the Kundalini, we can look at how she has been portrayed in world religions. Within these religions, reference is made to the dual nature of the universe. In essence, the universe comprises consciousness and energy. Universal consciousness is the divine mind which lies behind all of creation. While the whole of creation is made up of universal energy. In eastern philosophy, consciousness and energy are two parts of the one whole. You can't have one without the other. When personified, in the east, they are depicted as Shiva and Shakti. Shiva is the male aspect and Shakti is the female aspect. The Kundalini as a transformative energy is therefore considered feminine and an aspect of Shakti.

It was mentioned in a previous chapter on Search for the Self that our human awareness is far from the divine awareness from which we came. Nevertheless, for some reason, we needed to experience life in form, an experience that differs greatly from our original awareness as divine beings. Then, at the appropriate time, when we have fully experienced ourselves as individuals immersed in this world of form, the return journey begins. This, of course, has always been the plan. However, we can't do this on our own. It is the Kundalini that will take us through this process at the right time. Until then, the Kundalini lies dormant within us. The aim of creation is for Shiva and Shakti to once again merge in cosmic union. This is described in eastern philosophy as a divine marriage when Shiva and Shakti will once again join in beautiful harmony. The amazing part of this is that we are part of this. We will eventually experience the divine marriage within us as we return to the blissful awareness from which we came.

When humanity has evolved to where the majority are experiencing this marriage within, then rather than being the fourth kingdom in nature, the new humanity will be regarded as the fifth kingdom. Such is the magnificent goal of human birth. Of course, many will have moved beyond the physical plane of existence to continue the path of return on higher planes of existence. But, just as the individual is evolving, so is the group in which the individual forms a part.

As the created universe is Shakti, the female aspect of divinity, then the whole of manifestation is also Shakti. Likewise, all energy is Shakti and all of nature is Shakti. We are Shakti. Every aspect of our created being is Shakti. So, Kundalini is also Shakti. As the whole of creation is Shakti or divine energy, then the only difference between one aspect of creation and another is the rate of vibratory energy. Different rates of vibration account for the different forms of manifestation, and the slower the vibration, the denser the form. Matter can be considered as Shakti in its lowest rate of vibration. Therefore, the Kundalini is Shakti at a higher rate of vibration. Kundalini is an aspect of Shakti in a person which has the power to transform all aspects of the person to a higher frequency. With a higher frequency of vibration, we are more equipped for higher levels of awareness. Thus, the Kundalini is the divine energy working within to transform us to an energy level where we can attain soul awareness and later awareness of Self or Monad. Imagine the divine union or marriage of Shiva and Shakti taking place within our own selves, for such is the purpose of our existence. It is said that the first and second initiations contain a divine enticement, while through the third, fourth and fifth initiations, the marriage takes place. As a result, the nectar of this union of Shiva and Shakti is the perception of, and unity with, divinity gained. This is the ecstasy of the union, the higher consciousness gained and the purpose behind creation.

Accordingly, Shiva and Shakti are the source of power and the power itself. For there to be spiritual energy, there has to be a source from which it comes. From another perspective, the source of the universe, God, cannot be discovered or known unless something emanates from Him. By creating the universe, God could know and love Himself. When a person realizes his divinity during the meditative state of Samadhi, he realizes he is one with God. He is God. Thus, the creation of human beings was to enable God to be conscious of Himself through the form He created. As Self-realized beings, we are aware of our own Divinity.

This is not the end, though. Once we have moved beyond the need for human form, we pass through many higher levels of awareness as we progress through even higher expansions of consciousness. This continues as greater awareness of our Oneness continues until, finally, we are the One from which we came. However, understanding of these levels of awareness is far beyond the comprehension of our human minds. We live in a world of maya or illusion and yet when we see through the veils of illusion and perceive true reality, we realize we were never anything other than the One.

At the human level, consciousness has the threefold function of will, perception, and thought. At the divine level, this threefold manifestation is Atma, divine will; Buddhi, divine love and understanding; and Manas, divine mind or creative intelligence. Consciousness, although a result of the merger of the Father and Mother, still contains the Father and Mother aspects within it. In fact, there is no part of creation which does not contain the totality of the universe within it. This is the concept of Hylozoism. This is behind the theory of the Holographic Universe and the Holotropic Mind.

Purpose of the Kundalini

It is considered by many that at the soul level, we have divine consciousness, but this has yet to be realized in form through our personalities. Before this can take place, however, our personalities need to be refined as suitable "vehicles" for soul consciousness. The final transformation is carried out by the Kundalini, which has lain dormant until the appropriate time for this purpose. It is incredible to think that every human has this potential within. For this reason, human evolution may not be an accident of evolution, as Darwin thought. That the Kundalini lies dormant within each of us, awaiting the right time to carry out its transformation, shows a divine plan for every one of us. A new theory for future human evolution is that our existence is not an accident, but planned right from the very beginning.

At first, we seek world realization and want to be happy and successful. To gain happiness, we try to be successful in what we do and add more and more material comforts. Eventually, we realize that there must be something more. The search begins and a realization that world realization, which is temporary, does not bring happiness. Happiness comes through Self-realization. Knowing that we are divine beings, we seek a return to that awareness. Not only do we seek Self-realization but are assisted in this by the Kundalini. We have experienced living in the material world, and this was a necessary experience. We have realized a way of being that is not who we really are and with this knowledge, we are better able to experience who we really are. We fully realized who we are not so that we can more fully realize who we are.

Is There a Physical Basis to the Kundalini?

Gopi Krishna believed the Kundalini to be a superphysical substance like the mind but having a tangible organic medium through which it acts on the nervous system, effecting a gradual change or transmutation until it is receptive to higher energies. He believed that a nectar like substance is extracted by the nerve endings from the surrounding tissues. This substance has the form of a radiation as well as a subtle organic essence. Some of this energy streams into the reproductive organs, stimulating them into extra activity. In men, semen is produced in increasing abundance, which rises in a tiny stream up the spine to the brain, providing sustenance for the brain cells which have been stimulated into significant activity. In women, the fuel is provided by sexual energy and the secretions involved in sexual arousal. It is the energy used for sexual pleasure and reproduction which is used to nourish and transform the inner self. For this reason, this physical link between sexual and spiritual experience is not to be underestimated. It provides the link between science and religion and will bring forth a major change in Western psychology. The raising up of sexual energy into spiritual energy is the basis of most spiritual disciplines.

Kundalini and Spirituality

There is a common belief that if we arouse the Kundalini through various techniques, such as yoga or pranayama, our spirituality will increase. However, premature arousal of the Kundalini through such techniques is dangerous and can cause many mental health issues. The experiences of Gopi Krishna and Swami Muktananda, for example, show that even when Kundalini arousal has been activated at the right time, there can still be incredible suffering. We have identified with our ego and, for soul awareness to take over, the ego needs to be replaced. In being replaced, the ego believes it is dying, and that is how we feel when we are still identified with the ego. Towards the end of this process, our consciousness alternates back and forth between ego awareness and soul awareness. When aroused at the right time, though, no matter how difficult the process is, the Kundalini is being guided by spiritual will and, consequently, we do not receive more than we can handle, and eventually Self-awareness is attained.

Many accounts of profound Kundalini awakening show these continual fluctuations, from moments of utter despair and thoughts of imminent death to moments of bliss and connection with the soul. This is a process which can last for years and is individual to the person concerned. Sometimes, it passes with little trauma. Thus, a lot depends on how ready the person is for a transformative process which will dig to the depths of their being. The conflict only ends when the personality has completely been prepared and has become a true instrument of the soul.

When the energies involved in the rising of the Kundalini cause overwhelming symptoms, we know it as a spiritual emergency. Spiritual emergency can exhibit the symptoms of psychosis or schizophrenia at varying degrees of intensity, but rather than being a mental health disorder, it is a crisis of spiritual transformation. Caution is needed, therefore, to distinguish between spiritual emergency and mental health disorders. During a spiritual emergency, unconscious material with strong emotional charge emerges into consciousness. This has powerful, spontaneous healing potential and needs to be supported. The person needs to realize the healing nature of the crisis and be encouraged to allow the process to unfold and to co-operate with it. The spiritual energy is trying to work through and transform the personality. As very few people have gone through this process, very little is known about it. One day, the process will be far more common as humanity evolves and, with a better understanding, appropriate support will be available.

Symptoms

There are many symptoms of an awakened Kundalini ranging through the entire spectrum of physical, emotional, psychological, and super-conscious experience. Beginning at the base chakra, the Kundalini ascends, stage by stage, until the crown chakra is reached. This journey is accompanied by various physiological symptoms in the reproductive organs, the nervous system, and the brain. The Kundalini energy can take months or years to work its way up to the head, and physical sensations may be found affecting different parts of the body.

Physical symptoms may include an itching, tingling sensation, which may start in the feet and progress up to the head and crown center. Or the sensation may be localized in one or two parts of the body. Other symptoms are dizziness, pressure or pain in the forehead, or the top of the head and pressure felt along the spine. There may be a burning sensation in the eyes, diminished vision or blindness, and there may be a pain in the left or right side of the chest resembling a heart attack. Further symptoms can include spasmodic breathing, lapsing into meditation, a feeling of intoxication, an increased pulse rate, nausea, backaches, a pain in the spine, numbness in the hands, arms or feet, electrical sensations in the head or the hearing of deep inner sounds or a sensation of vibrations within the ears. There may be sensations of heat or cold, either localized in different parts of the body or throughout the body. At night, one may wake up sweating all over. These are just some of the many symptoms and, as mentioned earlier, what you experience will be unique to you.

As the Kundalini works its way towards the crown chakra, there may be a variety of spontaneous bodily movements which are very similar to those practiced in various forms of hatha yoga (kriyas). These include involuntary jerks, contractions, especially of the anus, abdomen, and throat (chakra locations), involuntary dancing, hopping, spinning, head movements and other sudden movements. It appears these movements facilitate the Kundalini's journey. Therefore, many yogic postures were developed to help an active Kundalini. The person may also experience the intense devotion of bhakti yoga, the detachment in action of karma yoga or the spontaneous knowledge of jnana yoga. It is not uncommon for the person to recite mantras, chant, make various animal sounds, compose poetry, all known as mantra yoga.

There are also emotional and psychological symptoms as well, which can resemble the psychotic episodes found in mental health disorders. It can be difficult to distinguish between the two. An awakened Kundalini may also trigger any emotional or psychological disturbances that already exist. This can make diagnosis very difficult. Various emotions, such as depression, anxiety, anger, guilt, intense emotional swings, mental confusion, and so on, can also arise. Often these stages of intense depression, etc., fluctuate between periods of elation and bliss and could consequently be confused with manic depression or bipolar disorder. However, the periods of bliss are far more spiritual and healing than the periods of elation associated with bipolar disorder.

Psychic experiences associated with Kundalini awakening include pre-cognition, mind reading, ability to leave the body, seeing auras, remembering past lives, channeling, and other paranormal experiences. These abilities, though, are considered of secondary importance and should not be dwelt on, as doing so can hold you back. Spiritual experiences, as such, are more associated with higher levels of consciousness and awareness. The bliss states and expansions of consciousness associated with some Kundalini awakenings, either suddenly or at later stages of awakening, produce states of awareness that are so enlightening that they go well beyond the normal levels of consciousness possible even for people that have meditated for many years. Once the Kundalini awakening has completed itself, the person may find that he or she is in this state of expanded consciousness most of the time.

Therapy

With so many symptoms related to the Kundalini, a balanced approach is required and medical tests should exclude a medical condition prior to seeking any therapy. Even if medical tests reveal no organic basis to a psychotic condition, as found in spiritual emergency, it is still necessary to distinguish between a functional psychosis and a spiritual emergency. A spiritual emergency shows the person to have been well adjusted prior to the episode, able to consider that what is happening may originate from within the psyche, and to co-operate with appropriate support received.

It is important to allow the Kundalini to run its own course and to acknowledge that it is a self-healing process. After a phase of Kundalini activity, the person is psychologically and spiritually more whole than beforehand. It is important, therefore, that a therapist adjusts to whatever level of experience the person has and uses techniques which can assist the person to flow with the process. A person undergoing Kundalini activity requires understanding and a supportive environment.

Chapter 5

Chakra Awareness—Awareness of the Seven Major Centers

In the west, our knowledge of the chakras is limited and most of what we know has come from eastern philosophy. Consequently, this chapter contains concepts and descriptions that will probably be unfamiliar. I present it for the descriptive content it provides, and which will hopefully give you an insight into a complex yet fascinating subject.

Within our physical body, there is a subtle energy system known as the etheric body. The etheric body delivers the life force or prana throughout the body by a system of 72,000 nadis. There are also a multitude of chakras which are vortices of energy which help to distribute energy to all the nadis. Of these chakras, there are seven major chakras, which I will look at in this chapter. I will also refer to a few lesser chakras, as they are of value to advanced meditators.

As we evolve in consciousness, there is a subtle and gradual shift in perception from instinctual awareness through to divine awareness. This change in awareness moves through seven stages, each corresponding to one of the major chakras. For most people, only the chakras below the diaphragm, the base, sacral, and solar plexus, have significant activity. However, as we expand in awareness, the higher chakras increase in activity. These are the heart, throat, brow, and crown.

The chakras are powerful energy centers which are not at our command. As a result, we should not try to manipulate the energies, but allow them to unfold naturally. We are best witnessing the process that unfolds within us following its own intelligence. Such an approach is safer in the long run. Over time, each chakra is brought to its own point of spiritual responsiveness and connectedness with the whole. Our attitude should be that of a grateful witness. Each chakra is also associated with a physical gland within the body's endocrine system, and each gland controls one of the seven major areas of the physical body.

Energy within a person is distributed by four means:

1. The etheric body which underlies the physical body of a person. Specifically, the seven chakras are found within the etheric body and are the focal points of reception and distribution of seven types of energy. We know these as the Seven Rays or aspects of divinity covered later in the book. The etheric body is the mediating point between the physical and spiritual aspects of a person and their respective energies.

2. The nervous system is the outer expression of the network of energies and forces of the etheric body.

3. The endocrine system is the exoteric expression of the etheric body and its seven centers.

4. The bloodstream carries the life principle, and the combined energies and forces of the etheric body and the nervous and endocrine systems.

Together, these four systems form one integrated whole and are the manifestation of the four aspects of matter: fire, earth, air, and water. Each of these four systems is essentially dual in nature and corresponds to the soul and personality rays of a person. In addition, each has a positive and a negative aspect combining matter as the static negative quality and spirit as the fluid positive quality that underlies it. Eventually, these will reach a perfect synthesis in the perfected person, when the soul has been initiated into physical plane existence and represents the appearance of the fifth kingdom of nature, the Kingdom of God on Earth. This happens at the third initiation. It can be looked at as a dual initiation, the realization by a person of the soul and the realization by the soul of the art of functioning as a human being.

Discussing the seven chakras, I will look at their full potential, a potential that blossoms as the chakra becomes increasingly active and energized by an awakened Kundalini. In addition, the five lower chakras will also be looked at in relation to "speech," as the Kundalini is considered in Hindu philosophy as the "Goddess of speech." Each of the lower five chakras also has rulership over one of the five senses. The words center and chakra are synonymous, and both can be used. However, when I refer to a chakra, it is specifically that chakra vortex. When I refer to a center, it is a field of energy surrounding and including that chakra. So, for example, there is the heart field which surrounds and includes the heart chakra.

The word OM, with the associated will and purpose behind it, created, and continues, the manifested universe. In fact, at a deep level of meditation, the sound of OM can be heard. It is referred to in the Bible with "In the beginning was the Word, and the Word was with God, and the Word was God. He was in the beginning with God; all things were made through him, and without him was not anything made that was made" (The Gospel According to John, vs.1–3). Essentially, every word or sound has power, and it is believed that in the ancient Sanskrit language, the sound of each word has meaning according to the object or idea represented. The power of words can be seen in ancient mantras which when repeated over and over, accompanied by meditation on their meaning, invokes the "deity" of the mantra and consequently produces the desired effect. For instance, the Gayatri mantra, which is considered the most powerful mantra of all, invokes spiritual light. Its repetition can stimulate the higher intellect and ultimately lead to spiritual fulfillment.

Speech relates to communication and understanding. The power behind the word or any form of communication is

Shakti or Kundalini. In the eastern tradition of gurus and their followers, an individual mantra can be given by a guru to a follower that will be appropriate to the "note" of the person, a repetition of which assists spiritual growth. It is like being given a key to unlock the doors to increased spiritual awareness.

In order to function within the physical realm, we have our five senses. These operate regardless of our level of awareness. Each of the five lower chakras controls one of these five senses. The higher levels of sense awareness increase according to our level of Self-awareness.

Many of the descriptions I will give for each chakra are taken from ancient texts, referred to by Goswami (1999). Colors and descriptions of chakras vary, so a consensus is given here. Each chakra is symbolically depicted as a lotus flower and the central part is enclosed in a pericarp, just as the seeds of a flower are enclosed within a pericarp. The essence of the chakra's qualities is symbolically shown within the pericarp.

There are many descriptions of chakra systems given in the ancient texts. The three major groups are:

1. Pouranika system,
2. Waidika system, and
3. Tantrika system.

The Pouranika systems are based on descriptions given in the Puranas. These are not as detailed as the other system. There are several Waidika systems:

1. Narayana,
2. Yogachidamanyupanishad,
3. Maheshwara, and
4. Yogarajopanishad.

Together these form the Waidika Chakra System.

The Tantrika Chakra System is more complete than the others. It is based on the Tantras. This is the one I mostly refer to.

There are 13 Tantrika systems:

1. Six are expounded by Shiva, A, B, C, D, E, F;
2. Bhairavi;
3. Rishi Narada;
4. Mahidhara;
5. Brahmananda;
6. Jnanananda;
7. Lakshmana Deshikendra, and
8. Brahmananda Giri.

Details of the chakras which follow are based on several sources, while the descriptions are based on the Tantras, supplemented by the Waidika and Pouranika accounts.

The Base or Root Chakra—Muladhara Chakra

Figure 2 Base Chakra

Found at the very base of the spine, this chakra supports all the other chakras. It is controlled by the will-to-be in incarnation and directs the life principle in matter and form. At the right time the will-to-be of the base chakra is activated by the higher will of the crown chakra causing the Kundalini to awaken so that it can pass through the prepared chakras in the etheric body to meet in spiritual union at the crown.

The base chakra is therefore where spirit and matter, the duality of manifested divinity, meet, and life is connected with form. The Kundalini at this chakra has slowly been transformed from the energy within matter to the transforming energy of the active Kundalini and ultimately into the divine light within. All of this takes place while nurtured by life and energy coming down through the etheric equivalent of the spinal cord. While this down-pouring happens, there is a simultaneous uprising of life, too. Together, they produce a gradual awakening of the chakras according to how the person responds to the Seven Rays or qualities of divinity. These are described in Chapter 9. Thus, increasing the person's consciousness according to their needs and ultimately in the service of humanity.

The base chakra controls the sense of smell. Smell is important for recognizing the aroma of food, such as the appreciation of good food or knowing that something is off. At the instinctual level, the sense of smell can assist the sex impulse.

Talking with no conscious awareness of any power in the words to communicate ideas, thoughts, motives, and desires represents speech at the level of the base chakra. Speech, however, not only refers to what is said but also to how it is said. The tone of voice can be expressive of a whole range of emotions, both in the giving and in the receiving. Silence and control of speech, alternatively, can be the reflection of a power greater than one's own.

In the diagram of the muladhara chakra, you can see that it has four petals arranged in the NE, SE, SW, and NW corners, just like a normal compass layout. The color of the petals is blood red or molten gold (shining red) but also referred to as gold or shining yellow. Each petal is labeled with one of four Sanskrit letters व (va), श (śa), ष (ṣa), and स (sa). On chakra petals, Sanskrit letters are shown clockwise in alphabetical order and used just like we would label the sides of a geometrical shape with a, b, c, d, etc. However, as the letters have the bindu dot they are called matrika letters rather than letters of the Sanskrit alphabet and are pronounced differently. The dot adds a nasal sound. This applies to all the chakras. These letters can be chanted as a mantra to aid in concentration. The other shapes and symbols in a chakra illustration also help to aid concentration on the chakra's meaning. Above each Sanskrit letter is a bindu dot which represents the creative point of that Sanskrit letter or mantra. Additionally, there is also a bindu dot above the Sanskrit bija letter for the chakra. Here, it represents the point at which the creative process for the chakra begins. The letters are given as a mixture of shining red or gold colors. Each of the four petals represents a vritti or tendency. Specifically, they are greatest joy, natural pleasure, delight in the control of passion and blissfulness in concentration. The square in the chakra is known as the "earth" region and is mostly given as yellow. The earth mantra is ल (la) and is also yellow. It is pronounced as la with a nasal "m." Repetition of the mantra gives rise to the Goddess Indra. As already mentioned, the mantra in the center of each chakra is a bija mantra. This means a seed or core mantra. The triangle in the pericarp (body of the symbol) represents will, knowledge, and action, or the deities Brahma, Vishnu, and Shiva. It is the seat of the Kundalini power as love-desire (kama) and the seat of the deity Shiva.

When we take a closer look at the deities and their symbols for this chakra, we see that the bija deity for the muladhara is Indra, who sits on a white elephant. The elephant represents physical development and as the elephant is white, this represents spiritualized physical development. Indra, therefore, represents the base chakra. There are two other important deities associated with the base chakra. The presiding deity representing the Kundalini power in the base chakra is Dakini. The deity representing an aspect of Shiva associated with the chakra is Brahma. Remember, Shiva and Shakti are the two polarities of creation, so in the base chakra, Shiva, and Shakti are represented by Brahma and Dakini.

As we continue to look carefully at each of the six chakras, from base to brow, we see that each has deities representing the distinct qualities of Shiva and Shakti found in each of them. For Shiva these are respectively Brahma, Vishnu, Rudra, Isha, Sada-Shiva and Itara-Shiva. For the power of Kundalini, these are respectively Dakini, Rakini, Lakini, Kakini, Shakini, and Hakini. Because of this connection, advanced meditation on the base chakra is done on both deities, Dakini, and Brahma.

The Sacral Chakra—Svadhisthana Chakra

Figure 3 Sacral Chakra

The sacral chakra controls sex life and the generative processes. It is related to conception and form building, whether a human being, an idea, an organization or higher. It is the chakra through which the forces of Impersonality will eventually express themselves and the problem of dualism be solved. Thus, the link with the throat chakra through which a higher creation is achieved.

There is a flow of energy between the spleen, the sacral chakra, and the chakra at the base of the spine. This triangle of force is connected with creation, vitality, and form building within matter. The higher correspondence of this triangle is between the pituitary gland, the throat chakra, and the pineal gland. The pituitary gland is associated with the brow chakra and the pineal gland with the crown chakra.

The sacral chakra and the brow chakra together create a functioning duality productive of the personality. The sacral chakra has its physical externalization in the gonads.

The sacral chakra represents an increased refinement in speech coupled with a greater awareness. For example, we may talk of divine mind, which although we may not understand exactly what it means, we know it represents a level of awareness far different from that of the human mind. Likewise, it would not be accurate to refer to a prayer as a mantra or even to assume that the love of a child for its mother is the same as that of the devotee for his guru. Accordingly, the language needs to be penetrated to some extent to understand the deeper meaning. This requires a degree of intuitive perception, a listening within for the meaning behind the words. In other words, of a higher level than gained from ordinary speech.

For example, how often have we found that when we try to communicate our beliefs to another, it is met with criticism or hostility because of a misunderstanding? How can we communicate our beliefs or ideals to another completely when the means of communicating this understanding is mere words, and then relying on the other person's understanding for interpretation of what you have just said? For instance, if someone asks you "Do you believe in God?" and your reply is "Yes," what understanding has actually been communicated? There comes a point when communication needs to go beyond the actual words spoken, or at least we need to be aware of the inability of words to communicate completely what is being said.

The sense of taste is controlled by the sacral chakra. As well as taste in relation to food and drink, there is also taste in the sense of a discrimination in our dress, manners, appreciation of art and so on.

The sacral chakra has six petals. In different accounts, the color is given as vermilion red, fire-like red, lustrous red, whitish red, or gold. The Sanskrit letters on the petals are from Ba to La, each with a bindu dot as in all the chakras. They are ब (ba), भ (bha), म (ma), य (ya), र (ra), and ल (la). In the middle is the bija mantra व (va).

The color of the letters is given as diamond white. The six vrittis or qualities of the petals are affection, pitilessness, a feeling of all destructiveness, delusion, disdain, and suspicion. However, the order given for these varies. These petaline processes radiate from the center of the chakra into the ida and pingala subtle energy channels located alongside the spine connecting all the chakras. Inside the pericarp is the "water" region, shaped like a crescent moon. From the bija mantra of the chakra, va, emerges the deity Varuna, who is white with four arms sitting on a Makara, similar to an alligator with a fish's tail. This symbolizes the immense power found in the watery, circulatory medium of the body, leading to good health. In addition, Varuna also represents sexual energy linked with the endocrine system. In Varuna's lap (represented by the bindu dot) sits the deity Hari (a name of Vishnu). According to the different levels of deep concentration or meditation, different forms of deity may appear, representing different levels of spiritual experience. These levels of awareness were personified in ancient India by different deities, and vivid descriptions were given of these different deities. Consequently, a deity could have many forms representing his or her many aspects. For example, from the mantra va arises the deity Varuna in the form of Hari. In the lap of the deity Varuna, sits Vishnu. Another aspect of Vishnu is that of Narayana and, in a very deep state of meditation, Narayana appears as Krishna. Having an incredibly deep understanding of deep meditation levels and experiences, the sages of ancient India could personify these energies into highly symbolic deities.

For example, imagine you have had a meditation in which you felt slightly blissful and yet, at the same time, you felt some discomfort. In meditation, this is an example of an integrative peak, meaning you are experiencing a peak of awareness associated with bliss, but relevant clearing is also taking place. If you want to portray this experience as an image, how will you do this? One way to do this is to personify the experience. To illustrate this, you might decide to do this by drawing a person with two heads. One head is happy and looking left, while the other head is sad and looking right. If the experience is felt in the heart chakra, then if the heart chakra for you is associated with green, then you could draw the person in the image dressed in green or sitting cross-legged on a green-colored lotus with twelve petals. In effect, you have created an archetype or thoughtform for that experience and you could share that thoughtform with others. One day, that image may appear to you in meditation associated with an experience and you instantly know what it means.

As mentioned earlier, Rakini is the goddess in the sacral chakra, personifying the Kundalini energy. The bija deity for the sacral chakra is Varuna. Through deep meditation on Varuna, Shiva, in the form of Vishnu, appears.

The Solar Plexus Chakra—Manipura Chakra

Figure 4 Solar Plexus Chakra

For humanity, this is the most active chakra. It has a special relationship to the heart and brow chakras. Notably, there is a downflow of energy to the heart from the soul via the brow chakra. This is facilitated by the advanced development of the solar plexus. At the same time, there is an evocation of the crown chakra.

The chakras below the diaphragm, of which this is the highest, are related to the personality. The solar plexus is the clearing house for all the energies below the diaphragm. It is located in the navel region.

The solar plexus is the important chakra through which the average person lives most of the time, conditioned by desires and ambitions. It is also the chakra through which most mediums and clairvoyants work. When mediums and clairvoyants are eventually polarized in the brow chakra, then they will have clear perception rather than clairvoyance.

The continual disturbance going on in the area below the

diaphragm is the major cause of stomach and liver complaints. Transference of energy from one chakra to another puts strain on the physical body and the organs related to the chakras, which leads to many of the difficulties affecting those on a spiritual path.

In the solar plexus chakra, the level of speech takes on more of the color of our needs. We may compulsively criticize, compulsively demand attention and seek gratification of our needs. Specifically, this chakra represents language born of the unconscious mind. Our unconscious needs and desires are often expressed in our words. This is the level at which most people operate and is reflected in the counseling approaches that attempt to explore these unconscious drives. For example, psychoanalysis relies on the power of words to reveal the unconscious processes, particularly through free association of words or dream analysis.

The solar plexus also controls the sense of sight. With our increasing awareness, there is a difference between "looking" and "seeing." To what extent does the mind interpret our visual impressions, and to what extent are we influenced by our emotions?

On the ten petals of the solar plexus are the letters ड (ḍa), ढ (da), ण (ṇa), त (ta), थ (tha), द (da), ध (dha), न (na), प (pa), and फ (pha). This has been accepted in all the Tantras. The bija mantra is र (ra). The ten qualities or vrittis of the petals are spiritual ignorance, thirst, jealousy, treachery, shame, fear, disgust, delusion, foolishness, and sadness.

Petal colors are given ranging from dark green, dark blue, golden red or black. Black is the most widely accepted. The color of the matrika letters is given as dark blue, black or like lightning.

In the pericarp is the "fire" region, which is triangular and red. The bija mantra, ra, is red lightning in color and its form, the deity Vahni, sits on a ram. In its lap, in the bindu, is the deity Rudra. Rudra is shown as sitting on a bull. A Shiva-Linga is also found in the "fire" region. The presiding deity representing the power of the solar plexus is Lakini.

The Heart Chakra—Anahata Chakra

Figure 5 Heart Chakra

The heart chakra is located in that part of the spine corresponding to the physical heart. A fully opened heart chakra enables us to think with the heart rather than to feel with the heart. This happens when the desires of the solar plexus chakra are transmuted into love through highly developed mental faculties. As soul and personality are integrated, personality consciousness is gradually replaced by soul and group consciousness, allowing the inflow of divine energy.

The heart chakra is involved with the meaning of words. The definition of words such as consciousness and spirituality require an ability which is severely limited without direct experience. The real meaning of the words cannot be limited, only our understanding of them. So, a refinement of our senses leads to the expression of speech through poetry or sometimes prophetic poetry. To illustrate this, in cases of spiritual emergence or Kundalini arousal, we often find an automatic desire to express a heightened awareness through poetry on the splendors of creation and divinity. Consequently, words are from the heart and expressed through the refined senses.

The highest expression of word power is the mantra, the sound of which purifies the mind and our immediate environment. This area of influence expands with time as the mantra is repeated. Eventually, a point is reached where the mantra's power becomes self-generating, and waves of joy and peace engulf the aspirant along with a great surge of energy as feelings of devotion and surrender to divinity are experienced. The heart chakra is our temple to divinity, and it is here that this communion with the divine takes place. However, if the ego is allowed to gain control, the loving feelings subside.

The heart chakra controls the sense of touch, but also has a special relationship to air. At this level, touch is particularly associated with a kind of feeling, not to be mistaken with feeling as an emotion which is more indicative of the solar plexus. Likewise, touch is more in line with the effect one has on another without the need for any return—a spontaneous action from the heart.

The matrika letters on the twelve petals of the heart chakra are क (ka), ख (kha), ग (ga), घ (gha), ङ (ṅa), च (ca), छ (cha), ज (ja), झ (jha), ञ (ña), ट (ṭa), and ठ (ṭha). However, there are also accounts of the heart chakra having 8 or 16 petals.

The twelve qualities represented by these petals are lustfulness, fraudulence, indecision, repentance, hope, anxiety, longing, impartiality, arrogance, incompetency, discrimination, and an attitude of defiance. The bija mantra for the heart chakra is य (ya).

The petal colors have been given as deep red, yellow, dark blue-yellow and white. The consensus is for deep red. The matrika letters have also been given different colors but usually shown as variations of red or white. The difference in color seen by advanced meditators in the classical literature is because of the method of concentration used and the nature of the power radiations emanating from the chakra. When a Kundalini connection is made in meditation, it is usually seen as green in its less evolved state or yellow in its more evolved state. Specifically, we are referring to the "flashing lights" seen in meditation rather than the chakras seen in advanced meditation by spiritual yogis.

The bija deity is Vayu. Deep meditation on Vayu gives rise to the bindu deity of Isha. Isha is a form of Shiva, who is the conqueror of death. The presiding deity representing the power of the heart chakra is Kakini. Isha is shown as white while Kakini is shown as white or yellow.

The heart is the center of one's individuated consciousness and has a close connection with the crown chakra, which is the center of one's universal consciousness. When the heart is balanced in duration, a connection is made and there is a download of conscious energy from the crown to the heart from universal to individual.

The Throat Chakra—Vishuddha Chakra

Figure 6 Throat Chakra

This chakra is related to the mind or mental aspect and is powerful and well developed in the average person. It is related to the thyroid gland. The throat chakra is related to the first initiation and is highly active once a person has passed through the initiation. For more detail on the initiations (expansions of consciousness) see the chapter on Transpersonal to Transcendental awareness.

The creative energy of the third ray of active intelligence now has the throat chakra as its primary focus whereas, before, its focus was on the sacral chakra. After the third initiation, the focus of the third ray will be the brow chakra.

The throat chakra is related to the personality by the creative thread, to the soul by the thread of consciousness and to the Monad by the sutratma or life thread. Once a person's creative life is centered in the throat, then the first stages of the building of the Antahkarana are possible. Now, the intelligence aspect of humanity focuses creatively through the throat chakra. The throat chakra is the organ of the creative WORD registering the intention or creative purpose of the soul.

When one's awareness has reached the throat chakra, perception beyond words is achieved. This may be indicated as a "knowing of the heart" or simply a "knowing." Someone who speaks from the heart may use words, but there is an added dimension to what is being communicated. The receiver of the communication might likewise hear words but be aware of the deeper meaning as well.

When one's awareness is largely from this chakra, others may be receptive to the sound of your voice as their natural form of knowing. Even the movements of your hands and other gestures will instill in others an awareness of strength and energy.

Before a full realization of the Kundalini's creative energy is possible, it is necessary to give up all worldly desires, and to shift our focus from the solar plexus to the heart and brow chakras. When our gaze is fully on divinity, then all karma has been burnt up. It is impossible to put into everyday speech the realization we have from this level of awareness, thus the misinterpretation made by people of the timeless truths written in all the sacred scriptures.

Spiritual experience is beyond the mind and beyond the control of the aspirant, even though there may be stimulation of the senses and accompanied background noises in the mind. In addition, there may also be psychic experiences, yet these are still of the mind. Spiritual experiences are an encouragement to go on and create enthusiasm to do so. They are not an end in themselves. They cannot be repeated at will and should be approached with surrender and humility. These experiences are not yet of the Kundalini. They indicate times when the habit of mechanical thinking, habitual responses, and reactions has momentarily ceased.

Hearing is controlled by the throat chakra. At the level of this chakra, hearing would reach awareness of the cosmic sound AUM,[1] the peak of experience for this sense. The difficulty we have in truly hearing is the interference of our own thoughts. Likewise, there is a real skill in really hearing what another has to say without distorting it with judgment, our own experiences, self-defense, and self-justification. Similarly, listening to the still small voice within also depends on our ability to quieten the mind.

The throat chakra is a shining smoke color. It has 16 petals, and the vritties or specific qualities of these petals are a mixture of mantras, musical tones, and the quality of deathlessness. The matrika letters on the petals are the 16 vowels, आ (ā), इ (i), ई (ī), उ (u), ऊ (ū), ऋ (ṛ), ॠ (ṝ), ऌ (ḷ), ॡ (ḹ), ए (e), ऐ (ai), ओ (o) औ (au), अ (a), अः (aḥ), and अं (āṃ). The pericarp region of the chakra is shining white and inside this is the bija mantra, ह (ha). The deity of the bija mantra is Ambara. In the lap, or bindu, of the mantra is the deity Sada-Shiva. In the pericarp of the lotus is the presiding deity Shakina, representing the power of the throat chakra. The throat chakra has a special relationship to the Void (akasha).

The Brow Chakra—Ajna Chakra

Figure 7 Brow Chakra

The ajna or brow chakra is located in the forehead, slightly above and between the eyebrows. It expresses the integrated personality, fully functioning at the time of the third initiation. The brow chakra distributes the energy of the third aspect of divinity, that of active intelligence, and is related to Spiritual Love, or Buddhi, and also to ray 2, love-wisdom.

Through its relation to the personality by the creative thread of life, the brow chakra is closely connected with the throat chakra, which is the center of creative activity. Together, the active interplay of the brow and throat chakras produces a creative life, expressing the divine idea. Specifically, the brow chakra focuses the intention to create, whereas the throat chakra is the organ of creation. It also fuses these creative energies with the true love of the heart. This produces the highest manifestation of the Kundalini. Whereas the crown chakra relates the Monad and the personality, the brow chakra relates the spiritual triad (Atma-Buddhi-Manas, or spiritual will, intuition, and higher mind) to the personality.

The brow chakra is referred to as the eye of the soul. When the crown chakra, brow chakra and alta major chakra, located at the base of the skull, are operating together, then one can see with the "eye of the soul." Then all three eyes see together, the initiate has insight into divine purpose, and later intuitive vision of the plan. The physical externalization of the brow chakra is the pituitary gland.

The name ajna refers to the guru's ajna (order), which takes place in this chakra. Also, the first divine form of the Supreme Being is centered in the guru chakra, which is immediately below the crown chakra but above the cranium. This power radiates from here to the brow and rouses the OM. OM is the form of Kundalini.

The two petals, which are of shining white color, are two radiations of power. One radiation is downward into the lower chakras and the other radiation is upward through the upper chakras. On the petals are the two matrika letters हं (ha) and p (kṣa), which are usually white but have also been noted as red. The OM symbol ॐ is also found in the pericarp. It is moon white or shining white. It is the first bija mantra, the sound from which creation manifests.

The deity Hakini is found in a triangle within the pericarp of the brow and represents the power of the brow. The pericarp also contains a triangle (not shown) which is the seat of Itara-Shiva, Shiva with full control over desires. Itara-Shiva takes the form of a lingam. When the Kundalini is awakened in the base chakra, it moves upwards to the brow chakra, where the OM is absorbed and consciousness becomes of the Kundalini. In addition, the brow chakra has a special relationship to mind (manas).

The ida and pingala nadis end in the brow chakra, forming a junction with the sushumna called the Tripathi-sthana. It is a red, six-cornered region found in the pericarp but not shown in the diagram. In this area is also found the seat of the Supreme Power as Kundalini. The sushumna and the brahma nadis terminate in the nirvana chakra, which is also known as the Brahmarandhra.

The Crown or Head Chakra—Sahasrara Chakra

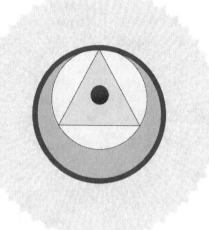

Figure 8 Crown Chakra

The crown chakra is located just above the top of the head, just outside the cranium, and is often known as the sahasrara chakra. It is the highest chakra and is related to spiritual will, the atma, the Monad, or transcendental self. Likewise, it is the eye of the Father or Monad and is related to ray 1, will and power. The crown chakra functions after the third initiation, distributing Monadic energy and the will aspect of divinity.

The crown chakra is related to the personality by the Antahkarana, which is fully operational after the fourth initiation when the causal body, the vehicle of the soul, has been disintegrated, and the Monad is consciously embodied in form. It is dynamic in quality registering purpose.

The pineal gland is the physical externalization of the crown chakra, which is active during infancy while the will-to-be is established and again towards the end of man's evolution when the will energy of established Being reaches accomplishment.

The lotus of all the chakras, except the crown, face upwards.

The crown lotus faces downwards like an umbrella. However, the pericarp of the crown faces upwards. The crown chakra lies in the void region above the cranium where there are no nadis. It is connected to the chitrini nadi by a power bridge. Within the chitrini nadi is found the vajra nadi and sushumna nadi.

The pericarp of the crown is endowed with many powers, and all knowledge lies within it. Specifically, Supreme Being or Parama Shiva, and Supreme Power or Shakti Kundalini are seated within it in union, and it is the center of immortality. The Supreme Bindu lies concealed within a triangle within the circular moon region in the pericarp. The Void is without mind or matter. Consequently, it is a Supreme Void with no form at all. So, mind and matter are absorbed, and all that is left is Shiva in union with Shakti.

The crown lotus is white and has 50 matrika letters on the petals. Different accounts say the letters are from "a" to la or from "a" to ksha without la. The petals are arranged in 20 layers of 50 petals and the matrika letters are repeated on each layer. The most common account is that the matrika letters are similar in color to the petals. Although given as white, there are also accounts of the petals being yellow, red, smoke-colored, etc.

At the top of the head is the Brahmarandhra, which is the endpoint of the sushumna, chitrini, and vajra nadis. This is linked to the crown by a power bridge known as visarga, and through which the Kundalini passes to reach the crown. In the lotus's pericarp is Supreme Spirit known as jivatman. Inside the pericarp is a golden color. Shiva and Shakti reside in the crown as One.

It is in the crown that union of Shiva and Shakti takes place. The crown is like an umbrella above the top of the head, and just below it, laying within it, is the guru chakra. Therefore, the guru chakra is also above the cranium and covered by the crown. It is referred to as the lotus feet of the guru or guru who is in the crown. It is the lotus on which the umbrella of the crown stands. All the chakras from the brow upwards form the ajna system. If you include the smaller chakras and the seven major ones from the base to the crown, there are actually 13 important chakras.

Notes

1. AUM is the correct spelling as there are three sounds, A, U and M. This is usually shortened to OM.

Chapter 6

The Mechanics of Consciousness

Creation and the Relative Field

What is the purpose of creation? There are many creation stories in the many traditions in the world. In the scientific tradition, for example, Charles Darwin says life as we know it has taken hundreds of millions of years to evolve to where it is now. He talked about natural selection and adaptive radiation as processes that allow species to grow. Whether Darwin was right or wrong it still begs the question, why are we here? As humans, we are looking at this question from a human perspective. That we are even asking proves we are experiencing something, even if our perception is limited. So how did we get to where we are now? And how, if it is relevant, do we get back to where we came from?

As you observe your world, the world around you and the world within, notice that there is a continual perspective that there are a multitude of forms. More precisely, there is you as the observer, and everything else. We know this as duality. So, what would a more truthful reality be? In the classical traditions, the most truthful reality is that there is only One, there is no other. You are that One. We are all that One. Therefore, observing a world with a complexity of forms, billions of forms, and all separate from you is, in reality, an illusion. Perhaps you can now gain an insight into just how far you must have come from an awareness of your true being, a being that only perceives Oneness in everything, to your current perspective that you are just an infinitesimally small part of an immense universe or perhaps 50 billion simultaneous universes.

The experience you are having now is because you experience more than One. The only way you can have any experience at all is by being aware of the other. You are consciousness, seeing itself as a separate, individuated consciousness. To maintain this illusion of separation, or fragmentation, from the whole, an illusory construct called the ego was created. As you can see, the ego has done a fantastic job of perpetuating this illusion of separation. Not only has the ego maintained this belief in separation, but it has also enhanced it. It continually adds to itself through belongings and attachments, to increase its importance, its relevance, while its biggest fear is to be unimportant and disappear. Its very existence is based on fear. The ego's role is to take you further down the involutionary cycle. For this reason, to return on the evolutionary cycle, it is necessary to dismantle the ego, to change your perspective from the egoic doer to the trans-egoic Self. Consequently, as you increase in awareness of Self, you increase in recognition of the One until, ultimately, you are the One. However, in truth, you have never been other than the One. That's why in the eastern religions they refer to all as being maya. Maya means illusion. We live in a world of illusion. The purpose behind Self-awareness meditation is to see through the illusion and ever more fully be yourself, to be the One.

As a result, through this experience of being what you are not, not the One, you will more fully experience yourself as what you are, One. By some twist of reality, One can more fully Be itself as the One, by experiencing itself as not the One.

That you are reading this book suggests you are on the path of return. You are moving toward Self-awareness and ultimately Oneness. This path is known as the evolutionary cycle as opposed to the one you were on for eons, which was the involutionary cycle, the path of descent into matter. Religion refers to the involutionary cycle as the Fall of Man. It was, however, a necessary experience, or it would not have happened, and with the experience gained, you now return to where you came from. The return path requires a complete transformation of yourself from an egoic doer to the trans-egoic Self. Fortunately, we have already been "wired" for the return path, so Mother Nature, or the Divine Mother, the creative principle within us, knows what to do and the transformation is carried out by the Kundalini fire within us. This internal fire cleanses our meridians, clears all the egoic data built up through many lives, and delivers us to the high estate to which we belong and from where we came. It is a much quicker path and begins at the first awakening at the base chakra. Correspondingly, the gradual clearing of data shows in our conscious experience through a five-fold cyclic process and is part of the mechanics of consciousness. You could say regular meditation encourages your part in this process. It would be more truthful to say that meditation happens to us when we are ready for it.

The Relative Field

In creation, everything has two polarities, positive and negative. It is because of this that we experience duality and ourselves as being separate from other people and other things. In the denser dimensions of a multi-dimensional reality, the negative polarity dominates the positive polarity and there is imbalance. This leads to a greater experience of separation. In the subtler dimensions, there is more polarity balance. The experience is therefore of greater wholeness or Oneness.

The experience of duality takes place in the relative field in which all experience is based on relativity. It is only possible to experience something relative to something else. Examples are light and dark, happy and sad, contraction and expansion, good, and evil, etc. These opposites are known as polarities. Each polarity, of course, requires the other for its existence. The positive exists because there is a negative, and the negative exists because there is a positive. They are comparative. In an evolutionary context, the two polarities represent either that which is more illusory and divisive or that which is more truthful and holistic.

Given that we live in a dense physical dimension, the

default dominant polarity is the negative. The challenge for us, therefore, is to reduce negative polarity dominance and enhance the positive polarity; to reduce illusion and increase truth, creating more balance. We realize that illusion leads to suffering; truth leads to peacefulness. So, by creating more balance, we can rise to more unified, truthful levels of awareness. This doesn't mean eliminating the negative to enhance the positive, as you can't have one without the other. The negative needs to be embraced and accepted for what it is at the same time as enhancing the positive.

Evolution is a movement towards the truth and Oneness. But remember, in the relative field of experience, for there to be truth, it must be relative to illusion and for there to be Oneness, it must be relative to diversity. Without opposites, there is no comparison, no subject, and no object, and therefore, no experience. These two polarities are found throughout creation, from the universe and galaxies, through to the smallest particles, as well as every other aspect of our experience; emotions, feelings, thoughts, the dense dimensions, the subtle dimensions, and all the vibrational frequencies which we can't perceive with our five senses.

When positive and negative are equal, there is balance. Balance leads to the next peak, and so the cycles continue. The foremost technique for enhancing balance is meditation. By default, the negative polarity is dominant in our experience, so balancing techniques usually involve enhancing the positive polarity. These include creating positive thoughts, positive emotions, positive affirmations, joyful songs, and mantras. To grow, we need to incorporate balance into all levels of our lives. For example, balance in the physical dimension is enhanced by eating healthy food with appropriate proportions of protein, carbohydrate, and fat which the body requires for optimal health. Exercise helps increase balance by keeping the body fit and by removing built up tension. Exercise also releases endorphins in the brain, making us feel good. Balance on the emotional level is gained by focusing on positive emotions, and balance in the mental dimension is gained by thinking positive thoughts to reduce the default negative thoughts. Since thought and emotion often work together, techniques which balance one will also balance the other. Feeling and belief, thought and emotion go together. It is also feeling or emotions that empower belief. Emotion, as the fuel, brings the intention or belief into manifestation. They always go together. Even at the highest level, as in spiritual mastery, there is still emotion, but at that level of awareness the emotion is more a celebration of the moment whose time has come, its magnificence, how profound and beautiful it is, how wonderful it is. It is celebration and joy in the present moment for what is.

As you increase your detachment, you can witness the two polarities, both positive and negative, without getting too caught up in either. It is increasing balance that leads to a witnessing consciousness from which one can watch the play of consciousness.

The Five-Fold Cycle

In order to evolve, we need to increase our experience of the positive polarity and bring about more balance. A move to increasing balance, and from dense to subtle dominance, takes place through a cyclic five-fold process of peak experience, evolution, illumination, processing and integration. As this process continues, and we move to greater balance, a gradual clearing takes place of our habits, conditioning, enculturation, etc.

Peak experience

Through meditation, balance increases. When there is balance, there is expansion in holistic awareness, known as peak experience. We may be aware of the peak experience or may not be aware of it.

Evolution

With each peak experience, we are more whole than we have ever been before; we are more whole and fulfilled. This ever-increasing wholeness is an evolution beyond what we have been before.

Illumination

Consequent to our evolution, we experience illumination as inspiration, insight and revelation.

Processing

For the new level of experience to substantiate itself, old out-of-date data needs to be replaced. This comes to the surface for processing and clearing. When old data is being processed, it may be experienced as thoughts arising, or as discomfort at the physical or emotional level. In an earlier lesson, much attention was given to the psychology of Self-awareness and the different stages of self. So, what needs to be cleared over time are the reactions, desires, and delusions we have formed within ourselves as a response to our enculturation from an early age. These were formed in our childhood as we attempted to make ourselves acceptable within the world. Processing can be seen to take place on all three of our physical levels: mental, emotional, and physical.

For example, on the mental level, we may experience unconscious, habitual, exaggerated, undirected thoughts, daydreams, dullness, or fogginess and "blanking out." On the emotional level, this may be experienced as moods, anger, fear, jealousy, sadness or exaggerated joy. On the physical level, there can be physical discomforts, specific aches and pains, sensations of heat and cold, involuntary movements, restlessness or reappearance of symptoms from old injuries.

Regardless of the symptoms of processing given, they should be acknowledged as proof that meditation is working and allowed to pass. They are an important part of the meditator's journey. If the symptoms are extreme, then contact should be made with someone who understands the process.

Integration

In addition to processing, the new level of experience gained through illumination also needs to be integrated or assimilated in terms of a greater awareness, and then the complete cycle begins again with the next peak experience.

The five-fold process works on many levels, from unconscious through to major experiences of awakening. Likewise, many cycles may happen at the same time.

Your external world is not separate from you. As unwanted data is removed, it doesn't just simply dissolve and go away. The data you have has been built up through complex psychological processes which have led to the psychological patterns that are now an intrinsic part of who you are in the world. Consequently, for this to be removed, it may require complex interactions between you and the world around to facilitate the removal. You will find events or happenings in your world which challenge you to view them from a more holistic perspective. Likewise, you will get caught up in these events and likely find it difficult and uncomfortable. However, it is through this process that the data is cleared. Eastern traditions will say this is your karma which you have to work out. You reap what you sow. The key to knowing this has happened is that once the process is complete, you will be more whole than you have ever been. You have cleared some baggage and can now travel lighter.

Thoughts and emotions work together, so when our mind gets caught up in its illusory negative thoughts, it is accompanied by illusory negative or fear-based emotions. So, when we shift negative thoughts, negative emotions will also shift from fear-based to love-based.

Egoic versus Trans-egoic Perspective

When you believe that everything happens in your life.... Good or bad, according to the will of God, you will always be satisfied.
Shirdi Sai Baba.

Throughout the involutionary cycle, a conscious awareness of self as the ego has taken place. Animals are instinctive and do not have an awareness of themselves in the same way that we do. They may have character but do not think, "I am separate from you," and act accordingly. Humans, however, develop the ability to see themselves as separate, unique individuals. Each individual ego sees itself as separate and responsible for everything it does. The egoic doer, however, is an illusion, whereas universal consciousness is the real doer. Universal consciousness has a holistic, unified perspective, but as part of increasing entrapment in the material world, it created a limited fear-based entity: the ego. Along with this limited perspective came all the actions and beliefs such a perspective creates and all the psychological issues that go with it. Let's look at the difference between an egoic level of awareness based in illusion, and a trans-egoic level of awareness based in truth.

The biggest issue an egoic perspective creates is lack of self-worth. You do not believe you are good enough, you are not whole and complete, there is always something more you need to be fulfilled, and so on. When you do something, you then judge how you have responded to what has happened. From birth, you have adjusted how you think, believe, and behave so that it can be acceptable in the world. With this, you are constantly being judged by others and likewise, you are critical or judging of them. Similarly, you see things as not being as they should be and you strive to make things better. Then, not feeling complete, you add to yourself belongings, ideas, beliefs, etc., and are constantly trying to make the world a better place to live in. But it never works, and it never works because it is an illusion.

However, the truth is you are complete. Everything is exactly as it should be, and the bottom line is, you are not actually running the show. It is exactly as it's meant to be, and everything is appropriate. This is the trans-egoic perspective. So, all the changes that happen to you on the evolutionary cycle, all the happenings, are all there to get you to change from the egoic perspective to the trans-egoic, from illusion to truth. This is the experience you are having, and it is necessary for your growth.

Your only responsibility in what is happening is to stay wakeful. The more wakeful you are, the more your perspective will be truthful. The driving force behind wakefulness is meditation. Whatever happens, who do you choose to be in relation to what is happening? When you think it should be other than it is, or you are other than you should be, then that is egoic illusion. If, however, you simply witness what is happening and say to yourself, this is all just the happening of consciousness, it is exactly as it is meant to be, then that is a trans-egoic level of awareness. An egoic awareness leads to self-worth issues as you judge how you have responded to what has happened. Taking a trans-egoic perspective provides an opportunity to allow things to be the way they are without judgment. This is a very healing perspective and allows the offloading of karma.

This doesn't mean you let things be and do nothing about them. Rather, you act responsibly according to the mechanics of consciousness, maintaining truth and not slipping into illusion. Do whatever is appropriate for the evolution of your consciousness without getting caught up in egoic stories about it. Keep to truthful stories and do whatever is needed to support and fully experience the experience that's happening. So, trust and watch as consciousness orchestrates the show. Be aware and inclusive of the mechanics of consciousness; peak, process, and integration.

Sometimes things seem to move more slowly than you would like them to. Consciousness may slow things down so you can integrate more. But from a trans-egoic perspective, it is all perfect. So, allow it to be the way it is and know that through the experience, you are growing and evolving. You are moving from dense to subtle, from negative dominance to subtle dominance. It is as it is, and it is all appropriate. Similarly, your vibration is increasing, and you are growing in the light. It is all about wakefulness, and every reminder you get is always about that. Your wakefulness is validated and acknowledged, or you are being told you need more.

An Everyday Life Example

For example, let's assume you take a special focus to enhance your loving awareness. So, you repeat affirmations; you try to view the surrounding environment from a loving perspective, you may even try to see the love coming back to you from everything around you. Because of this focus, you may feel blissful. This focus has focused your amplitude of power and delivered you to peak.

Perhaps things are not going well at work, though. A colleague or client who seems to make life very difficult challenges you. They disagree with your decisions and complain to your supervisor about what you have done, who then turns round to reprimand you for the action you took. As a result, you get caught up in this negativity and try to react or respond, blaming the other person and trying to justify what you did.

Try to look at this differently. Although it may seem totally unrelated to your loving focus, what has really happened is that in relation to the peak you created earlier, you have entered the processing phase of the cycle. From your unconscious, the data that is incongruent to your loving focus surfaces and is projected onto the world around and the current situation you find yourself in. Therefore, the question is, can you maintain your loving focus, or do you get identified with illusion projected onto the world around you? If you can't stay focused on the loving essence of all and everything, particularly when it is challenging, then you will project your stories, your commentaries, onto the situation. As a result, your illusory experience is then stressful, difficult, and depressing.

So, really, a more loving focus has produced the necessary experience to challenge this, pointing out what is interfering with your ability to maintain a truthful, loving focus. It has been brought to your awareness so you can learn to dis-identify from it. Consequently, by accepting this, dis-identifying from your illusions, you become clearer and have grown proportionally.

The mechanics of consciousness here, is that it is taking you to peak, and then the incongruent data related to that peak arises. Then you move through the data so that the integrative aspect of the peak is restored. When bliss returns, it is then greater than before.

Another aspect to this is that in the situation given, the peak experience that was created related to the heart field. It was a love focus. It created a nice expansion of the heart field. And yet the data that came up related to the mind or mental dimension. In reality, what happens is the mind field interferes with the heart field. The heart field is the gateway to true reality, but mind field gets in the way: the mind field with all its data, illusions and stories that it tells about what is happening. So, the sequence is, peak experience opens the heart, followed by the data which moves you back into the mind field until the data is sorted out and then integration happens in the heart field.

The reason you cannot experience the truth of reality is illusion or illusory data. Getting identified with illusory data leads to a miserable, limiting experience and illusory separation. In reality, it is the experience of illusory separation that leads to issues of self-worth, self-negation, and inability to love oneself. Look at the experience you have when you get identified with the illusory data and say to yourself, who would I be without this data? Know the data for what it is, dis-identify from it and remain a witness. When you can experience yourself without your stories, you can experience yourself as you truly are. Remember, all your data got programmed into you during the involutionary cycle. It was a necessary part of your experience. In the evolutionary cycle, it is time to dismantle the data, as it is no longer congruent with who you are. After all, you gained a valuable experience in who you are not during the involutionary cycle, so now you can more fully experience who you are during the evolutionary cycle. It is, and has always been, perfect. It's a beautiful process. It's just illusion that sees it otherwise.

Life happens, consciousness happens. So, who are you choosing to be in relation to it? If you are going to have stories about what is, then try to keep them truthful in relation to the happening of consciousness. Can you love everything just the way it is? Not as your stories tell you it should be. Everything is appropriate, so stop telling yourself it should be other than it is. For example, why is your client the way he is? Why is your boss the way he is? Why is this person the way she is? Why is this situation the way it is? It is as it is because that's the way it is!

It's easier to love plants and animals because they don't talk back to you. But with people, you project your own data onto them and what you get back is harder to deal with. So, say, hey, bring up my data, confront me with my data, let me see it for what it is, and let me dismantle it.

The more awareness you have, the more it can be focused. Practicing focused awareness becomes easier. So, if you don't have enough awareness and that awareness is not focused, consciousness will always wander to the default dominant negative, illusory polarity. Only focused awareness can interrupt or reverse the wandering mind out of illusion and into truth.

All meditation techniques are based on focused awareness to take you out of the default, habitual regurgitation of unconscious data to a more balanced, expanded, truthful perspective of reality.

Because belief and emotion are intricately combined, when your mind wanders into illusory, negative thoughts it is combined with illusory, negative emotions. Negative emotions are essentially fear-based rather than love-based. So, when focused awareness shifts thoughts from the default negative polarity, it also shifts emotions from fear-based to love-based.

An egoic perspective gets identified with what is happening. It tells many stories based on separatist, illusory data. A trans-egoic perspective, on the other hand, is a witness consciousness watching what happens and not getting identified with it. Another name for this is unified witness consciousness. It doesn't mean you do nothing, though, it's not an escape. Rather, it's watching what happens and then responding accordingly. It is the happening of consciousness at that moment and is exactly as it should be. It is your stories about it that say it should be other than it is. Regardless of whether it is a person's behavior, an illness, an accident, your favorite sports team winning or losing and so on, it is the happening of consciousness. Are you going to flavor the experience with all your stories? Such as, she doesn't care about me. He was so inconsiderate of his staff. It's painful, it's horrible, they should have won, they were cheated; the referee was biased. I should have been more careful. I didn't deserve that. Regardless, just be with the experience that's happening, enjoy watching players perform at their best, take suitable medication for your illness, accept that the other person behaved the way they did because that's what they did, and so on. Don't create misery for yourself because of your illusory stories. Why invest your ability to be happy or sad based on your team's performance in a game? So, the key is, flow with it, allow it to happen just the way it is, resolve it, and not invest in stories that make you miserable. The trans-egoic perspective is that whatever is happening is the way it is and whose time has come. Whatever is happening is the same consciousness that I am. The watcher and the watched are the same one consciousness, and a witnessing consciousness watches both with equanimity.

What does your consciousness want out of the experiences you have? Do you really know what's happening? What does your consciousness really care about? In reality, what it really cares about is that you are presented with all these experiences as a means of greater evolution. Look at all your experiences like that and use them as opportunities for evolutionary growth and a means of greater awareness.

Breath focus always works well to bring the heart field into coherence and maintain that coherence. A coherent heart field is in a state of relative balance and when this is maintained, it is more able to link with the crown field. Coherent fields can interact with each other, and when the heart field and crown field, individual consciousness, and universal consciousness interact, the crown field can download expansive subtle awareness and witness consciousness into the heart field. Conversely, the mind field is an incoherent field and usually blocks access to the heart field. That is why all meditation practices begin with focusing on the mind. With breath focus and a consistent balance of the mind field, it is possible to remain focused in the heart field.

When you face difficulties and you approach them with more of a detached, witness consciousness, then you can complete whatever it is and dissolve the limitation associated with it. As a result, your awareness expands proportionally.

Finally, if you have an object of your devotion, whether it is a divine personage, an archetype, a guru, or some form of Master, then the more you evolve the less contrast there is between you and the object that represents a unified state of being for you.

Chapter 7

Meditation Pointers

Beginning Meditation

Meditation is foremost a balancing technique. Through balance, we become more whole or unified, which leads to a holistic experience of reality. Beginning meditation practices work on the mind field, as this is the dominant focus for beginners. Focusing techniques or exercises are used to rein in the mind "I cannot meditate because I can't stop my thoughts," is a common reason given for not meditating. However, even advanced meditators think at the start of meditation. You can't just stop the thoughts at will, it takes practice to reduce thoughts and detach yourself from them. Until the hold of thoughts is reduced, it is not possible to gain the balance required before the next level of meditation is achieved.

It is important to consider the environment for your meditation, such as where meditation will take place, where to sit or lie down, posture, use of incense or other aromas, quietness, or the use of meditation soundtracks, to name a few. Once a suitable environment is created, next come techniques to focus the mind. The traditional method is to focus on your breath, a candle, the third eye between and just above your eyebrows, music, affirmations, mantras, or a guided meditation.

You will find you have favorite focusing techniques you use most of the time. Occasionally, it is good to alternate focusing techniques so that they become less repetitive. The more "newness" in the moment a technique has, the more productive it is. A habitual pattern is less productive. You are more present, more in the Now, when you use a new technique. A habitual technique leaves more room for repetitive thoughts to enter. Therefore, the key is to be as much in the Now as possible.

It also helps to keep a regular pattern of timing and ritual to meditation, as this creates a structure or pattern which the unconscious understands. So, when you sit to meditate, the subconscious knows it is time for meditation and can easily settle into it. Your consciousness evolves most efficiently when your pattern of meditation is regular.

If you choose to get up and meditate during the night, then first ensure you have had at least 4 hours sleep to take away sufficient tiredness and then, because your biorhythms say that it is sleep time, sit for the whole meditation hour. Likewise, if you feel discomfort because of the processing part of the meditation cycle, then rather than lying down for the second half, which you might do during the day, get up, move around, shake it out, and sit again.

Focusing techniques enable you to maintain a single point of focus. For example, if you focus intently on your breathing, it is more difficult for unwanted thoughts to interfere. Focus, therefore, increases balance, so using a breath focus, for example, increases the positive polarity.

Starting with breath focus, it takes a while to reverse dominance from negative to positive. As it does so, it increases witness consciousness, allowing you to witness the mind and observe whether it is thinking or still.

By default, thoughts are fragmented, meaning they are based on perceiving a world of exterior objects separate from oneself. They are negative as opposed to holistic thoughts, which are positive. To create balance, therefore, negative thoughts need to be replaced by positive ones. A good way to do this is to repeat positive affirmations to yourself.

Thoughts are usually based on the past or the future. Thoughts which take you out of the present moment are also considered negative. The negative polarity of thoughts is always the default dominant and leads to imbalance and a state of disharmony. Rarely, unless you maintain focus on a current activity, are thoughts based in the present moment. But even then, when the activity is repetitive, the mind is usually thinking about something else, maybe something you did before or something you are hoping or planning to do in the future. Focusing thoughts on the here and now moment increases the positive polarity. Thoughts can go over and over the same problem or issue, such as things should be different or better than they are. In sharing such thoughts with others, it can lead to gossip.

As you become more balanced in meditation, your thoughts slow down and you find yourself increasingly witness to them, your awareness becomes more subtle, and you find it easier to move into stillness. This is the purpose of meditation techniques.

When you maintain a focus, such as the breath focus, the balance created pushes your consciousness to a tolerable peak. When you are at peak, your frequency of vibration, and your amplitude of power, are the highest they have ever been. Balance allows a holistic expansion of awareness, known as witness consciousness, to increase. This is a detached observation of your presence. As you watch with witness consciousness, stillness increases, time seems to move faster, and you shift to a more subtle dimensional focus. Continued practice increases the time of stillness until stillness in duration results. This is stillness relative to the noise of an active mind.

Clearing and balancing the mind field leads to stillness in duration and a gradual opening of the heart field and a more subtle dimensional focus. When you are in the heart as opposed to the mind, you are more self-aware, more present, more wakeful, and more whole. You are more in the Now. A dense dimensional focus is characterized by linear time and space, while the awareness of Now characterizes a subtle dimensional presence.

During the day, you may look and see the surrounding objects, yet you know that these are all forms of consciousness. So, you, as consciousness, are aware of all the other forms of consciousness around you. In this situation, you are the positive polarity of consciousness and all the objects around are the negative polarity.

Experienced Meditators

It is advisable for beginning meditators to sit upright. If you are sitting on a chair, it helps to sit without leaning on the back support. Sitting towards the forward edge of the seat can help to keep your back straight. Maintaining a straight back helps to keep you more present and wakeful. As you become more advanced in meditation, the various channels and meridians in your subtle body have been well actualized and cleared, then sitting posture is of less importance as you are more able to go beyond the body, relax it, and move more subtle quickly. The entire purpose of maintaining a straight back is to assist the Kundalini energy to rise upwards. Eventually, this will happen quickly, so posture is of less significance.

As your meditation deepens, your awareness develops further into unified witness consciousness, an even more subtle level of consciousness in which you are watching what's happening from the perspective of consciousness watching consciousness, and an increased awareness that all is one. This then moves even more subtle into absence, which is positive polarity dominant. As the word implies, you are only aware of absence before and afterwards, but not during it. Often you realize your meditation seems to have passed quickly. That's because you were not present for much of it. Presence and absence are opposite polarities to each other. Presence, as in the waking state, is the negative polarity and absence is the positive polarity. Similarly, the positive polarity is unified and subtle, while the negative polarity is diversified and denser. Absence, as the term implies, means you are not present to what is happening. It is like you are asleep, but is an important part of meditation. Just because you're not present to what is happening does not mean you have fallen asleep. It is a subtle, unified state of awareness which you can't cognize with your mind. Absence is stillness, silence, emptiness, and nothingness in duration.

The best approach to meditation is to be a witness to whatever is happening and flow with it. Rather than trying to change what's happening, be more accepting of it. As you increase subtle dimensional dominance in meditation, the more you will find yourself at peak. Then you will find yourself drawn into absence, which shows positive polarity dominance.

As you become more advanced in meditation, you may notice little change, even though you are becoming increasingly subtle with increasing Self-awareness. You find that the peaks you have in your meditations are continually pushing the evolution of your consciousness more and more subtle. The typical parameters for an advanced meditator are a quicker access to witness consciousness, a quicker ascent from dense dimensional dominance to subtle dimensional dominance and by the end of the meditation, in the transition, noticeably more opiation or bliss and, a greater holistic saturation within your consciousness. The word bliss refers to everything from baseline contentment through to radical, opiated, intoxicating bliss, the innate joy of consciousness. Whatever your state of being and current level of awareness, this is your baseline. Whenever you use your focused awareness in meditation, your baseline is magnified and expanded, as is your wakefulness and bliss. This corresponds to peak experience.

The more awareness you have, the more you can focus that awareness to control the mind from wandering to its default illusory data and direct it to truth. From an egoic doer perspective, by doing more focused awareness techniques, you can increase your Self-awareness. Yet, from a non-egoic doer perspective, your increased amplitude of power and thus increased Self-awareness leads to more presence and focused awareness.

Peak is the cutting edge of your evolving consciousness. This new frequency of vibration affects your whole multidimensional being, resulting in everything within your database that is incongruent with the new frequency to surface in order to be released. This is clearing and can be uncomfortable as your database is being re-scripted. With this in mind, if you are inconsistent with your meditation practice, then you are more likely to have processing. Regular meditation helps to build the integrative cycle with peak and process happening at the same time. Should you feel discomfort because of your meditation, then it is good to exercise as this helps to move the energy through.

World Realization or Self-Realization

Let's look at self-esteem. Most people have low self-esteem. This is because your self-worth and its associated data lead you to negate yourself. Consequently, you don't feel you are good enough and it holds you back. This relates to the most primal of your data. It stems right back to the beginning of your journey into form. It results from a contraction in consciousness, from a subtle state of awareness to the limited, dense, fragmented awareness that you are now in. It is this contraction in awareness that led to the formation of your ego. However, your ego had a purpose. It has given you an experience of what, in truth, you are not. As a result, self-worth got lost in the process. You forgot your original holistic awareness of being One to becoming a small, separate, insignificant self. Identified with ego, the story you tell yourself is that things should be other than they are, and you should be other than you are. You compare yourself with others and rarely like what you see. Think of it as a circle. The journey into form was the first part of the circle beginning at the top. We know it as the involutionary cycle, the descent into dense material form. A point comes at the bottom of the circle when this has achieved its purpose and you have fully experienced the material world.

It may have been satisfying for a while, but compared with your true inner nature, it is an illusion.

Eventually, an awakening takes place, and the path of return begins. You are now on the post-awakening path, the evolutionary cycle. All the limiting, negative, false data must now be unpacked and replaced with the truth of who you really are. You needed all this to get you where you are now. You have fully experienced what you are not and now it's time to experience what you are with the benefit of the incredible lessons you have learned. Because of being in the realm of duality, you now have experience, which will provide a comparison. As a result, you can more fully appreciate and delight in the gradual unfolding of who you really are, having fully experienced what you are not in the realm of illusion, or maya. Honor your experience for what it is, have a broader perspective of it, understand it, and allow it to be.

React, fight, win and you may rise to greater heights in the world. There may be promotion, recognition, dominance, more egocentric power, and greater world realization is achieved. However, the question is, do you want world realization or Self-realization? Are you on the involutionary cycle or the evolutionary cycle? Step aside and observe with your increased Self-awareness or wakefulness. Respond appropriately and don't react. Accept all challenges as being placed there for you to grow in Self-awareness and the resultant expansion in your Self-awareness will be far greater than anything the world can offer.

Re-scripting the Ego

You often hear it said that you are destroying the ego, getting rid of it, and when you are fully Self-realized, you will have no ego. That's an oversimplification, though, you never totally get rid of the ego. It is based on your database and contains all your recorded experience to date. Overall, most of the data you have in your database is illusory because the ego is all about separation and an illusory duality that doesn't exist. However, as you progress on the evolutionary cycle, you gradually dis-identify from all your illusory data so that you are no longer unconsciously bound to it. So, instead of habitually acting out your data, you become a conscious creator of your reality, re-scripting your data to that which is more truthful. You are rewriting your data and replacing it with truthful data. You are no longer a writer of fiction; you are a writer of non-fiction. Through meditation, you gradually return to an experiential truth of who you really are, a truth that there is only one. Your egocentric level of data gets replaced with a trans-egocentric level of data. The trans-egocentric data is truthful data, such as "I am blissful consciousness," "all is one," "there is only one."

Egoic Doer or Trans-egoic Doer

From an egoic doer perspective, you may think that by doing all your focused awareness techniques, you have increased your Self-awareness to reach this point in your evolution. From a non-egoic doer perspective, it is your increased amplitude of power that has increased your Self-awareness; it is this that has led to more presence and ability for focused awareness. So, did you, as someone separate from consciousness, decide what to do? Was it you as separate from consciousness that did something? No, you, as separate from consciousness, don't exist. It is consciousness that has brought you to where you are now, and consciousness that moves the Kundalini within you. The Kundalini fire moving within you is moving through your chakras, clearing your meridians, dissolving patterns and issues, and transforming you from within. Meditation is an experience whose time has come. It is a certain level of awareness that we call meditation. When you have an evolved consciousness, you are naturally a meditator. Correspondingly, along with that level of evolution, there is also a level of Kundalini activity. The entire show is being orchestrated by consciousness. Maybe you had an awakening experience, perhaps not. Perhaps the Kundalini within you was triggered by a guru. Perhaps not. Regardless of what brought you to where you are, be grateful and celebrate. It is the experience whose time has come. Your judgments about what you have or haven't done to be where you are now are futile. The fact is, as my teacher used to say, "you couldn't be more on schedule if you tried."

An Experience of Wakeful Emptiness

As an advanced meditator continuing your journey, you notice meditation to be more noumenal, empty, nothingness. Similarly, you notice more wakeful stillness or wakeful nothingness sustained in duration. It is a very non-phenomenal experience, dominantly empty, almost absent, yet with some awareness within it. Rather than absence, though, you are still wakeful with it. The following is an example of how it can appear in meditation.

"As I sat there, I felt I was separate from everything, including other people in the room. In fact, I could see in my mind's eye the person sitting in front of me who was also facing the front, and they were translucent. It was as if the person was there, but almost not there. I felt alone. If I wanted to cry, I couldn't. There was no emotion. I felt separate from these too. It was like I had been totally emptied out and was very detached, ready to be filled anew with love, light, and joy."

This was a most profound meditation experience known as wakeful emptiness or wakeful nothingness. It is a very subtle dominant, unified state of consciousness, so subtle, it's beyond the mind's ability to cognize it. Consequently, there is no feeling or emotion associated with it. And yet you are wakeful to the experience. The fullness of this experience is wakeful emptiness, yet full of love, light, and joy. Love, light and joy are the very vibration of the soul at the center of your heart field. This is a much more subtle perception of reality. Within it, empty consciousness and empty nothingness are experienced as translucence. Likewise, it is a detached, unified state of witness consciousness, an experience that there is no other. It shows positive polarity dominance, being over becoming. It's like a witnessing consciousness dominantly watching emptiness and nothingness. The Gnostics referred to it as the closest one could get to the ultimate mystery.

The Divine Feminine

Universal consciousness is often represented as the Blessed Mother or Divine Mother. The divine feminine archetype represents the unified level of consciousness in your experience. In many traditions, she is worshipped as a deity and the form she is given varies according to the tradition or culture.

Once you have tasted unification with Source or love, it will haunt you from then on. The data of separation and longing will keep surfacing to be cleared. The illusion of separation causes this. With the data of separation that we carry, this longing will look for the Beloved in others. But we will not find the Beloved in others we can only find it within. One's own universal consciousness is the Beloved. Ultimately, you and she will merge in a divine marriage or union.

The Five-Fold Cycle

Every time you meditate and through balance and stillness bring yourself to peak, you go through the same process of peak and process, and through this, you are gradually evolving your consciousness to be more than it has ever been. However, having discomfort in meditation is not pleasant. You would obviously prefer meditation to always be blissful, but for meditation to be ever more blissful, all the baggage, all the unwanted data, must be cleared, and that's a long process. When advanced in meditation, a single sitting of meditation can include several cycles of the five-fold cycle. The full cycle is peak experience, evolution, illumination, processing, and integration. In short, it is peak to process and integration. Clearing is related to processing and is the removal of unwanted data. Deep meditation really pushes the peak. It has its benefits and its discomforts. It exacerbates the tolerable peak and elicits more of a depth clearing. So, don't expect all your meditations to be the same. Some days peak will come easily while other days because you're processing, balance and stillness required for peak will be more difficult to achieve. Likewise, where you are in the five-fold cycle has a significant impact on your meditation.

You won't experience many phenomena in meditation, though. It is during the day that the results will show. Observe your experience during the day and during your waking hours. This is where the real growth is noticed, as regular meditation practice will increase your wakefulness and your power of presence.

Constantly Moving Kundalini

The Kundalini is awakened when your evolving consciousness has reached an appropriate point. When this happens, you move from the involutionary cycle to the evolutionary cycle. Eventually, on the evolutionary cycle, meditation becomes a way of life which is appropriate for your evolving awareness. You feel the need to meditate because you feel the need to be more truthful about who you really are. Meditation is not just your sitting practice; it is a state of being who you really are.

When the Kundalini gets activated, she can be a wild crazy energy causing big oscillations between the peaks and troughs of the five-fold cycle. Discomfort, processing, and clearing result from this Kundalini activity, and this can lead to a lot of upheaval. The Kundalini is the transformative energy within and moves upward from the base center towards the crown and transforms you as it does so. The Kundalini is constantly moving between chakras and through your energy meridians.

Lights, which may be seen in meditation, particularly near

the start, can indicate where the Kundalini is now. It may just be a pin prick flash of light, but its color shows which chakra the Kundalini has just moved to and is a message from the unconscious showing this to you. For example, the Kundalini might be in the crown or the gonads, the heart or the third eye, and so on. As it moves, it continues to dilate the meridian system; it does this by clearing the data in them, which restricts that dilation. Correspondingly, this can also lead to many symptoms or sensations in the body. Finally, when all the meridians have been totally cleared, the Kundalini has an uninterrupted flow throughout the meridians and chakras, and one experiences a unified state of being. So, in meditation, when you start to feel discomfort after a while, it is usually because the Kundalini energy in your meridians has reached a point requiring clearing and the resultant processing takes place.

The Kundalini slowly actualizes the subtle dimensions and increases its amplitude of power. Even during the day, as an advanced meditator, prolonged focus can also activate the Kundalini. For example, you may be attending a seminar or driving a car. When focus is steady, you can feel the blissful energy and a mild intoxication. You can also feel a little thirsty as the Kundalini energy creates a little friction and heat to which the body responds by using up water in your system. The purpose of Kundalini movements or kriyas are because of meridians being cleared. However, a regular, advanced meditator is less likely to have this happen as the frequent peak and process of meditation clears meridians appropriately.

Lights in Meditation

When you see lights in meditation, it shows the third eye has been actualized and can witness what is happening. Color is a vibrational frequency, so the color is a barometer on which chakra your consciousness is focused on at the time. It can be one or more chakras simultaneously. Usually, the lights appear and disappear quickly, and because they are subtle phenomena, any focusing on them will cause them to disappear. For example, when you see a flash or flashes of blue light in meditation, it shows the Kundalini connecting with the subtle dimensions from the third eye to the crown.

The Kundalini oscillates backwards and forwards to deliver more. This is experienced as peak and then it backs off a little for processing and integration. If a color is seen, it is correspondent to where the Kundalini is at the time. The third eye is an indigo blue which is between blue and purple. The crown is violet. A blue with a lot of red in it may represent inclusion of the red of the base chakra. This is because the base chakra is the seat of the Kundalini and from which the crown center is actualizing. Therefore, they are experienced in combination. That several chakras can connect at once makes color interpretation difficult. When I refer to blue, I am referring to blue colors to avoid confusing the many variations.

Before you consistently see blue or violet, you are likely to see black. Black represents the causal level and is halfway between the third eye and the crown. As the causal level actualizes, it is seen as a black light. At first, this is tiny and then it enlarges and takes form.

The Blue Pearl and the blue light are synonymous. When seen in meditation, blue light represents peak experience. Lights don't always appear, though, even when you have reached the point of seeing them regularly. If not seen for a day or so, it is because of clearing or processing taking place. Occasionally, saffron orange is seen and is the aura of the Blue Pearl. This is like the orange seen at sunset and is also the color worn by many monks in India to represent this aura.

The heart is usually seen as green, and the solar plexus is seen as yellow. However, these can change places on the evolutionary cycle. Here the heart is green when there is processing, otherwise the heart is yellow, a pinkish yellow. The solar plexus also shifts between yellow and green. To determine if the yellow and green are heart or solar plexus, you need to look at your current experience and determine based on that. If you are extremely peaked and processing and you see a lot of yellow, it is more likely to be solar plexus and its corresponding issues of self-worth. If it is a benign integrative peak and you are seeing yellow, it is more representative of the evolutionary heart field. These are the predominant colors seen, but others are possible. Seeing pink, for example, is related to the heart chakra and results from the interaction between crown and heart. Mauve represents the throat chakra and primary orange represents the sacral chakra.

Muktananda often talked of four lights that were significant to him and represented the four bodies of the individual soul. Red represents the gross body, white the subtle body, black the causal body and blue the supra-causal body. What you see is highly individual and a reflection of your own progress.

B.S. Goel also saw a red aura within which he saw many of his visions. Likewise, there were other colors that he saw, including blue and white. These represented the five elements of fire, earth, air, water and akasha and the associated colors are crimson red, yellow, green, white, and blue.

Other ways the colors can show themselves are in your visions and your dreams. For example, if you see a black mandala, it is likely to represent a connection with the causal level. Likewise, if you dream of a yellow car, it could represent a balanced heart chakra on your current journey.

Phenomena

Meditators want more phenomena in meditation to show there is something happening. However, little changes in meditation. The more noumenal the meditation is, the fewer phenomena the meditation has. The ultimate meditative experience is wakeful nothingness where you are a witnessing consciousness watching nothing, watching emptiness. Your consciousness, however, will occasionally give you some phenomena as a reward for your progress. For example, you might see patterns, shapes, and mandalas, hear voices, smell lavender, or some other experience. It is not a regular occurrence but is a kind of encouragement to keep going, a reminder of the truth of what's happening. The visuals and patterns you see may or may not have meaning to you, it is not important other than that's the state you are in. Just delight in the experience. Your proper goal, however, rather than looking for phenomena in meditation, is through your practice to observe a greater amplitude of power, wakefulness, and greater bliss in your daily life.

Somewhere in your meditation, maybe once a month, for example, there will be a peak experience of a more phenomenal kind that stands out, validating the truth of what's happening from unified levels of consciousness.

The Blue Pearl

At first, the Blue Pearl shows up as a blue light (flashes) or diffused blue light, then progressively it takes shape with the form of a tiny circle. This is a gradual progression of the supra-causal represented by the crown. Later, the Blue Pearl will be more violet, as this is the true color of the supra-causal level, the crown. The bluish light, or bluish hue, expands over time and is seen in the waking state. Then everything you see will have a vivid bluish or violet tint. All your vision is bathed in the lucidity of subtle dimensional dominant consciousness. The more this increases, the more you feel one with it, the more bliss you feel and the more peace there is. You recognize it for what it is, the substratum of all and everything, as one vibrating, scintillating, sparkling consciousness.

The Blue Pearl may be seen as a progression forming within the black of the causal level. Once you are established at the causal level, you will gradually see the Blue Pearl appear within the black, as if you are seeing through the causal level to the crown. When you get to see the Sourcepoint, or Blue Pearl, it is an iridescent blue. Surrounding the Sourcepoint is an orange or saffron glow, a kind of aura around the Sourcepoint. These colors denote the relative polarities. The iridescent blue represents universal consciousness, the subtle dimensions, and the positive polarity. The saffron orange represents individuated consciousness, the denser dimensions, and the negative polarity.

The Guru Principle

In the Tantric tradition, there are two primary principles. The first is the Kundalini principle, the second is the guru principle. The tantric system acknowledges a connection between the guru and Kundalini energy. The Tantric system is really a form of Kundalini yoga. However, Kundalini awakening is going to happen at some point, regardless of whether a guru is involved. In the Tantric tradition, it is said that the guru will appear, to assist, but the individual is at choice to accept a guru disciple relationship.

The mark of a true guru is in the guru's ability to modulate the effects of an awakened Kundalini. With the help of an authentic guru, the oscillations between peak and process reduce. This eventually leads to an integrative peak in which peak and process happen at the same time. Even with the help of a guru, it takes time to experience integrative peaks in meditation. So, an ongoing integrative peak in meditation shows an advanced meditator's profile and is validation of the guru disciple relationship if you are in one.

If you have the help of a guru, you may not be aware of this process happening just as the guru may not be consciously focused on the process happening to you. It is an energetic experience that comes about through the guru's very subtle energetic field. In other words, it is entrainment, rather like the well-known magnet and iron filings experiment in physics. As it is a very subtle energetic field, it can operate regardless of physical distance. The guru disciple relationship is the physical form correspondence of the subtle connection between universal consciousness and individual consciousness or crown to heart. They continue to oscillate until one day they merge into one.

Processing and Clearing

In processing, the result of an increased amplitude of power, caused by the peak, ripples through your database with its higher frequency. Any data in your database that is incongruent with the new frequency must surface to be cleared. This can cause discomfort or an overactive mind. When the mind is overactive, thoughts are prolific. Your only responsibility when this happens is to accept that this is processing and be aware that these thoughts are also forms of consciousness. Try not to get caught up in them. You may feel you have to sort out whatever the issue is and to solve whatever problem has surfaced. But that is not the case. Your judgments are unnecessary, as it is being worked through by the Kundalini. Stay with it and observe it as your consciousness wants you to be more present to it. Consciousness will keep you more present to it anyway, so that it can process. Consequently, processing is a good thing. It shows that you are evolving. There is always more to evolution, so there will always be more processing within your multi-dimensional consciousness. It may become more subtle, but it will always be there. But remember, at the end of each cycle, you are always more than you have ever been.

While you are clearing, you are less balanced, less blissful, more present than absent. Being wakeful to the clearing that is happening facilitates the clearing. After clearing, integration takes place as you adapt to the new level of you that you are. Clearing is most effective when you are present to it. When you are processing, it makes you a little more present, but your consciousness contracts a little and you feel less opiated. If you have a choice between sitting up with the discomfort or lying down and probably going absent, sitting would be preferable, as you have more Self-awareness of what is going on. Intermediate or advanced meditators can sit for longer periods than beginners, but everyone is unique in how they handle their energy. So, remember, if the clearing gets too much, then either get up and exercise, walk around, move, or end the meditation. Occasional day-to-day thoughts in meditation are of little significance as far as clearing is concerned.

As an advanced meditator, you may feel, particularly in transition, both bliss and discomfort at the same time. The bliss is nice; the discomfort is not. However, it shows the entire process is working. Over time, the processing, or clearing, becomes more subtle, but it is always there until you have cleared it all. As you become more subtle in awareness so your processing also becomes more subtle.

Another thing a meditator often finds is that anything that requires extra focus during the day can cause the brain to bring up a similar pattern to meditation, as the brain identifies focus with meditation. The brain switches to a meditative EEG, which is balancing but can also cause the Kundalini to move up. Therefore, a little care helps when focusing on anything, whether it be watching television or using a computer, etc., as the meditative EEG opens your database, the subconscious and unconscious, so the content you are focused on goes straight into your database, programming it. So be wakeful about what you watch and focus on.

In many books, you will read about an individual's journey to Self-awareness and the final stages often seem to be extremely difficult, with intense depth processing. But remember, this process is leading towards the end of the ego, so for some people, this experience is much like dying. But this is not always the case, for many it may hardly be noticeable.

The reality is that it's a mixture of these two extremes. It is a shift from egoic consciousness to trans-egoic consciousness or dominant illusion to dominant truth. It is a gradual process with oscillation between the two. Eventually, the ego yields to the truth. The continued oscillation back and forth is because there is a huge amount of egoic experience with associated data and habit that needs to be cleared.

Absence in Meditation

Absence is when you appear to go to sleep in meditation and is often mistaken for sleep; one minute you are sitting meditating and the next thing you realize that much time has passed. In effect, you have had periods of absence without knowing it. Likewise, it is possible to have dreams in this state. What differentiates this from normal sleep is that you have gone absent because of your meditation, and your brain EEG shows this. You are at peak, and when you come out of absence, you can feel blissful. Conversely, because peak leads to process, you may feel discomfort after your absence. When you go absent in meditation, you find that there is both presence and absence. It is a subtle dimensionally dominant experience in which both polarities are oscillating so fast that your brain can't distinguish the difference between the two. The brain then assumes that the dominant of the two polarities is the only one that is happening. However, in relative reality, you can't have one without the other. You can't have presence without absence, and you can't have absence without presence. In absence, it is the positive polarity of the absence/presence duality which is dominant. You move from presence to the Sahaja state and then quickly on to the Nirvikalpa state where it appears there is no presence; it is nothingness in duration.

Going into absence will take the emphasis off the denser dimensions of physical, emotional, and mental, but in other ways, it may exacerbate them. So, if there is strong processing and it is uncomfortable, it is better to get up and exercise, to move the energy through. Absence in meditation corresponds to peak experience. This results because when you reach a peak in meditation, you have maximized your level of amplitude of power. What then happens, rather than frying you with this increased level of power, consciousness places you in absence, which reduces the amplitude of power so that it can maintain a tolerable peak. Maintaining a tolerable peak, with peak and process happening at the same time, is an integrative peak. Even though it may not seem that much shifting is going on, there may be a lot of shifting taking place on the subtlest levels of your consciousness. Correspondingly, absence is used to sustain the integrative peak in duration. It is an efficient way of evolving your consciousness.

Heart Centered

People often talk about being in the heart. So, what exactly does this mean? Being in the heart refers to the heart field, which is centered on the heart chakra. The heart field is the center of your individual consciousness and when the mind field is out of the way and the heart field is balanced in duration, it connects with universal consciousness in the crown. Then you have an interaction between your individual consciousness and universal consciousness, or the dense dimensions of your being and the subtle dimensions. This interaction gradually leads to wakefulness. It is the gateway to the universal and true reality in the eternal now of its happening. Along with this comes downloading of a greater amplitude of power and you become more whole. As the greater amplitude of power and energy downloads into the heart field, the meridians surrounding it dilate and open more. Remember, as the Kundalini is working in the crown, it is also working in the heart because the two chakras are intimately connected and coherent. It is this dilation that results in data being relinquished and cleared. Universal consciousness is the "all possibility" of consciousness and the "all possibility" of experience. When you interact with it through the heart field, you interact with it self-referentially based on the current evolution of your individual consciousness and download the possibility that becomes your experience in this moment. The actualization of that connection, or the interaction between the two, leads to wakefulness in the Now, the eternal Now. The heart field is, therefore, the gateway to the universal and true reality in the eternal now of its happening. When the energy of the throat chakra comes into this interaction as well, it allows the expression of it.

The more balanced and coherent your heart field, the more able you will be to notice these downloads. This may include signs, visions, voices, et cetera. The third eye enables you to perceive or witness the interaction between universal consciousness and individual consciousness. It is your awareness of what is happening.

It's easy to say you must balance your heart to gain access to the crown, the heart being the gateway to the crown. However, to balance and actualize the heart, the mind must be balanced and settled before this is possible. That is why all the great meditation teachers teach you to work on the mind, to balance and settle it, in order to gain access to the heart. Breath focus opens the gateway to the heart field, while duration in the heart field creates a coherent heart field which then links with the crown. Interaction between the heart and crown, individual and universal, progressively substantiates a universal or subtle awareness and this leads to a greater amplitude of power.

Energies in the heart can feel pleasant, unpleasant, or a mixture of the two. This is because of the oscillating polarities between fear and love. Ultimately, there are four quadrants to balance, horizontal balance as in positive and negative polarities, and vertical balance as in individual and universal polarities. When there is balance in the horizontal, maintained in duration, then the vertical polarities are actualized as in individual and universal or dense and subtle through the heart chakra. This leads to the experience of Now. Your innate essence is joyful energy, joyful essence, and bliss. When the amplitude of power increases in your denser dimensions, your biochemistry is affected. Your hormones and neurochemicals produce more opiate, which makes you feel more opiated or blissful.

When the heart is connected with the crown and meridians are being cleared, it can be felt as edginess, nervousness, or anxiety. This shows the peak is being pushed and resultant clearing is taking place. Correspondent with actualization of the crown is an associated actualization of the pineal gland. This can sometimes be felt as a sensation at the back of the pallet and progressively increases. As it does so, more neurochemical opiates are secreted, predominantly DMT. Some of the secretion will trip through the back of the pallet as a kind of nectar which in Sanskrit is called Amrit.

Amplification of Power

When there is sustained absence in duration, a deepened absorption, it can effectively increase and store power. This power is downloaded from universal consciousness to be used through increased wakefulness during the day. Consciousness is very efficient in how it does this and the more power that is created for expression during the day, the more Self-awareness is built for your evolution.

Absence links the crown with the heart and a download from universal consciousness to individuated consciousness takes place. This builds power and stores power, which is gained as you move to deeper meditative states, such as the Sahaja state, which is the ultimate unified absorption. Increasingly, the Sahaja state gets experienced during the waking hours of the day as meditative experience deepens. The Sahaja state represents alternating presence and absence, which, when advanced oscillates so fast, a unified state of awareness is experienced by combining the two.

During absence in meditation and during normal sleep time, power is built up. The key is to build more power during sleep and meditation than is expended during the day. This provides the fuel for the evolutionary cycle. Over a period of many years, an increase in Self-awareness or wakefulness is noticeable. As the evolutionary cycle progresses, this increase quickens, and it quickens because you are more able to build the power through your deeper meditation. Another way of looking at it is to say "Being" stores power while "Becoming" uses it. The renunciates and mendicants of all traditions knew this. So, they lived a lifestyle of silence and seclusion. A lifestyle of being rather than becoming, where power was expended through the five senses. Thus, they continued to build and contain power. The more power you can build and sustain, the more you increase the amplitude of power. It has more impact. In the presence of a very spiritual person or Master you can feel the power. It is entraining. Likewise, the more conservative you can be with the building and expenditure of your power, the more it is available for increasing your own Self-awareness. Meditation is like plugging yourself into Source, recharging the battery and keeping it topped up. This is then shown in the power's dispersion through the waking hours in terms of wakefulness. Occasional focusing techniques or balance breaks throughout the day also help to maintain your presence and wakefulness and increase your power.

Talking is one of the worst ways to expend your power. However, when talking or teaching with a very focused awareness from a level of unified consciousness, it does not expend power. Instead, it is more a case of what you give is what you get. Great mystics could teach, and their power was reflected back to them, rather like an infinity symbol, and was magnified in the process. Not just in teaching, though, but in interactions with others, if you can teach, talk, or discuss from a level of awareness, particularly when it is a topic that you have created, and you are watching what you present, then energy will be increased and come back to you. Therefore, it evolves, bringing with it more insight. The entire process won't be depleting for you.

As your evolution increases, your amplitude of power in meditation also increases. It doesn't just stop when meditation stops. This increased amplitude of power affects every dimension of your multi-dimensional consciousness. In addition, this increases the length of the transition after meditation to maintain that level of power longer because it is so saturating and transformative to all the dimensions of your consciousness. This allows you to remain subtle dominant longer, as your subtle dimensions are more actualized. This increasing amplitude of power is your presence. It is this presence, or Self-awareness, that can permeate the formless, noumenal aspect of the experience. So, the task of the advanced meditator is to build that power, contain that power, and to increase the amplitude of power. The increasing amplitude of power is proportional to wakefulness and is experienced as palpable bliss. Another key point of Self-awareness is that whatever level of Self-awareness you have, informs you of your perception of reality, and thus the choices you make within your experience of reality.

As you become more wakeful during the day, wakefulness also increases during meditation. It is important not to confuse wakefulness with simply not being asleep. You find that as you go deeper and more wakeful in meditation, with greater amplitude of power, visionary experiences become more vivid, more alive.

When you go very subtle and therefore beyond linear time and space, the meditation may seem very short, but in fact, a long time has passed. Presence and absence are combined, making it difficult to differentiate whether present or absent.

This is a hypnogogic Sahaja experience.

By maintaining an integrative peak through regular meditation practice, you are constantly increasing the amplitude of your power and, at the same time, increasing your Self-awareness and its associated bliss. Increased bliss is because of the effect your increased power has on your pineal gland and the release of opiation causing neurochemical changes shown in peace, delight, contentment, and wakefulness. You notice an ever-increasing Self-awareness and bliss. An EEG, or neuromap, will show a gradual increase in amplitude and symmetry in the EEG graph, particularly in the alpha, theta, and delta levels.

Initially, bliss is usually felt around the heart area. However, it can also be felt in the head area and eventually is felt throughout the physical and multi-dimensional consciousness.

Finally, group meditation has the benefit of amplifying the power of all the members of the group, providing benefits for all present.

Samadhi or Absorption

In meditation, there are three levels of absorption, or samadhi. These are Savikalpa, Nirvikalpa, and Sahaja. These are experiences of unified holistic awareness. Savi means with and kalpa means thought or form, so Savikalpa means with thought or with form. It is a unified state of awareness where the negative polarity of presence is dominant over the positive polarity of absence. So, in meditation, it would represent a balanced awareness but with presence dominating absence. This can also happen in your normal waking state. For example, in your daily activities, you are speaking, thinking, or listening, but at the same time, you are aware you are doing these things and that they are all forms of consciousness. All are experienced as the same one. This is a unified level of awareness, but with the negative, thought field level of awareness dominant. This is the Savikalpa state.

In meditation, the next level of absorption is when absence dominates presence. Thus, the mind is still. There is emptiness, nothingness, and a unified awareness. This is Nirvikalpa samadhi. Nirvi means without, so Nirvikalpa means without thought, or without form. In Nirvikalpa samadhi you are sitting in meditation with stillness of mind, nothingness, emptiness, in absence. As a result, you are absorbed in formless consciousness.

Beyond these is the Sahaja state, which is a combination of the previous two. Sahaja means naturally flowing or naturally happening. Coming out of absence into the Sahaja state is when you are subtle enough to experience both polarities, being and becoming, and perceive the interaction of the two. Thus, in this state, the two polarities are oscillating so fast you can't cognize the difference. It is a unified awareness. It is positive polarity dominant, but unlike Nirvikalpa, it is an absence in which there is a lucid awareness of form. In essence, it is wakeful nothingness. In the waking state, the most advanced spiritual Masters can go about their daily activities constantly flowing unified awareness as a constant. Whether they are eating, sleeping, walking, coming, going, they remain absorbed in unified awareness no matter what. Likewise, in meditation, they are deeply absorbed in the Sahaja state. For a spiritual Master, there is absence, but not in the sense of total absence. As you progress, the absence becomes more lucid. It is like a saturating absence in which there are glimpses of awareness and glimpses of lucidity. Awareness permeates the absence. It is wakeful nothingness. There is nothingness, but occasionally within the nothingness you are aware that's what you are experiencing. So, it is dominantly the positive polarity, which is noumenal, a formless consciousness with small amounts of lucidity. The incredible Self-awareness and amplitude of power of a Master can permeate the absence in meditation. Furthermore, there is no time when a spiritual

Master is not Self-aware. That is why they say, "a spiritual Master never sleeps."

Advanced meditators can only experience this occasionally. For example, the Sahaja state is experienced when coming out of meditation, in that brief transition between absence and presence. Then, you are holistically aware and so are briefly in the Sahaja state between absence and presence; it flows spontaneously and naturally. For the advanced meditator, this state will also progressively reappear throughout the day when least expected, it just appears. Over time, it increases, and to help this along, you can use little focusing reminders, balance breaks or whatever to regain wakefulness. Sleep time slowly becomes more lucid, as in wakeful nothingness. The bliss increases and becomes more palpable, both in and at the end of meditation, as well as during the day. This oscillates because of the five-fold cycle.

Increased Clarity

Occasionally, because of peak experience in meditation, you will notice a slight increase in your level of Self-awareness or wakefulness as increased clarity. This is then noticed during the day as a contrast to the way things usually are. They are clearer, more present than before. Then it gets integrated and remains more substantiated in your consciousness. The evidence that you have of the evolution in your consciousness is your ever-increasing Self-awareness or wakefulness and the ever-increasing amplitude of your power with the resultant palpability of your presence. All you need to do is to remain a witness to it as much as possible. Increased wakefulness enables your perception of reality to be more non-dual and unified, and increasingly see reality as one. So, as you evolve, you will observe changes to how you perceive things. It keeps progressing into more and more of a holistic experience.

Transition

When you come out of meditation, in the transition between absence and presence, you are in your most subtle dominant state. It is the most palpable part of your meditation, and when you are most likely to see visions or patterns which appear briefly and then dissolve. This is when you have a unified, subtle, dimensional consciousness. Therefore, as subtle dominance gives way to the mind, the mind can organize the subtle experience and represent it as a vision.

It is a good practice to note your experience in the transition after meditation, as you move from an interior dominant meditation to an exterior dominant waking day. Observe and identify with your state of being. You will find you feel more whole and more present. For this reason, utilize your transition time to enhance the benefits of meditation. Observe your state in transition, perhaps use a focusing technique to enhance it. If you have a heart field awareness, focus on that. Give gratitude, identify with your holistic awareness, experience your own presence, and then carry that throughout the day.

If meditation is followed by sleep time, particularly if you have gone from absence straight into sleep, then your sleep time is effectively an extension of your meditation. Likewise, when you awake from such sleep, it is the same as transition from meditation. As your transition time expands with ongoing meditative practice, wakefulness during the day increases and meditation increases from an hour or two to an eventual 24-hour day meditation. Thus, it is an unbroken awareness of yourself as consciousness.

Dreams

Dreams during your meditative sleep time can be particularly diagnostic with all the symbols of negative polarity dominance, positive polarity dominance, balance, peak, processing, et cetera. In fact, the complete cycle can be shown in a dream. Dreams are therefore another way of looking at, and diagnosing, your

117

experience. A separate chapter is given to dreams.

During a meditative sleep, dreams are more likely to be lucid, easier to remember and related to the evolution of your consciousness, as they are combined with your meditative awareness. Dream scenarios also give a good indication of wakefulness and of how you respond to challenges. Therefore, it can be beneficial to meditate before and into sleep time as it extends the meditative brainwave frequency. And of course, it encourages meditative dreams.

Your Day Reflects Your Meditation

Things will happen to you during the day that seem totally unrelated to your meditation or your ever-expanding awareness. Someone does or says something to upset you. As a result, you might react to this and hit back. Your work environment might even become an unpleasant place to be. The key here is that you create your own reality. This might be the next learning experience for you to respond to, consciously deal with, and to grow in your evolution as a result. It can, however, be very difficult. Look at your thoughts and your emotions about the problem. Unpack them, observe, and witness them. Look at the mechanics behind them. Try to take a more trans-egoic perspective. Allow your thoughts and emotions to be and simply watch. Clouds come and go, but the sky is forever the same. You are here to grow, and these challenges are here to help you with this. It may not seem like it at the time, but if approached correctly, you will grow, and your state of awareness will expand as you jump yet another hurdle. Try to invest in wakefulness as your most important life path. Truly, the path you are on, your current life experience, is the happening of consciousness for you. So, be wakeful of it, be aligned with it.

To go on a meditation retreat, or stay in a spiritual center, is a wonderful experience. Your soul delights in the experience, the energetic and the holistic experience of the sangha (community). But really, what is the sanctuary? The sanctuary is wakeful, focused, holistic experience, so if you can live this within yourself, wherever you are, then the sanctuary is within you and will always be with you.

During the day, view all your personal connections to be as they are and maintain truthful wakefulness toward them. Acknowledge that this is all the working out of karmic history and by being accepting and honoring, many so-called difficulties can reach completion, meaning that you no longer need to repeat them. Honor your connections, particularly the deeper connections, with others and try to see them in a unified awareness. View people from an essence to essence or consciousness to consciousness perspective and try to move away from illusory separation and attachment. All connections are evolving towards completion. Once attachment is dissolved, you can see each other from the Oneness that you are. To reach a harmonious completion in your relationships, you simply need to recognize that others are the same consciousness that you are. All those around you are forms of consciousness, and what you see in them is a reflection of yourself. Our connections are often egocentric but moving to a trans-egocentric perspective, others are just seen as reflections of the same consciousness that we are. So, that way, there is no attachment, no duality and therefore no stress.

So, try to avoid the egocentric level in relation to anyone or anything. From an egocentric perspective, you look in the mirror of another person, see separation, and then maintain separation. This is duality and perpetuates your journey with them. A trans-egocentric perspective harmoniously completes your journey with the other person and removes conflict. I'm not saying this is easy, it requires a lot of practice. The more you become wakeful, because of your increasing amplitude of power through meditation, then the easier this becomes, and you gradually move towards meditation as a 24-hour a day experience. The Masters always say you are here to learn how to love. First, you must learn to love yourself as the consciousness that you truly are, and then you learn to love the consciousness in everyone and everything around you. So again, you need focused awareness, focusing on moving from an egocentric perspective to a trans-egocentric perspective of reality. Meditation delivers you to a true holistic experience of reality.

Supra-Causal

We are all multi-dimensional beings. At the denser level, we talk in terms of layers or bodies. At the subtle levels, however, it is increasingly difficult to talk in terms of such layers. Both universal and individual consciousness are multi-dimensional, just different ends of the spectrum. Looking at it another way, the supra-causal is the Sourcepoint at the center of which is the soul. It is a more individual level of universal consciousness and located in the crown. Likewise, this also has a denser component known as the soul body, which corresponds to the causal level and, thus, it is often referred to as the causal body. This is the vehicle for the soul operating through the denser dimensions. In short, individual consciousness ranges from the most subtle unified level at the supra-causal through the causal, subtle, mental, emotional, and physical dimensions.

Brain map

A neuro map, or EEG, when configured appropriately, will show your progress in meditation. This brainwave profile shows your evolution in consciousness from non-meditator through to advanced meditator and beyond. Usually, the EEG is taken while you are in a normal waking state, showing the wakefulness which has been gained because of your regular practice of meditation. Obviously, when you are meditating, it will show greater coherence, therefore it is usually taken outside of meditation in order to see the results of your regular meditation practice and thus your wakefulness during the day.

The neuro map, or EEG, for an advanced meditator, compared with a non-meditator or beginning meditator, shows increased coherence, or balance, between the left and right hemispheres of the brain. There is also a greater amplitude of power in the delta and theta frequencies. These frequencies correspond to a substantiation in wakefulness or holistic experience. In addition, as the delta and theta levels increase, spikes appear in the gamma range too, which show an increase in subtle dimensional dominance or wakefulness. Therefore, the gamma spikes are proportional to the denser delta frequencies. Theta and delta represent heart field dilation, while gamma represents actualization of the crown.

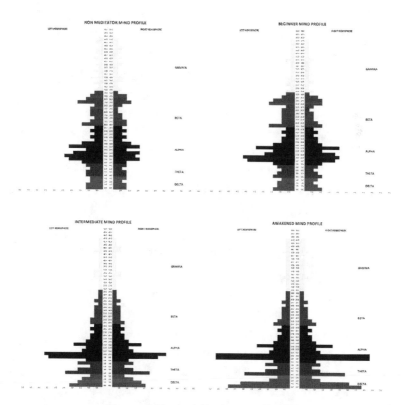

Figure 9 Typical Brainwave Profiles

Awakenings and Satoris

An awakening or satori experience is like an extreme peak experience. Such an awakening experience occurs rarely, like a crack has briefly opened in the veil, to let the light or truth of where you are going slip through momentarily. Then the window closes again, and you walk the path of continuing actualization of that experience. From then on, tiny glimpses may occasionally be received as this awakening experience gets slowly incorporated into your being.

In the classical tradition, there are three major awakenings corresponding to major evolutionary shifts. These initiate three major paths through the chakras. The first is from the base chakra to the heart, the second is from the heart to the third eye (brow center) and the third is from the third eye to the crown. In fact, each of these supposedly corresponds to the last three incarnations. However, as we are now in the very dense Kali Yuga Age, it is most likely to be longer than this. The third and most noticeable, as far as evolutionary experience is concerned, the third eye to the crown, is known as the Royal Road. This culminates in enlightenment. Additionally, there is a significant point between the third eye and the crown, which represents a level of awareness not connected to a chakra. This corresponds to the causal level.

Symptoms of the three levels of awakening are correspondent with the chakras involved. From the base chakra to the heart relates to egocentric levels of experience. Evolution here involves a gradual dismantling of illusory doership. However, even when the higher awakenings have taken place, there is still work to be done at this level. But when sufficient clearing has been done, one moves on to the higher awakenings. This level is related to such experience as found in relationships, sexual experience, you and the other as separate from you. It involves the gradual replacement of egoic, dualistic separation with the dawning of trans-egoic, unified levels of non-separation.

The next awakening, which is at the heart, continues the development of trans-egoic awareness. Hence, it includes increased awareness of one love, one consciousness, and one Source that is all and everything. Likewise, remnants of exclusion are replaced with inclusive awareness and increased trans-egoic unification, corresponding to opening of the heart.

The journey from the third eye to the crown leads to a total reversal of polarized dominance, from dense egoic awareness to subtle trans-egoic awareness. It is a journey from separation to trans-egoic unification. So, the entire journey, through these three major awakenings, is from the base chakra to the crown. Everything in between is the progressive process of dismantling the illusory level of awareness and substantiating a trans-egoic level of awareness.

Summary

I have aimed in this chapter to give ideas about what you can expect to experience as your meditation proceeds. But it is important to point out that everybody's experience on this journey is different because everybody's karmic debt is different based on their previous experience in form. No two journeys are alike. Comparison is useless and discouraged by the Masters. The section I have given on lights in meditation, for example, may apply to you or it may not. Not everyone sees lights and if they do, it may be barely noticeable and may only be one color such as blue. Some people see vivid images, others see none. The only real measure of your progress is your increased wakefulness during the day, increased amplitude of power, bliss, and palpable presence. Even that may not be obvious to you for a long time.

The key things you should look for are your ability to sustain stillness and emptiness in duration in your meditation and, as you do this, the more your holistic awareness expands. The third eye is the gateway to the subtle dimensions and is witness to what is going on and provides the occasional reminders or confirmations coming from your heart crown connection. It is at the end of meditation that your most subtle state of being is found. This is when you are most likely to notice interaction with multi-dimensional consciousness and a more consistent Sahaja state happening naturally and spontaneously. Likewise, this will increase during the waking state, too. Finally, be grateful for the occasional confirmations and reminders you get to show you are progressing.

Chapter 8

Understanding Dreams

Dreams are a valuable indicator of your spiritual path and evolutionary process. However, at first glance, this is not obvious, as dreams appear to comprise stories related to everyday matters. A deeper look will show the influence of childhood conditioning, enculturation, life experience, and your current experience in your dreams. Although the past is valuable in a psychological context and provides an important tool for understanding how this has conditioned your present, it is not the only focus in dream analysis. There is another layer to dreams which we will look at based on the mechanics of consciousness and the five-fold process. Rather than looking at how the past is influencing your present, this layer looks at what is happening now, as you develop and grow in Self-awareness. Dreams also contain symbolism in the form of archetypes, and this provides deeper meaning from the unconscious, providing clues to what is happening in the here and now. You can even receive direct messages in dreams from a higher level that can provide further guidance on your journey.

Dream interpretation takes practice, so to help with this, many examples are given to cover the many types of dreams you can have. Once you record your own dreams and learn to interpret them, you will gradually gain confidence in your own ability. Through a process of conscious dreaming, you will find you can influence dream content beforehand and receive answers.

As mentioned, the narrative provided by a dream contains two layers of meaning. The first layer applies to your life experience to date and provides the context and content of the dream. Because we are conditioned so much by our past, this dream analysis provides a useful tool showing you why you are the way you are and why your current experience is the way it is. However, this is not the primary focus of dream interpretations given in this book, but provides a backdrop. The next layer of dream interpretation applies to where your feet are now and your current response to daily focus and challenges. So, the dream points to how you are managing this through reference to an ongoing five-fold process. This process represents the mechanics of consciousness which play out on the evolutionary cycle, slowly removing the psychological layers which form the ego. You could say that the second (evolutionary) layer of meaning in dreams is showing how the first (life experience) layer of meaning is being re-scripted!

Before we look at how to interpret the content of dreams, let's look at how dreams and dream symbolism come about? It all starts with the pineal gland, which is in the center of your head. This is the physical externalization of the crown chakra, which is your connection to universal consciousness. The pineal gland is sensitive to both light and vibration, so when you close your eyes to sleep, the pineal gland secretes a neurochemical called melatonin. It is melatonin that causes you to fall asleep. Once you are asleep, another neurochemical is released, known as serotonin, which is closely linked to an opiate known as DMT. DMT acts as an interface between universal consciousness and physical consciousness. Serotonin is hallucinogenic, and it is this property which allows downloads from universal consciousness into physical consciousness and is responsible for the dreams in sleep. When "messages" are received as dreams, they are cloaked in symbolism. This symbolism is a blend of images relevant to the waking state and daily activities and to a more universal symbolism such as is associated with beliefs.

Our conscious existence in the world is a "play of consciousness," and in this play of consciousness, we have invested in the illusion of separation. This illusion is the fragmented belief that we are our individual ego identity, an ego with needs, fears, and drives to maintain the separate identity which it believes it is. Once we awaken to this illusion, the journey back to wholeness begins as sourceful awareness gradually replaces ego. This begins the stage of the spiritual seeker wherein drives of becoming are gradually replaced by recognitions of Self, faint at first with only small glimpses of Self, but increasingly, with greater awakenings or satoris. Small realizations gradually gain momentum and build a realization of the Self until ultimately Self-realization is attained. It is a long but necessary process achieved by few. Fortunately, dreams provide us with insight into this process. They show us how the ego has created a false reality around it, as well as the cycle of increasing awareness out of this false reality.

The Psychological Context of Dreams

The first layer found within dreams is the life experience layer. This layer represents your psychological makeup and is widely used by psychologists to help understand why you are the way you are and why you may face current issues. I will look at this level of dreams based on the psycho-analytical approach adapted by B.S. Goel in his book *Psycho-analysis and Meditation*. Dr. Goel underwent a spiritual transformation followed by many psychological difficulties. As a result, he spent many years undergoing psychoanalysis to understand what was going on. He also meditated deeply, so could see the benefits of both methods and could compare the two approaches. Eventually, Goel developed his own approach to gaining Self-awareness which he called Psycho-analytical Meditation. Dream interpretation was an important part of the process. He later became enlightened and received the spiritual name Shri Siddheshwar Baba.

The second layer of dream interpretation I will look at is based on the mechanics of consciousness as taught by Master Charles Cannon, a modern spiritual teacher and founder of the

Synchronicity Foundation for Modern Spirituality. I call this the evolutionary layer. The advantage of this layer of dream interpretation is that it is focused on the Now. Accordingly, there is no need to go into a deep psychological understanding of why you are the way you are. But I present the psychological context to help understand the background content in dreams.

At birth, the spiritual Self takes form as a human baby. The baby has three essential needs: the need for security, the need for food, and a spiritual need to return to the original spiritual source from which it came. Along with these needs come reactions based on these needs. The need for security results in the reactions of fear and possession, hunger results in the reactions of greed and possession, while the spiritual need results in the reactions of attachment, lust, sex, or desire of a love object. Thus, we see that there are three content clusters found in dreams based on these needs.

When there is a denial of these needs, emotional pain leads to a fourth powerful reaction, which results in anger or violence. This anger or violence is directed towards the denier of the essential need, whether a person or other cause. So, this forms a fourth content cluster of dreams.

The various needs an infant is born with, along with reactions to these, gradually lead to personality adaptations made to be acceptable in the world. The personality develops through stages. The spiritual self is the first stage. The animal nature with its needs and reactions is the second stage, and the adaptations made to be acceptable in the world form the third stage. Once the third-stage self has been formed, most of the desires and reactions become repressed and are acted out unconsciously. So, we see that the third-stage self is an artificial self, developed to be acceptable. It is a learned response to the world to "fit in." Success at this is what can be called world realization, as opposed to Self-realization which comes later. We continually strive to be better with ongoing success or failure, and, as a result, psychological issues arise such as low self-esteem, depression, and anxiety when, somehow, we believe we are not adequate. The third-stage self, the artificial self, makes up the fifth cluster of dreams.

You will find these clusters are all interconnected and can be conscious, subconscious, and unconscious. Together, these five clusters form the first type of dream, which are dreams referring to your psychological makeup. This "database" provides the content and context for dreams. Therefore, we see dreams reveal to us unconscious material that is not easily realized during the waking hours when we are living from the third-stage self, the self that is acceptable in the world.

A second type of dream about which little is known relates to data accumulated from past lives and resides deep in the unconscious. It can be said that the personality a child develops in this life results from karma from this and past lives. As the sixth cluster, this is based on hidden memories from previous lives. Hence, if they appear in dreams, they often get distorted or disguised because of the current personality.

Although in dreams one or all of the clusters may get activated, one is usually dominant over the others. Also, the face-saving need of the third-stage self often interferes to change things according to the need to be acceptable in society. The most fundamental need of a person is the underlying spiritual need to be connected with one's original spiritual source. This is the deepest unconscious desire of humans. As a result, this forms the most predominant cluster in dreams.

Finally, there is a third type of dream which can be considered a transmission from a guru or another wise and revered person. In these dreams, a message is received from universal consciousness to guide or encourage you towards greater wakefulness or wholeness. The personification of the carrier of the message is selected from an authority figure held within your own database. This type of dream is quite rare and is shown as part of the second layer, the evolutionary layer, of dreams covered in the next section.

The Evolutionary Commentary in Dreams

As mentioned earlier, the spiritual need cluster of dreams is the most common. According to Freud, deeper spiritual needs result in reactions of attachment, lust, sex, or desire of a love object. When these arise in dreams, the face-saving cluster converts these reactions into symbols, thus making them more acceptable and a replacement for otherwise unacceptable behavior. Freud believed these symbols were often phallic and related to sex; symbols such as going up a staircase, swimming in a river, and so on. Unlike Freud, however, the second, evolutionary layer of dreams interprets the same symbols as a rising in consciousness, gaining more wholeness, the flow of consciousness, etc., rather than purely sexual. We notice here that there is a close relationship to the Kundalini, the internal energy we have. We can see, therefore, a link between the two dream layers, with a similar fundamental cause based on the need to return to Source. A critical point here, though, is that from Freud's perspective, these symbols show an avoidance strategy of the third-stage self, while from the evolutionary perspective, they show the way of return.

This second layer of dreams, based on the mechanics of consciousness, uses the content and context from the first, life experience layer, and then shows your current progress. To do this, it uses a unique symbolism which is easy to miss if you're not looking for it and don't know how this layer works.

Dream symbolism, as usually given in books, takes the symbolism, and applies it literally. It is a densified level of perception. However, dream symbolism is never that literal. Dream symbolism is not about the people and objects your unconscious selects for dreams, but about the archetypes they represent from a holistic level of awareness. The symbolism and interpretations are similar for an average person or an advanced meditator, but the dream content is based on the person's level of Self-awareness or wakefulness. Consequently, the more balanced you are as a constant, the more wakeful you are, then the more truthful your perspective, and the more wholeness there is. This will show in your dreams. Wholeness disempowers illusion and this will show as a diminished negative polarity dominance.

The people presented to you in your dreams are often family members, friends, close associates, lovers, etc. But it is important to remember that your dreams are not about these people. They may have importance for you in your unconscious database, but that's where the symbolism ends. In dream interpretation, this is the most important concept to remember. Everything, everyone in your dreams, are merely symbols. Your dreams are only ever about you.

When we talk about the two polarities, positive and negative, these are not just horizontal balance as in left brain and right brain, dark and light, and so on. They are also multidimensional, from the densest, fragmented, materialistic perspective to the most subtle, unified perspective. As we evolve, we are moving from a materialistic, individual experience to a unified, holistic experience. So, again, we move from a negative polarity dominance to greater positive polarity and balance. To do this, we learn to be more wakeful, conscious, and inclusive in our reality.

Dreams show you where you are today in this process. They provide a commentary on where you are on your life's journey and the evolution of your consciousness. Therefore, the task is to understand this symbolism and what the commentary is about. Symbolism provided by the unconscious can be ingenious, and the more this symbolism is acknowledged and the lessons learned, the more likely you are to receive this symbolism. Importantly, dreams bring your awareness to the data you have. Mostly, this data is about self-worth. Try to remember that, by virtue of existence, you have all self-worth. As a unique expression of consciousness, no other worth is required. To believe otherwise is an illusion, and to compare yourself with others is also an illusion. Likewise, you have all worth by virtue of being conscious. Any other worth you give yourself, any self-negation or self-rejection, is ego-centric illusion.

Self-worth pops up constantly in dreams and so it will continually remind you of this. Dreams show repeatedly your lack of acceptance of who you are. They show that your ego-centric perspective is flawed, and how you are mired in illusion. But when you wake up from a lovely dream you want it to continue, you interpret the dream from your normal daily experience and think, *It is true, she really cares for me? I will tell her I dreamed about her. It must be a sign we should be together.* Consequently, your interpretation is based on your desires. In such an interpretation, you have totally missed the point. You have colored a symbolic representation about where YOUR "feet" are now with your usual data and misunderstood what your unconscious was telling you.

The ever-evolving play of consciousness plays out in our individual experience as each of us continually grows to greater levels of awareness of our ever-increasing wholeness and Oneness. This entire process is ongoing and cyclic, moving ever higher. Each cycle contains peak, evolution, illumination, processing, and integration, with each cycle higher than the one before. For this reason, it is known as the five-fold cycle, and is the process by which our mind evolves. Likewise, there are major cycles and minor cycles, some we hardly notice and others that seem extreme. This is no different in meditation, and sometimes it can even be enhanced. So, meditation isn't always calm and blissful. Occasionally, it can be so uncomfortable that the best thing is to get up and move the energy through before returning to your seat. As we meditate, balance is created between the left and right hemispheres of the brain. Balance increases wholeness and this leads to peak experience. This new frequency of vibration is felt throughout our multidimensional being. Any data we hold within which is not in harmony with the new frequency must shift to be replaced by the new data. Thus, the discomfort as clearing or processing takes place.

Correspondingly, this process continually plays out in our dreams and shows where we are, one day to the next. Such cycles can take minutes or months, depending on the type of peak and associated processing or clearing that needs to take place. An advanced meditator may find that much of the time peak and process occur simultaneously, this is then known as an integrative peak.

Dream symbolism can also refer to Kundalini activity. Dreams symbolically show this activity in various ways. Two of the most obvious dream symbols referring to the Kundalini are fires and snakes. I have included a few such dreams in the examples later.

With a basic understanding of the mechanics of consciousness, we will look at how this is shown in dreams. It is amazing how precise the commentary shown in dreams can be. Dreams, therefore, provide an excellent way to look at your evolutionary process in a way that is unique to you.

Some Basic Facts in Dream Interpretation

Male and female persons in dreams represent the positive and negative polarities. This is the same regardless of whether you yourself are male or female. Usually, dreams will contain a mixture of the two polarities. Although one polarity may dominate throughout the dream, the dream may swing between the polarities, or the dream may show a progression from one to the other.

Male figures usually represent the positive polarity. This can be a father, brother, male friend, or any male. The positive polarity can also be shown as ascending a hill, a mountain, a tall building, going upstairs, going up generally or being high up. An increase in the positive polarity can represent rising to the higher chakras in one's subtle energy body or moving from individual awareness towards universal awareness. As such, the positive polarity represents you in a more truthful way, with less of the illusion of separation and with more wakefulness and wholeness. Correspondingly, on the evolutionary cycle, the positive polarity is always increasing its dominance as you are increasing your wakefulness and wholeness. However, if the male is a male from your childhood, e.g., father, then he could represent your childhood enculturation rather than the positive polarity. It all depends on the context of the dream.

Female figures usually represent the negative polarity. This could be a mother, sister, female friend, or any female. It could also be shown as descending a hill or mountain, or going into the basement of a house or building. Hence, the negative polarity represents your illusions, your virtual reality, as opposed to truthful reality, and the data you have stored in your unconscious about who you are relative to others around you. Mother can represent both the negative polarity and childhood enculturation.

As has been noted, a predominance of male persons in your dream shows positive polarity dominance. Positive polarity dominance means that your experience at this point is more truthful than illusory. Likewise, a predominance of female persons in your dream shows negative dominance. Negative dominance means that you are steeped more in illusion than truth at this point in the dream commentary. An equal number of males to females shows a balance between the two polarities. Balance allows you to expand your awareness, leading to peak experience and a greater awareness than you have had before. It is more holistic and unifying. If you are male and female together in harmony, e.g., happy to be together, hugging, arm in arm, etc., then this also represents balance.

There are exceptions to the general male/female rule. If the woman is an authority figure, then she represents the higher aspect of the negative polarity, which is more truthful and unified. This can be referred to as the divine feminine. A male authority figure also represents a higher level of truth and can be referred to as the divine masculine.

The first part of a dream tends to be more truthful, and then later, judgments of the "third-stage self" creep in and ruin what the initial part of the dream was showing. For example, if the dream started with positive polarity dominance or balance, then the second part of the dream often descends into past data and clearing, representing processing after the peak.

Let's look at an example dream:

Lady Friend and Work

I was at work and had a written task to do. A lovely lady friend of mine was there too and had a similar task to do. I suggested a couple of times that we did this work as homework rather than at work. However, she did not want to do this, saying it was easier to do the task at work. I think she had computer issues at home.

Next thing I remember is that we were walking back to her place. She put her arm around me and wanted me to do the same to her. I wasn't comfortable with this, as people may see us. Given that I am married, I would rather wait till we got to her place. Nevertheless, she insisted, so I complied.

Then, a young woman came up to me and asked if I knew what the Bible said about this, considering I was already married. I said I do, but then ignored her.

It was a pleasant dream and easy to interpret from my usual day-to-day perspective. But that interpretation is not what the dream was really telling me. There was a predominance of women in the dream, females represent the negative polarity. And yet, the first woman in the dream wanted to walk arm in arm with me. That was a good sign. It shows that I am currently achieving balance, with less negative polarity dominance. This represented a peak experience in this cycle. But having achieved the peak, the processing starts. My data gets in the way, I'm a married man, and this behavior is not acceptable. I am confronted by another woman chastising me. My enculturation does not condone this behavior. The other woman represents more data getting in the way, more fears. The dream is showing me I have been going through a cycle; I had balance, which led to a peak experience. Then came processing as some old data needed to give way to substantiate the new peak attained. One complete cycle was represented in the dream, which could have been reflective of a cycle I went through during the day or a cycle I went through while asleep. Regardless, it shows the five-fold process is ongoing and was reflected in this dream symbolism.

There is dream symbolism that we all share, and yet how that symbolism appears in our dreams is highly individual. What a symbol means to one person may not mean the same thing to another. Culture and beliefs have an enormous impact on the symbols we receive, and for this reason, symbols are uniquely presented to each individual and so is the interpretation. As a result, you need to learn to interpret your own symbolism and what it represents to you. Your "stories" are unique to you. So, be wakeful of them and be wakeful of your own data presented in these stories. As your experience, and your consciousness, is constantly evolving, so too are your stories. Your database is constantly being upgraded, so be wakeful to the changes which come about as your consciousness evolves.

As mentioned earlier, a dream will occasionally contain a figure representing your highest ideal of who you can be, whether this be a spiritual Master, guru, or authority figure. The authority figure could be mystical, spiritual, or even medical, etc. This will depend on your enculturation, whether religious, spiritual, or otherwise. Such a dream is a form of empowerment and along with the empowerment comes a message. The message is always an encouragement to be more wakeful in one way or another and pertinent to what is currently happening in your life.

As you evolve, the more you accept your own self-worth, you accept yourself just as you are, and you extract yourself from illusion. You have invested power in the illusion of who you, in truth, are not. So, as you dissolve this illusion, you take back this power and, as the amplitude of your power increases, you become more unified in your experience, more whole. The unified level of experience is blissful consciousness. It is pleasurable. When truth dominates, illusion gets disempowered. However, growth in dominance of the positive polarity, unified awareness, is not constant, it waxes and wanes. Sometimes it is easier to be more truthful than others.

More Dream Examples

Reticulation, Renovation

I dreamt my dad was working on the irrigation pipes in my garden. I hoped he knew what he was doing, as there was a lot of water gushing out after he had fixed it. So, it needed to be fixed again. Then I noticed he was attaching things to walls, but was not doing a very good job of using the wooden plugs used to screw into. The plugs were way too long for the holes he had drilled to put them in. I started to redo some of them myself and then noticed there were builders working on the house who were putting up large extensions on two sides. I realized they had been drilling the holes and didn't seem to know what they were doing.

To begin with, dreams are always about you and not the other people in the dream. So, even though my father is in the dream, the dream is about me and not my father. The building represents my physical body, or rather, my psyche. The dream shows where I am at, in the five-fold process. For example, irrigation pipes refer to the flow of consciousness as they carry water, yet my ability to flow with it is blocked. Somehow, I believe it should be other than it is. Consequently, this is a self-worth issue and stems back to my childhood, as represented by my father. Father, as male, usually represents positive polarity, but here reference is to my father as he was in my childhood. At that time, my father was judgmental or critical and I believed I was not good enough. If I was to take a closer look at my childhood, I might see how this information was programmed into my Self-awareness. Many of our current traits were programmed at that time. However, there is a lot of positive polarity in the dream, as it is all male figures, so it is showing that despite the apparent negative conditioning in my childhood, consciousness is still orchestrating the show perfectly. I may not understand how or why, but I should trust that it is appropriate. As for the men drilling the holes and my thinking, they didn't know what they were doing. That is my judgmental data and cannot be trusted as the work is being done by men and thus the positive polarity. It is quite common for judgments to enter the latter part of a dream.

My Father, and I Not Able to Meditate

I was in the back garden of my childhood home at night-time and I could see into the house where my dad was asleep in his chair in the living room. I needed to go to the bathroom, which was on the other side of the garden, but I didn't want to be seen by him. Suddenly, he woke up and proceeded to move out of the living room. So, I moved over to the toilet and realized that our small dog, Chloe, was outside, too. I wanted to do my meditation in the bathroom where it would be quiet. However, when I looked inside the bathroom, I realized how uncomfortable and dirty it was, so I decided it was not a good place to meditate. Then, I saw Chloe. She got excited and barked. My dad was then in the kitchen and heard this, so I went inside and pretended I had just been to the bathroom. Dad went up to his bedroom, and I realized that all my meditation equipment was in his bedroom, so I would have to meditate without it. Chloe pushed open the door and made a commotion. I thought she had caught a rat, but when I got closer, I saw she had caught a mouse, who, in turn, had also caught a mouse in its mouth.

Although my father is in the dream, it is about me and not him. My father in this dream represents my positive polarity. I am evading my positive polarity, so its dominance is reduced, meaning the negative polarity is dominant. The dream shows processing taking place, so this is currently happening in my daily experience. Correspondingly, the symbolism of the bathroom shows a place of elimination and clearing. I want to be meditative and balanced but can't because I'm processing. I can't meditate in the bathroom because it is too dirty. In other words, I can't be balanced while I am processing. My father, my positive polarity, goes up to my meditation room. The symbolism of going up represents increasing wholeness or rising to the higher chakras. In this case, I can't connect with the positive polarity, which would create balance, because I am processing, which, of course, is totally appropriate. The dog barking is a distraction. The dog itself is a distraction and represents my animal nature or my ego. In its mouth, the dog has a mouse, which also has a mouse in its mouth. Being familiar with Hindu philosophy, I know the mouse represents the deity Ganesha, who always has a mouse at his feet. So, the mouse has Ganesha symbolism and Ganesha symbolizes the removal of obstacles.

The dream is telling me that this is a processing experience, and the outcome will be that I will relinquish the obstacles which are distracting me from my wholeness. Furthermore, at the time of this dream, I had started a new pattern of meditation but was finding it difficult, as it was causing discomfort because of the processing it brought about during meditation. As always, this is appropriate, as process leads to clearing, resulting in a greater flow in consciousness and thus a greater Self-awareness.

Negative Polarity Dominant Dreams

Two Lady Friends and Flowers

I was walking along with a lady friend and I needed to go into a building to meet another lady friend with whom I was very close many years ago. As we go into the building, the lady friend I was meeting takes us to a particular part of the room and the accompanying friend starts to get very annoyed and says, "I know what all this is about." Then I realize that there are flowers on the table and the second lady has bought this gift for me. I can see there are two large bunches of flowers, with a light blue and white color, similar to irises. The setting seems quite romantic even though she has several children with her. However, I feel a little uncomfortable as I haven't bought a gift for her. I say to the first friend, "I won't be long, say half an hour," but she doesn't want to wait around. Instead, I say "well, go away for half an hour and then come back." She is still not happy and leaves.

Then, I sit down near my old friend and she pats on the seat next to her, as if to say come closer. I realize she is happy to make close acquaintance again, and something I want to do too, perhaps reigniting our old romantic acquaintance.

This dream represents a progression. Initially, two women show negative polarity dominance. Then, the flowers, the gift, the romantic gesture represent evolving or unifying of the negative polarity to a higher level. It therefore shows going from illusion and identification to more in the way of truth and balance.

Wife Misunderstands Situation with Female Colleague

I had been to a conference of some sort with a couple of colleagues from school. One of them was female. Then I remember being in a room in bed and a female colleague is changing her top and putting on a new blouse. At that moment my wife opens the door and sees the colleague putting her top on, and I am in bed, so immediately she jumped to the mistaken conclusion that we had been in bed together. She stormed off and wouldn't talk to me. Later, I noticed she had thrown my bed down the stairs.

This represents the negative polarity and the many illusions it presents. Still, in the dream, I wasn't really concerned about what was happening, showing some detachment and witnessing of what was going on.

Daughter-in-Law had a Baby

My daughter-in-law had had a baby. She was ill with something. In the end, I think she was okay.

Multiplying the negative or the negative was growing. All represents imbalance due to there being too much negative polarity. Here, the dream is calling my attention to that so that I can be more wakeful.

Phone Call about Mother-in-Law

I dreamt there was a long-distance phone call about my mother-in-law. My brother took the call and then passed the phone on to my wife. The person at the other end said "no" as if to say, "she didn't make it."

Interpreting this dream, I could make many assumptions about what is or will happen to my mother-in-law. However, this is just the context of the dream, which, as usual, is only about me. The dream represents the demise of the negative polarity, illusion, or ego. Again, I am an observer of this in the dream, which shows increasing Self-awareness. In essence, I am more wakeful, and the dream is pointing this out to me.

Canadian Girl

I dreamt I had just got to know a Canadian girl and was very attracted to her. She had little time left before she returned to Canada, but there was something about her and I really wanted to get to know her more before she went back. Further, I'm in my childhood home, myself and others were in the front room while this girl was in the back room. So, I made a point of seeing her.

Next thing I remember, I'm on what appears to be a school camp. I am very busy. Somebody mentions that there is a boy on top of the silo, but I don't have time to attend to it straight away. Then I get a phone call from somebody else telling me that a boy is not doing the right thing on top of a silo. So now, I go quickly over to the silo, and I climbed to the top. The boy is on the top where he's making rude gestures to people around. This boy is the Canadian girl's brother. I rush up to him and tell him not to do this and then this part of the dream finishes.

Next, I remember, I'm in the classroom and teaching students about lung disease. The Canadian girl is shaking her head as if to say, you don't know what you're talking about, because she actually has lung disease. I'm aware of this and after I finished talking, I get her and a couple of others to go outside with me. I can't really remember what happens then.

The Canadian girl represents my negative polarity and some illusory, subconscious information that is surfacing and being brought to my awareness. Somehow, this is attracting me to her. When this is established, the scene changes to show me from where this illusory data is coming. It is coming from my childhood, as represented by my childhood home, the time when I received most of my enculturation from my family.

In this dream, her brother, although male, does not symbolize the positive polarity. He represents data related to my negative polarity, as he is connected to the girl. He's a young boy, also representative of my childhood. What is he doing? He is using negative strategies to get attention, which must have been what I did as a child, using illusory strategies to get love. As I am interacting with the boy in the dream, it shows that I am interacting with my negative childhood data to bring it to awareness.

Then the scene changes again. The Canadian girl, my negative polarity, points out that the data is unconscious to me and says, "You don't know what you are doing." The negative strategies used in my childhood are being brought to the surface and show how I used manipulative strategies in my childhood to get attention (love). Such strategies are rooted in self-worth and self-acceptance issues. The dream is showing that this issue is being worked on now.

Woman Pours Boiling Water on her Head

I dreamt I heard about a woman who just poured boiling water over her head attempting to kill herself. She was in great pain and was plucking at her head as if she was trying to remove the cause of the pain.

The woman represents my negative polarity, and this is diminishing in dominance as shown by her trying to kill herself. Similarly, removing the ego to gain greater wholeness can often be painful. The water represents awareness, consciousness, or wholeness, which in this dream is disempowering the negative polarity which represents illusion. So, at the time of this dream, increasing holistic awareness is replacing illusion.

Positive Polarity Dominant Dreams

Buying a Small Safe

I dreamt I needed to buy something for the school principal (male). So, I bought a small safe.

As dreams are always about oneself, in this dream the principal represents me, my positive polarity. I am the principal of my life. The safe would be to safeguard something, to make safe, and to place something of value in it. The symbolism here most likely represents safeguarding or maintaining the truth. In dreams, when you buy something for somebody, you are buying or giving something to yourself, and this is particularly true when it is the positive polarity that the gift is for. So here I appear to be maintaining a truthful perspective.

Archipelago in Sweden

I dreamt I was in Sweden and was at the northernmost island of an archipelago of islands at the top of the country. It appeared very barren, but the weather was good and there were tens of ships entering or docked in the harbour, to transport minerals from all the mining there.

Next thing I remember, the dream changes and I'm with several others on a visit to Sweden. I have a fantastic travel book and am asked where I would like to go. I thought of Bodo, the northernmost island, but before I could say it, it was announced that the train I was getting on, goes to Bodo.

144

In this dream, Sweden represents travel, holiday, or ideal state of being. The northernmost island represents the crown chakra and my ideal of connecting with it. Ships taking away the mined resources represent the insights received from the crown chakra. Next, the train journey northwards could represent a journey up the spine (Kundalini) to the crown chakra.

Note: Bodo is actually a town in Norway and there is no archipelago of islands at the top of Sweden, but in dreams, things can get a bit confused. It is the symbolism that counts.

Praised by Father

This was part of a dream in which there was an object on my desk, perhaps a game, which needed repairing. However, my parents didn't want me to fix it, but I did anyway. Consequently, my mum wasn't happy, but when my dad came home, he was furious and started shouting at me. Surprisingly, I stood up to him and shouted back. "I am an adult now and I decide what is best for me. You want to control me, but you can't do that anymore." Rather than retaliating, Dad suddenly changed and started praising me. I was his beautiful boy, etc. He had never talked to me like that before.

There seems to be a bit of a test here. The positive polarity is represented by my father in this dream. He was quite strict in my childhood and was partly responsible for my enculturation and negative data. Nevertheless, at the same time, being male, he also represents the positive polarity and appears to be angry with me, but realizing that I'm now more evolved, he yields and praises me. Finally, he is happy with my progress.

Friend's Funeral

I went to the funeral of a friend of mine. It was strange as the coffin lid was off and I could see this friend moving. He started

145

talking and sat up in the coffin. Others saw this too, but didn't seem bothered by it. So, the funeral was going ahead, as usual.

Sometimes dreams can be absurd! My male friend represents the positive polarity. Trying to put it in a box shows the seriousness of life. Nobody seems to notice, and the funeral goes on. My positive polarity is waking up from the dream, but everybody else is asleep.

King Died

I heard from somebody that the king had killed himself. I already knew this, as I had read it somewhere earlier. I thought it was the King of Sweden, but I was corrected and told it was the King of Germany. Then I realized this was probably a coverup and he had probably been killed by someone else. However, we were being told he had killed himself. This was a conspiracy theory coming out.

The king, being an authority figure, represents the higher aspect of the positive polarity. We would call this the divine masculine. The divine masculine represents formless or noumenal consciousness. In that sense, he can't kill himself, so it is really a lie. So, in the dream, I am questioning this as a conspiracy theory which kind of validates wakefulness and ability to see through the illusion. I realize they are trying to stop him or get rid of him.

Loss of Wallets

I was driving along in my car. I checked and adjusted my speed when I saw a police car on the left. I slowed down almost to a stop and then turned into a car park, also on the left. I pulled over near the police car, but when I looked, the police car had disappeared and instead there were some people sitting at a table. I then walked into the store and realized my wallet was not in my pocket. I must have dropped it somewhere because I remember looking into the wallet just before going into the store. So, I went out of the store, checking the ground as I went, but my wallet was nowhere to be seen. A guy nearby said he saw a man take my wallet, like a pickpocket, and then the man had gone into the bar next door and sat somewhere on the left-hand side. The guy that was telling me, however, had the other man's wallet and gave me a look at the photo so I could see what the guy who had taken my wallet looked like. He was tall, slim and had white hair. So, I went in to talk to the man. When I got into the bar, the man was sitting at a table with a few other people, both male and female. I decided not to confront him in front of the others. Instead, I went up to him and asked if I could have a word with him outside. He agreed. I showed him his wallet and asked if it was his. He confirmed it was and reached out for it. But I didn't give it to him, rather I said, he needed to give me my wallet first. As he went for it, I noticed he had several wallets inside his jacket, and I left it at that.

This dream represents what I value, symbolized by the wallets. Doing the right thing by the police also represents manipulation of values, what is right and what is wrong, or rather what works and what doesn't. There is a lot of male symbolism, which represents the positive polarity, or the subtle dimensions, wakefulness, etc. So, I'm looking at my values relevant to truth as opposed to illusion.

Dreams Showing Balance

Cyclone

I was in a house, and my parents were there too. Apparently, there was a cyclone on the way, and I had a chart that showed its predicted path. Then the cyclone came, seemingly in two hits as it passed. A

couple of windows were smashed, but that was about it. I talked to
Mum about the cyclone and how its path was the same as predicted.

Here my parents represent my two relative polarities. The
house represents me and because my parents are in the house,
it denotes balance. As I am in balance, I am more holistically
or subtly aware and can predict what will happen such as
the path of the cyclone. When it had passed, I spoke to my
mother, the negative polarity, to point out what happens
when she's not dominant: there is balance. To sum up,
negative dominance means more illusion, and in this dream,
I can point out that one needs to see through illusion and be
more wakeful.

Dreams are highly individual to you as an individual.
Consequently, general symbols don't always work. It is up to
your skill, or the skill of the dream interpreter, to determine the
likely meaning of the symbols. It is important, therefore, not to
assume what fits for one person will apply for another, as this
can be misleading. So, be mindful of this when you interpret
your dreams and be open to alternative possibilities.

The next dream is very short, but highly symbolic. Again, it
will give you an idea of how dream symbolism can work well.

Group of People, Work Colleague, Fixing Something

I dreamt I was with a group of people. I was outside of the house
with a female work colleague. I think we were going to look at
fixing something to do with a frame for a window. We walked off.
It was very crowded, and we seemed very close.

The group of people at the house represents my multidimensional
personality. The woman represents my negative polarity, but
because we seemed close, there was a coherence or balance
between us. This could symbolize a coherent or balanced heart

field. The window frame needs fixing, which suggests the need to improve my perception. Prior to sleep, I had been contemplating the Vesica Pisces symbol, otherwise similar to a Venn diagram, which is a mathematical shape. So, the window probably represents this as well, as in the merger of inside and out.

Volatile and Valuable Packages

I was in possession of some important packages, which were hidden from obvious view. I'm not sure where these came from, but I think I was responsible for moving them from one place to another. One package contained highly volatile material, while the other package contained valuable jewelry for my wife. When I got to where I needed to take them, there were many people around who seemed to want to get hold of them while I was trying to keep them hidden. The Volatile package ended up in one part of the house and the jewelry in another. I hoped to keep the volatile package hidden. I gave the jewelry to my wife.

The volatile package and jewelry represent the exterior and the interior, the objective and the subjective. In this dream, I am trying to maintain a balance between the two as the world tries to encroach on it.

Membership Card for Restaurant

I was with my brother and maybe one or two others. My mum had given us a membership card for a restaurant that she enjoyed going to. So, we went there for a coffee. When we got there, at first, we weren't allowed in, but when we showed the membership card, we were shown to a table. It seemed a posh restaurant and was quite full. There were many people there for breakfast. It appeared the clientele who frequented the place were well off. I watched with interest. Soon, however, the restaurant was empty, and it was time for us to leave.

I am with my brother and other males showing positive polarity dominance. My mother giving me a membership card represents the Blessed Mother giving me entrance or holistic awareness expansion, and thus a more unified state of consciousness. This is followed by witness consciousness watching.

Car Needing More Petrol

My car was placed out in the open but undercover. I needed to get some petrol, so I found an old bath and used this to catch the petrol in. I'm not sure where the petrol was coming from. At the same time, it was pouring with rain, so along with the petrol, there was a lot of water getting into the bath too. In addition, the bath was muddy at the bottom. Somehow, the bath was connected to the car, and slowly, petrol was getting into the car. As some of the rain was also getting into the bath, not only was the petrol polluted with mud, it was also polluted with water.

Here, the car represents me and the fact that it needed petrol meant I had a low amplitude of power. I needed more power, but I also needed to be careful about the source of the power and the purity of the fuel. This could mean watch my diet and what I eat, or it could mean be careful of the energetic environment I find myself in. As a result, I need to be careful of anything in my energetic environment and how it affects me and my power. From a holistic point of view, it is calling my attention to balance because it is balance that fuels my wakefulness or wholeness. So, the dream is probably telling me I was a little low in power, and perhaps my experience was fragmented. I need to be wakeful to what I need to do to restore balance and wholeness.

Dreams Showing Peak

Attending Wedding with My Wife

A dream in which my wife and I had traveled somewhere to attend a wedding. It appeared we were staying in separate places. On the day of the wedding, I was not ready in good time. I was with some other men, and we were all a bit disorganized. In the meantime, everything seemed to go wrong, and I was running late. Increasingly, it looked likely that I would be late for the wedding. When I put a shirt on, it was the wrong shirt. When I shaved, the shaver shaved off part of my shirt. One thing after another was going wrong.

Self-worth data is being referenced in this dream. The wedding symbolizes communion or unification in consciousness and so represents peak. Subsequently, this was followed by processing.

My Car Stolen

I looked out of the window of the house and saw someone sitting in the driver's seat of my car with his elbow sticking out of the window. I went outside to see who it was, but he had driven off. Then I went back into the house and told the others my car had been stolen, including a bag with my valuables. When I tried to call the police, I struggled with remembering the emergency number. 000 or 999 or 911.

A male driver taking my car shows the positive polarity has taken control of my journey and represents peak experience. The rest of the dream represents the process following the peak.

Traveling in 747 with My Daughter

I was traveling with my daughter on a large plane. It was like a large adapted Boeing 747. We were flying over the mountains in somewhere like Italy. We had good seats with a view. Although we were not next to the side windows, we had an overview of the scenery because of the strange design of the plane. Next, we were traveling in a car with my brother driving. These were the same mountains we had flown over. He drove carelessly, sometimes over rocks, and I was sure he was causing damage to the underside of the car. He was probably getting punctures as well.

Following that, I went into a shop with my daughter. This was possibly a stationery store, or combined bookshop and stationery store. I wanted to buy an eraser while my daughter was looking for something else.

The first part of the dream in a plane, flying over mountains with an excellent view, represents peak experience. I was there with my negative polarity (daughter), but this was in a state of balance, allowing my holistic awareness to expand. It shows I was subtle awareness dominant with a good view, in a state of witnessing consciousness.

Next, I was in a car which represents my journey. Both my polarities were there, but the positive polarity, my brother, was in the driver's seat, so this is a continuation of the peak. He was driving recklessly, which represents pushing the peak and taking me to the cutting edge of the evolution of my consciousness. I was nervous because it is taking me beyond what I am comfortable and secure with.

This was followed by the next scene in which I was in the stationary or bookstore. This represents my database, all the information in my unconscious. The eraser is interesting because it shows that because of peak experience comes the evolution and illumination phases of the five-fold cycle, so that old data that is no longer congruent with who I have become, needs to be eliminated.

Dreams Showing Processing

Student Disruptions

> *A long dream in which I was at school as a teacher, but nothing was going as it should. Two big classes were combined in a large hall with a dividing screen blocking one class from another. Many disruptions made it impossible to begin the lesson. Eventually, some students walked out. I called out for them to come back, but they ignored me and eventually both classes walked out. Then I had another period with the class, but with more disruption. Finally, I was very annoyed and told them all to go.*

The dream started out with me teaching at the school and this represents peak experience. But then everything goes wrong and shows resultant processing after the peak. A closer look at the processing shows that the dream has something to do with self-worth. This represents the first layer, or context, of the dream. Self-worth is anchored in love, so a lack of self-worth goes back to the deepest root of separation from love, Source, Oneness, and wholeness as a small child. This is the primary illusion in our consciousness, the illusion of lack of worth, acceptance, adequacy, or self-love. This eventually transforms into self-negation. What happened in the dream is the worst thing for a teacher, when there are so many disruptions that it is impossible to teach, and then the ultimate fear of being rejected by the students.

Dad in Old Dilapidated House

> *My dad was living in a large, old, dilapidated house. He came back from work, and we talked a bit although he quoted something in French. Then a couple of female relatives of his arrived separately in new but old-fashioned cars. They were from the same time period as the cars, and the dream also seemed to be in the past.*

My dad represents the positive polarity. The dilapidated house represents me with my old conditioning. The women also represent the negative polarity and my past, while their new but old-fashioned cars show the journey of life as a joyous game. At the same time, though, I am witnessing all of this. This dream actually followed a peak experience in meditation, so represented the shifting of old data because of the peak. Father can represent some of your conditioning as well as your positive polarity. Context has a lot to do with this.

Spider inside Shirt

There was an insect moving inside my shirt at the front where my heart would be. I opened up the front to shake whatever it was out, and a spider fell on the floor.

This dream was related to the clearing process. Something inside needed to come out. It was related to the heart chakra.

Dream of Funeral

I was at my childhood home, when I saw a funeral procession approaching the neighbor's house. It was for a friend of mine who had lived there. The coffin bearers also comprised a couple of old friends. One said he had got a new job and was planning to move to Birmingham. It seemed all my old friends were moving away. I asked another friend what he thought, but he didn't want to talk, as he was still upset about the funeral.

This was another dream related to the clearing process. Also, in the dream I was understanding what was being cleared, as shown by some friends I could talk to and others I could not. I was changing, and the funeral showed this, a metamorphosis from illusion to truth.

Dreams Referencing Self-Worth

Family in Car and Deflated Tires

I was with my family in a car. We stopped at a shopping center, followed by a short journey home. However, when we got home, we noticed that all the tires were deflating and that they must have been punctured by vandals while stopped at the shopping center.

My journey had been interrupted or limited, shown by vandals and deflated tires. So, I am shown as a victim in this dream. The symbolism here refers to low self-esteem and issues of self-worth that are slowing me down.

Bus Deliberately Driven Wrongly and into Swamp

This was a dream which seemed rather disorganized and hard to know exactly what was going on. I was traveling on a bus and the bus driver decided he was going to do the wrong thing. He would drive on the wrong side of the road; he would go the wrong way around roundabouts. It was almost like he was looking to cause an accident. Eventually, he drove into a swamp. The bus went in and slowly sank. Everybody had to rush to the back of the bus to get out as it sank, and I had to do the same thing. When I got out, of course, I was sopping wet, muddy and smelly. Then later, during the dream, I seemed to meet up with somebody who looked after me and allowed me to be with them. I was caught between being dirty and smelly and wanting to clean up and needing to get home and this seemed to go on for a while. The big concern about traveling home on a bus or train was because then nobody would want to sit near me because I smelled. It all seemed to be awkward. It all seemed to be a problem.

This was another dream referring to self-worth, self-acceptance, etc. The male driver doing the wrong thing shows that consciousness, the positive polarity, is orchestrating the show, but my judgments get in on this. So, the bottom line is, who am I choosing to be in relation to this?

Dreams Showing Witnessing or Wakefulness

Aborigines and Kangaroo

I was on a camp, and we saw some aborigines putting a young kangaroo onto a barbecue. The kangaroo was crying out and I'm thinking, should we stop them? However, it was obviously their food. So, we didn't go over and stop them, and that was the end of the dream.

The fire represents Kundalini, and the kangaroo being barbecued represents something being processed by the Kundalini. Consequently, this dream shows witness consciousness as I was seeing something and allowing it to be the way it is rather than judging it.

In Hiding in India

Because of having done something, some people were out to shoot me. I had to go into hiding and went to India, where I was homeless and moving around. Then I bumped into a male friend who had also been in hiding and had settled down in a permanent place to sleep. He knew the ropes. I also had a carry bag of more important possessions with me.
Then there was a woman who seemed able to help me. I was given her name, Melanie.

People wanting to shoot me represent difficulties. The need to go into hiding or be more wakeful shows the need to be more detached and more holistic. Going to India also implies moving into a more subtle dimensional awareness, as in my belief system, India is a spiritual country. So, the first part of the dream is showing that I need to be more wakeful and view things from a more truthful perspective. Likewise, bumping into a male friend represents an encounter with the positive, more unified, truthful awareness. He's been there a long time, so he was wise. The woman helping me shows a more balanced, more conscious level of the negative polarity. Her name in the dream was not important.

Academic Project

During a night-time meditation, I found I had lots of thoughts going on about an academic project I was involved in. These ideas just kept coming through. Then later when I returned to sleep, I dreamt an attractive female colleague at work was helping me with this but it was difficult to get uninterrupted time to go over it.

When sleep time immediately follows meditation, it can also be considered meditation. So, this was a meditative dream. The attractive female colleague helping me represents the negative polarity and adds an element of illusion to what I was doing, which was materialistic study to perfect knowledge in the negative dominant, relative field of awareness. To summarize: illusion is always available, but do you buy into it or are you more wakeful? As mentioned before, dreams are always about you and never the other person, so the interruptions could be considered my wakefulness, preventing the illusion from continuing.

Dreams Referencing Evolving Consciousness

Train to Work in Basildon

I was on a train from my hometown to Basildon. I was prepared with my excuses for why I had the day off work if asked. But then

I thought to myself, "You don't need excuses anymore, you retired last Friday."

The train is the journey mirroring the evolution of my consciousness. Then I realized I don't need all the excuses or stories as the journey is the destination and all is appropriate.

Police Officers Can No Longer Carry Pencils

I dreamt that all police officers were told that they could no longer carry pencils. This seemed strange to me. Why should police no longer be allowed to carry pencils? I was sure this wasn't true and even tried to search on the Internet to prove this wasn't true. In reality, it made no sense to me. How were police supposed to write their notes?

This is not a simple dream to decipher, but I've included it because it seems like nonsense. Police represent authority, so it represents me as authority, as dreams are always about oneself. So, what is my true authority? Consciousness is my true and ultimate authority. Because of consciousness, I have all the authority I need. Pencils are used to write things down, to record things, to make notes. But from the perspective of consciousness, it's all just a flowing energy, happening newly in each moment. There is no need to write and record. That perspective is egocentric, while in this dream the police represent authoritative consciousness, which is trans-egocentric, always in the present moment, the eternal now of consciousness. Consciousness is orchestrating the show.

In a Small Boat

In another dream I was with others in a small boat and a large whale appeared, swimming alongside. Then it dived and surfaced so close to the boat I was concerned we might get struck by its tail.

The ocean represents consciousness. Being in a boat on the ocean shows I am holistically aware. The whale represents the depths of consciousness as a whale goes deep into the ocean. It is the most evolved of consciousness because it is submerged most of the time. Here the whale represents total unification in consciousness, or holistic awareness. Therefore, this dream represents peak experience. While my apprehension shows a shifting in data in relation to the peak.

A Wedding with a Chance the Bride Would Be Mine

It seemed there was a wedding taking place, and yet, strangely, it also seemed there was still a chance that the bride would be mine. Next, there were a few piles of wedding photos, and we all had to select a few. If I selected the right ones, then the bride might still come to me.

Marriage is an archetype representing unification of consciousness or wholeness. My consciousness has downloaded this archetype and shows me the possibility of actualizing that archetype according to my choices, which is shown by the wedding photos. When I choose the right photo, the truth, I will actualize the experience of communion and continue my journey of evolving consciousness.

Dreams Referencing the Play Consciousness

Holiday Tour with Family

My family and I appeared to be on a kind of holiday tour. As part of this tour, we were taken by the tour leader, and owner, to his house. It was an immaculate house, so he must have spent a lot of money on it. It also appeared his business was doing very well. He showed us through the house and there were one or two bedrooms. One room was full of family photos, not just on the wall but standing all over the place and on the floor. Then, it seemed we were lying down. I remember there was a kind of miniature train ride as well. While waiting for other activities, we had to spend a lot of time in the garden area, which was a decked-out patio amongst the trees, with lots of children's play equipment. The tour leader's wife was also around, but she didn't take part in the tour. I was impressed with the man's ability to set up and organize the company as he had done. And of course, it was doing very well. Although on this day, because of a shortage of numbers, he said a couple of times that he would run at a loss today.

In this dream, the tour leader represents the positive polarity which is guiding me through the play of life. The house represents me, and a lot of work has gone into improving the house. Finally, the room of photos represents memories.

Dreams Referencing Kundalini Activity

Lion Dream

I had a dream with a lion in it. The lion belonged to someone, or was being looked after by someone, and, for a short while, I had to be close to it. But presumably the lion was tame enough not to attack me. It was a male lion.

The male lion represents power, spiritual power. Consequently, the dream represents a peak experience. In the Hindu pantheon of deities, each deity has an animal mount. Shiva has the bull, Saraswati has the peacock, Krishna has the cow and the Blessed Mother, the divine feminine, has the Lion. So, this dream references the divine feminine, which is also the Kundalini energy.

Fireplace and the Queen

I remember part of a dream where it was necessary to prepare a fireplace. This was told to me as a joke and in the dream, it was very funny. But when analyzing it later, it wasn't funny at all. The joke was that the Queen arranged this large outdoor fireplace and because of her arranging, when it came to lighting the fire, it burned brighter and larger. Next, I remember trying to tell this joke to somebody else. First, it was difficult for me to remember the joke and even halfway through; I realized it didn't seem funny at all. But anyway, I tried.

The Queen represents the divine feminine archetype, and her job is to light the Kundalini fire. When she does this, it burns brightly. Some people think this is a joke, but it is not. It's an intense process.

Volcano Erupting at School

I was in a large, single story building with many other people and a volcano was erupting, sending lava and ash onto the edge of the property, so forcing us to keep moving. Then it is time to evacuate over a swamp, causing difficulties in deciding what items to take.

Here, the volcano represents Kundalini energy. She occasionally erupts and moves to ever more subtle levels, dismantling data as she goes. Consequently, I am trying to hold on to my attachments, but the Kundalini doesn't allow this.

Fire and House

I dreamt my house had been spared a bushfire, but then I discovered that under part of the side of the house there was still a fire burning a couple of weeks later. I spent a lot of time trying to put out the fire and discovered small burning patches inside the house (seemed like the basement). So, I cleared as much of it as I could to prevent the fire from burning further.

The house represents me, and the fire was in the basement, under the house, which represents the Kundalini which resides in the base chakra. The fire represents wakefulness or consciousness. So, I'm bringing my awareness deep into the unconscious and eliminating illusory data, and it seems I was succeeding in this. Peak experience increases the fire in the unconscious and brings more of it to awareness. This represents clearing because of the peak. Similarly, this shows the five-fold process. Process always follows peak and, in this dream, there is progressive integration as I was keeping it all under control.

Huge Bushfire Next to Large City

In this dream, I was with a group, and we were in a large city. Then I noticed there was a huge bush fire, so I told the group not to head where we were going, which was somewhere near the edge of town, but to move back towards the city center where it would be safer.

The fire represents the Kundalini, the internal, transformative energy, which gradually leads to unified levels of consciousness. By witnessing it, and adjusting proximity to it, represents consciously maintaining the peak experience at a tolerable level. A full experience of holistic reality would be too intense, and I couldn't handle it. So, consciousness tempers the experience with the mind to avoid me getting burned. In short, consciousness helps to maintain a tolerable peak so that my evolutionary progression continues responsibly.

Conscious Dreaming

A conscious dreaming focus is when you focus on a particular idea or theme as you drift into sleep. If you really focus on something, the focus can flow through into your dream experience and color the dream, or dreams, accordingly. Because whatever you focus on can affect your dreams, the idea is to focus on something positive so that the dreams will also be positive. For example, you could focus on loving yourself as you are, or focus on being blissful consciousness. You could also repeat an affirmative statement such as "I am one and free," or "I am ever expanding in blissful consciousness," or "I am perfect just as I am." Whatever you focus on is likely to appear in your dreams, so the key is to keep your focus positive and uplifting so that your dreams reflect that too.

Can Dreams Refer to Past Lives or the Future?

As far as your dreams tap into the unconscious, which can include the collective unconscious of past lives, it is possible that some content from past lives may appear. In my experience, though, this is very rare, and if it happens, it is likely to be distorted by this life's data. I had a dream once in which I was getting married. I remember the woman clearly and, in the dream, I knew her as well as would be expected of someone I am about to marry. When I woke up, however, I could still remember the face of the woman, but now it was the face of a stranger. It was not someone I knew in this life. Perhaps it was someone I had known, or even married, in a past life. Other than that, from the mechanics of consciousness perspective, the dream represented balance or harmony.

By tapping into universal consciousness in your sleep, it is also possible that as far as the future is known in this level of awareness, such knowledge could make its way into the dream. I have had transmission dreams in which I have been told that something will happen, such as a leap in conscious awareness.

But caution is needed here, as the future is not set in stone and can change. It is also unlikely that you will be told anything that was not appropriate for you to know now and will usually be couched in symbolism, as the time spent focusing on a future happening is likely to hold you back from fully living in the Now and may really only have been a possibility rather than a definite fact, anyway.

Chapter 9

Personal to Transcendental Awareness

For many people, there seems to be a lack of meaning in life. Meaningfulness in life refers to a kind of aliveness that gives life a feeling of being more worthwhile. When you are in contact with the soul, there appears a center of meaning and order. When you are disconnected from your soul, there is a feeling of despair or chaos, whereas when you are connected, all is well again. This fluctuation continues and relates to a duality caused by the distinction between the personality and the soul. The soul is the center and totality of the psyche and can, therefore, reconcile all opposites. Once you have reached a certain level of development, the dualities start to disappear as more or less conscious interchange occurs between the personality and the soul and, ultimately, soul personality fusion is attained.

There are two primary energies affecting a person: the energy of the threefold personality (physical, emotional, and mental) and the energy of the soul. The energies of the personality and the soul will express themselves according to certain ray characteristics. There are seven rays or qualities of divine manifestation, and the whole of created manifestation comprises a tapestry made up of these seven qualities of divinity. The Seven Rays comprise the following qualities:

Ray 1 Will or Power,
Ray 2 Love-Wisdom,
Ray 3 Adaptability or Intelligent Activity,
Ray 4 Harmony through Conflict,
Ray 5 Concrete or Scientific Knowledge,
Ray 6 Idealistic Devotion, and
Ray 7 Organization or Ritual Order.

The other energies affecting a person are those which control the seven centers or chakras. These are also determined by ray potencies and are dominated by either the energy of the personality or of the soul. It is the conflict between the different energies that results in good or bad health.

The conflict between the soul and personality is ongoing— it is the basis behind religion, mysticism, and spiritual understanding. One understanding is that after countless lives, a person has experienced more and more of the world of form. The material world has been attractive with attendant desires, happiness and pain. This has been referred to in religious literature as the "Fall of Man." Although usually perceived as a bad thing, a sin, the reality is it was a necessary and valuable experience to be had, even though in the process man has totally forgotten the original high estate he had. This has been described as the Garden of Eden. Eventually, after countless trials and tribulations of living a material life, comes an inkling that perhaps there is something more than this. Perhaps a faint recognition, but it is a turning point. The involutionary cycle of ever-increasing materialism ends and there is a reorientation, leading to the journey back. So begins the evolutionary cycle. If there is a purpose behind all of this, maybe God, as man, had to totally forget his divine heritage so that he could more fully experience who he is on his return. It is a play of consciousness.

Now, on the path of return, the evolutionary cycle, conflict manifests physically and psychologically and assists in the evolution of man's consciousness. The early stages of the path are a gradual contact of the personality by the soul. This can cause stress and strain in the physical body from the effect of the soul energy contacting the person and vitalizing the centers in a rhythm according to the soul ray. However, the personality works against soul control. The personality is experienced mainly through the throat center and the centers below the diaphragm, so it is here that many of the problems are found.

166

At different points in a person's evolution, different objectives materialize so that the person can progress. The working out of these objectives brings with them their attendant difficulties, a process that can be quite complex and presents difficulties in determining various illnesses and states of consciousness which result.

As the various crises occur, it helps if the person can have some understanding of what is occurring and that these are a normal part of evolutionary growth. Through these crises, the person learns wisdom. Although the person suffers, he can draw on inner resources, one of which is knowledge. This is a stage in which the glamors of the world no longer hold sway. When you realize that the world is an illusion, it becomes meaningless.

In the initial stages of the evolutionary cycle, the principal aim is to experience growth and gradual soul contact in the physical, emotional, and mental bodies. This is achieved through living a full life and experiencing basic desires and emotions. The chakras involved are sluggish and semi-dormant, and the energies at play are all below the diaphragm.

The average intelligent person has the aim of responding fully to the need to develop an integrated personality for the soul to control and use. At this stage, a person is still not consciously aware of the need for soul contact. Now, the energy of the chakras below the diaphragm is more intensified, and the person operates largely from the solar plexus chakra and responds to the forces of the personality. All the chakras are brighter than before.

First Initiation

The first expansion of consciousness, or initiation, takes place when there is a dawning within the person of the need to look more towards the life of the soul. This initiation enlivens the heart chakra. Control has been gained of the physical body and now a re-orientation takes place within him to break away from past beliefs and old patterns. The person needs to step out of the crowd and independently seek his own path. There may be a feeling of being "born again" because of the soul-oriented attitude and a feeling of the need to repent of old ways. The person may also look at a healthier lifestyle and work towards personal wholeness. Increasingly, the person will feel the need to be honest with himself and look at how he can be helpful to others. Essentially, there is an aspiration towards a more spiritual life. Changes made in life will depend on individual ray makeup. A predominantly ray-one person may cut connections to old friends, whereas a ray-two person is more likely to change the type of conversation he wants to have with them.

The person will become more in charge of his emotional body and more mentally focused than he was before. The personality is still very much in control and only glimpses of the soul life are likely. The first threads of the Antahkarana are being built as a conscious line of connection between the aspirant and the soul. Also, changes take place to the physical body to purify it, but the person is not usually aware of the processes going on.

The same changes occurring in individuals at this stage can also be seen happening to groups. Groups and individuals have a separatist outlook believing that "my way" or "our way" is the correct way. The focus is still very much on the form and the divinity outside of oneself, whether it be the sacred text as the word of God, the saint, or the guru. At the same time, your religion, guru, or path is believed to be the right one, the better one, or even the only one. A group focus is, in reality, a soul impulse and yet at this stage it is in its infancy with personality goals clouding the, as yet, faint glimpses of soul awareness.

Between the first and second initiations, more and more light is revealed and there is an understanding of what is going on. The light of the soul is increasingly illuminating the personality vehicle. This light makes its presence felt through the mind.

As an "aspirant" on the spiritual path, the soul energy has

drawn the personality magnetically towards it. The forces from below the solar plexus are transferred via the solar plexus to the higher chakras. Eventually, all the energies are transferred as follows:

Base chakra—Head chakra,
Sacral chakra—Throat chakra, and
Solar plexus chakra—Heart chakra.

The person then has a much higher level of creativity and becomes aware of group consciousness. So, each of the first three initiations shows mastery of the three "vehicles" of the personality. At the first initiation, it is mastery of the physical body that has been attained. There may be many lives between the first and second initiations.

Second Initiation

The next expansion of consciousness is the second initiation. This initiation enlivens the heart chakra, and the aspirant becomes more of a disciple. The spiritual light that has been experienced through the mind has helped the person to control his emotional nature and he has become increasingly mentally polarized. Now, the throat chakra has become the primary focus, and the brow chakra has become more active. Ray 6 rules this initiation, as the goal is to know what love is. To get there, however, ray 6 needs to be worked through. The focus on the form of divinity evidenced in the first initiation is now replaced by the search for divinity within. The ray 6 quality of devotion and sometimes fanaticism is replaced by its ray 2 aspect of unconditional love and a search for the formless divinity. There is an increasing focus on an expanding consciousness, and the need for another is replaced by the search for unity in all. Although the higher attributes represented here are not achieved until the third initiation, there is more focus on achieving them. Increasingly, the mind is used as a revelation of the soul. As with the first initiation, the person may not be aware that he has undergone a change, as it is such a gradual process.

After the second initiation, the person learns more and more what love is, and the consciousness withdraws more and more from personality concerns, being used more and more as an instrument for the soul. The personality does not control the person so much and likewise, neither does it disturb his peace of mind. The problem of mental illusion is a strong disturbing factor, but increased use of the intuition can help to overcome this. Further along the path, intuitive wisdom can be used increasingly to dispel the glamors of maya.

Control of the chakras by the soul is promoted through a process of stimulation, elimination, and stabilization. Such a process affects the organs and substances near the chakras. Transference of energy is towards the brow chakra. Personality integration is at its peak and soul control is taking over. The person is now an intelligently powerful and creative person. At the second initiation, mastery of the emotional body is shown.

A new factor now enters in, the discriminating faculty of the mind. By means of it, the disciple can bring the mental life under control and dedicate it to the life of the kingdom of God, which is consummated at the third initiation. Through the correct use of the mind, the disciple is led to make right choice, and to balance (with wisdom) the endless pairs of opposites.
(Bailey, 1989b, p.100)

Third Initiation

The third initiation usually follows soon after the second and it is possible this can happen in the same lifetime. The third initiation, ruled by ray 5, is powerful, transforming and of incredible proportions. From the point of view of the Hierarchy, it is the first major initiation. More and more people today, particularly those who have undergone the second initiation, have the goal in mind that they want "Self-realization." This is the achievement to be gained by the third initiation as this is when consciousness has reached the point of personality synthesis and regular contact is maintained with the soul. More correctly, this is Soul-realization. As Self refers to the spiritual, Self-realization is not attained until the fourth initiation. The soul is sometimes referred to as the personality of the Spirit or Monad. The prime impetus for the transfiguration of this initiation comes from one's guru, or Higher Self.

The focus of life is now towards the soul and the group. Because of soul contact, the person is engaged in service, a natural expression of the soul. The person also has a conscious awareness of "being," has control of the personality and exerts dynamic will and purpose. Soul/Personality synthesis has taken place, and the person becomes an embodiment of the soul. Now the initiate has the purpose of mastering the science of soul/personality integration so that more and more the will and purpose of the Spirit or Monad can be manifested through form. By the third initiation, personality endeavors are repulsed and replaced by soul purpose, particularly as expressed by the soul ray. This initiation is referred to as the Initiation of Transfiguration. The important chakra at the third initiation is the brow chakra.

Finally, the initiate has the goal of ensuring that all the chakras respond to the ray energy of the soul and the other ray energies are subsidiary to it. The crown chakra is now radiant and beautiful. The person is energized from three sources, the energy of the lower chakras is lifted into the head, the soul energies are pouring into the crown, and the energies of the crown and base chakras are merging.

Control by the soul's energy is not complete until after the third initiation, by which time the physical vehicle has been transformed and is not subject to the health problems that are often experienced in the previous initiations. That's not to say there are no health problems, but rather, not those caused by the gradual integration of soul and personality, as this process is almost complete. At the third initiation, mastery of the mental body is demonstrated and consequently all the bodies that make up the personality.

The third initiation marks the complete fusion of soul and personality. Light floods from above and a state of "being" is achieved. The Monad is now increasingly gaining control. Higher psychic abilities are now increasingly apparent and the ability to create clear, useful thoughtforms for the service of others. The soul infused personality is selfless enough and the intellect sufficiently refined to withstand a knowing not previously possible. This continues until the fourth initiation.

Fourth Initiation

The fourth initiation, like the third initiation before, is an initiation of immense importance in your spiritual evolution. The third initiation has incorporated soul awareness into the personality so that you are now a "living soul." There are still aspects of the personality vehicles that need to be mastered, and it is not until the fourth initiation that such mastery is attained. By the fourth initiation, the personality is totally given over to the soul. Now a person is "liberated" and is no longer bound to the cycle of birth and death and need not reincarnate any more. Not that you don't reincarnate, but you will only do so to be of service to humanity. After the fourth initiation, the crown chakra is fully open, and all the chakras are vibrant and alive. The Kundalini energy is fully aroused on the physical, astral, and mental planes and vibrant from the base chakra through to the crown chakra.

Higher Initiations

The fifth initiation is considered the initiation of the Master and it is at this point that the Kundalini is fully aroused, not only in the physical body but at higher levels, too. Now, Shiva and

Shakti have finally merged in the cosmic dance of creation. The Soul has served its purpose as the personality of the Monad, and it is now the Monad, or Spirit, which is embodied in form.

The Initiations as Experienced by the Different Ray Types

In Bailey (1991, p.163) it is stated that, "There is nothing in the whole solar system, at whatever stage of evolution it may stand, which does not belong and has not always belonged to one or another of the Seven Rays." What we are concerned with here is that an individual's personality will be found to predominantly express one of the rays, as will the soul, and that it is through the process of integration of the soul and personality, through the first to third initiations in particular, being affected by their respective rays that gives the unique experience of a person to these initiations. To begin with, when there is only minimal soul contact, as in the first initiation, the response will be mostly according to the personality ray. In due time, as the personality becomes more fused with soul quality, it is the soul ray which becomes more obvious. The following examples show the changes to be expected as soul fusion of the personality takes place, leading to the third initiation.

I will take as an example a person with a ray-6 personality and a ray-2 soul. The personality may focus on narrow personal devotion to an ideal, religion or cause. He may be passionate about what he believes in, even fanatical to the extent of insisting that others follow the same ideals. The ray-2 soul, on the other hand, is more concerned with an all-inclusive spiritual love and understanding, detached, forgiving, and experiencing itself as a center of divine love. So, as the evolution of consciousness moves from being totally personality centered to soul centered, this person will move from the purely personality interpretation of ray 6 to the soul-filled interpretation of ray 2. There will be a gradual evolution from one to the other in which the person will occasionally experience crisis, moments of "light" or "revelation" as the soul and personality become integrated until eventual fusion of the two takes place.

As we are concerned with a person's growth from the perspective of the soul ray, references given to how persons on different rays experience the initiations apply to the soul rather than the personality ray. All the rays are found within the soul and yet one will be more dominant. There will be ups and downs, times when the person feels separateness from soul and other occasions when the person really feels infused. Occasionally, when light and revelation are experienced, the personality may suffer delusions of grandeur and self-importance. This is all part of the process.

Throughout the process, there is movement between the stages of alignment, crisis, light, revelation, repulsion, integration, and fusion. Following is an example of the process for individuals on each of the different ray types. For ease of writing, the masculine gender is used.

During the journey from personality control to soul control of an individual, there are many minor cycles of backward and forwards. For the ray-1 individual, the process is essentially one of control, fluctuating between achieving control and being controlled. At first, the goal is separative achievement until an alignment with the soul is attained and then he sees how his use of power has been misused. This leads him into crisis as he is shocked and disbelieving of what he has done. Eventually, light is thrown on his distortions of power and, as he evolves, he receives revelation of the source of spiritual power within himself. As soul contact increases over time, he repulses worldly power, and integration of personality and soul proceeds. Ultimately, his goal becomes one of the use of power for achievement of the divine Plan.

For the ray-2 individual, the process is about the use of love. Initially, he is concerned with worldly love, but this increasingly seems to be lacking, particularly when love is lost, and he questions what love is really all about. Alignment brings about a faint recognition of a broader, more inclusive and unconditional love. He sees the loneliness that comes about when worldly love is taken away. He senses loneliness and feels there must be more to love. In due time, this calls for a detachment from worldly values, which at the same time leads to a crisis. Light reveals the fact that personality love is not real love. It is love misused. Then, he gradually receives the revelation of his loving soul showing him a vision of a love beyond anything he has known before. Worldly love and attachment are repulsed in favor of real love, attained more and more as integration of personality and soul gradually leads to soul fusion and he realizes he is love. Finally, the personality becomes an instrument of divine love and wisdom flowing through it.

For the ray-3 individual, the process is the use of intelligence. Initially, it is a manipulative use for the perpetuation of the glamorous forms with which he surrounds himself. However, never achieving the immediate objective, he is constantly planning for the future. Alignment eventually comes about when he learns to achieve a stillness through which he can disengage from worldly pursuits. This leads to crisis through a recognition of the futility of his action and entanglement. From time to time, he senses the need for more stillness and gains a determination to stand in spiritual being. Fear and emptiness, though, are felt when he attempts to stand still. The understanding that comes about from this crisis is the light which encourages him to follow the Plan and which is more clearly seen through revelation. Through repulse, all the snares are removed and responsibility carries him forwards. Eventually, with soul and personality integration, the personality becomes an effective instrument of acute, divine intelligence, aligned with the Plan in an adaptable manner. Fusion follows giving a conscious soul infused personality intelligently executing divine purpose.

For the ray-4 individual, the process is linked to the service of humanity which is also on the fourth ray. The fourth ray creates a kind of healing or harmony, bringing all forms to an ultimate perfection and atonement through the indwelling life. It is this realization that provides the incentive for alignment. Prior to alignment, the fourth-ray individual suffers from the ill effects of inconsistency, vacillation, self-centered creativity, and an unwise, unbalanced struggle with dilemma after dilemma. He delights in the dramatic life. However, it is the faint recognition of divine harmony and peace that brings about alignment. Crisis comes about through the recognition that life is nothing but irreconcilable conflict and that there must be something more than this which, as yet, is not happening. He feels isolated, torn and despondent, and yet is determined to stand. Light reveals where fighting is useless and unnecessary, but also where it is productive. Revelation shows the warrior within who is capable of victory as well as the inner Master. The two are known to be at-one. It also shows that both sides are one. The ray-4 individual then finds that repulsion of that which is beautiful to the personality eventually helps in integrating soul and personality, thus enabling the personality to be an instrument of divine harmony, peace, and beauty. With fusion, he becomes an agent of beauty and synthesis.

For the ray-5 individual, the problem is one of mental materialism and uninspired matter-of-factness. Eventually, matter and material expertise will fail to attract. More detachment leads to more alignment and eventual crisis. This crisis is particularly noticeable in the consciousness of the personality where a balanced point of view is achieved, which the individual finds difficult as it leads to an ending of the joy-life and of desire. He now finds this arid and has a sense of loss, as there is nothing left in the material world worth knowing. Consequently, detachment is needed from the preoccupation with the senses. The crisis leads him to consider that which is worth knowing—the all illuminating mind of light behind this world. Revelation shows the relationship between the soul and personality and then repulse leads him to throw out worldly knowledge in favor of the true knowledge of the soul. Eventually, he gains a mastery of the science of energy and becomes, more and more, an agent of the divine mind.

For the ray-6 individual, the problem is one of dissociating himself from his vision, his truth, his ideals and so on, which lack the wider love of God for all. As a result, he is lost in his devotion, driven by his idea and the glamor of his own thoughts. With alignment comes the realization of the ill effects of his frenzied following of ill-considered objectives. This is accompanied by a loss of savor of those things he was previously so dedicated to. Alignment is through the faint recognition of the divine pattern or ideal behind things. Thereupon, he learns breadth of vision and a right sense of proportion. Then, he senses a need for a peaceful standing still, which at the same time evokes a crisis. This crisis shows him that none of the ways he previously followed is the way. He also recognizes that there is something which unifies all the other ways. Yet, his attempt at restraint deepens the crisis. Revelation reveals the divine idealist who respects all paths. Repulsion leads him to reject all partial dogmatic views and thus exclusivity disappears. Finally, the integration that follows, renders the personality an effective instrument of inclusive idealism. The sixth-ray individual can then join the "group." Fusion leads to a soul infused personality who is an agent of the divine pattern and the embodiment of the divine ideal.

For the ray-7 individual, the problem is one of acknowledging the ill effects of building in the dark, manifesting forms without the light. To some extent, ray-7 individuals are entombed in their own work. Then, with alignment, there is a faint recognition or sense of the true recognition of the Plan. He senses the need to construct forms that can be of value to divine purpose. So, a tremendous inflow of power is induced. He faces crisis as he recognizes he has not built true to type and realizes that in future he will need to follow the blueprint of the Plan. As he waits for this pattern to come through, he suffers the pain of ignorance. Then, as the power flows in, he is in crisis on how to handle this power without losing balance. The light reveals how he has misused the power for selfish ends, but also how it can be used for divine purpose. The continually growing light leads to revelation of the design and plan, and the role his soul must play in the scheme of things. Repulsion of all building that does not fit the divine blueprint is followed by integration, rendering the personality an effective instrument of white magic. Fusion follows, and the individual becomes more and more a means for divinity to represent itself through matter.

Facilitating the Process

Finally, it is worth looking at how the various stages in this process can be facilitated. If you are intuitively aware of a change coming about, no matter how painful it is, understand that it is part of the process. Learn to accept these changes with the awareness that at the end of the process, you will be more whole than you were before. Energies may create many tensions. So, stay with it and try to be grateful for the change that is happening. As with spiritual emergency or other Kundalini activity, soul or Monad induced change is self-healing. Tension is needed to precipitate movement. Try to evoke a vision of the soul which encourages and affirms your highest understanding of your own being and which you will uphold at all costs. For example, "I am the light," or "I am love," or "I am one with the Master."

If appropriate, try to evoke help from the Master, guru, your soul, or an image of the highest level of awareness that you can perceive. Have courage and seek alignment with your own will, or whatever method seems appropriate to you for enhancing your well-being. Therefore, you need to call for, accumulate and strengthen the energy that will eradicate the obstacle. Also, encourage friends or relatives to be with you to support you. Explain to them what is happening according to your understanding.

If childhood memories are triggered, try to be the adult rather than the child within. Accordingly, use the adult you to look after the child to meet the need that was not met in childhood. Refer to the section on Psycho-analytical Meditation and use techniques given there to help through times of difficulty.

In the stage of crisis, it is important to understand that the pain of division is actually a sign of spiritual progress. As a result, the present pain is spiritually therapeutic. The pain will stop when a new pattern is set. So, take a light into the "dark place" and see that you are going through an important phase of growth.

Self-observation helps to throw a light on the problem. No matter what the light reveals, fearlessly look and see what is presenting itself. Use the mind to bring the light in, particularly as energy follows thought. To think is to create. The eye directs the flow, and the light reveals the personality for what it is.

The soul on its own plane is revealing itself. So, intensify awareness of your inner being, by asking yourself questions while in a meditative state. For example, "I allow this expansion/ shift/energy," or "What quality does this energy have for me?"

When revelation from the soul comes blazing through, all things of the personality will appear ugly or repulsive. Such is the law of repulse when the personality is repulsed by the soul, and yet, the soul aims to integrate with it and infuse it. As a result, one should not hate the things of the personality. Instead, drop them and build anew. Redesign your life.

Integration of soul and personality is the main essence of the process through which we are journeying. There is a lot of power in integrative words and affirmations, so they need to be used wisely. It is important to appreciate all of your qualities and to synthesize them. Consequently, the task is to increase integration, both within the threefold personality and between soul and personality.

In summary, fusion of soul and personality is the goal. We are the soul; the greatest gift is being able to be who and what we are. Being a conscious soul means that we will work in full accordance with the divine Plan.

Chapter 10

Self-awareness Meditation—
Building the Bridge

Prior to building the Antahkarana, a person is focusing on trying to eliminate major faults and developing virtues. Thus, the major emphasis of religions has been to encourage people to develop good character, often with the promise of an eternal life in heaven as the goal. Building the Antahkarana begins when a conscious reorientation has been made to seek a spiritual life, when the "desire" to pursue a spiritual path has become more than simply doing what is right or wrong.

The intricate movement of energies between the seven major and many minor chakras is ongoing but shows some major patterns during the evolutionary process. Until the first awakening from the involutionary cycle to the evolutionary cycle, the major focus of activity has taken place below the diaphragm from the root chakra to the solar plexus chakra. The solar plexus is the center of the personality which has been motivated by desire, the desire to fully experience life in the material world. In fact, in the process, our original nature is forgotten. The solar plexus operates in the realm of the lower emotions and lower psychic energies. The solar plexus is the clearing house for personality energies below the diaphragm, and the energies from here must always be carried to the heart. The heart is also a clearing house between those chakras below the diaphragm and those above.

Initiations and Awakenings

According to ancient Vedic writings, there are three awakenings which take place prior to the third initiation. The first awakening is when the person aligns with the spiritual path, the path of return, or the evolutionary cycle. The second awakening occurs at the heart chakra when the heart chakra aligns with the brow chakra. Finally, the third awakening occurs when the brow chakra aligns itself with the crown chakra. Once the brow chakra and the crown chakra are completely aligned and related, the third initiation can take place. Although three awakenings are indicated prior to the third initiation, or soul-realization, in Vedic literature, there are only two initiations (expansions of consciousness) indicated in other esoteric literature. The journey between the brow chakra and the crown chakra is known as the Royal Road. When the midpoint between these two chakras is reached, an awareness of the causal level has been attained. The Royal Road culminates in full soul awareness at the third initiation.

The third initiation is a major initiation as it represents complete soul infusion into the personality. The fourth initiation represents an awareness of Monad in the personality, with the soul as the vehicle for this. Complete Monadic fusion in form is completed at the fifth initiation. This is true mastery of Divinity in form and the culmination of the evolutionary process in form. Further expansions of consciousness, of which there are many, are referred to as cosmic initiations. These are beyond the realm of human experience.

Once the will to pursue the spiritual path on the evolutionary cycle has begun at the first awakening at the base chakra, building of the rainbow bridge begins. The initiate has passed through the door of the first awakening, and even if unknowingly, has commenced building a bridge toward another distant door at a later initiation. Likewise, there is a reciprocal will to build from the Monadic level. It is a creative process. The desire for spiritual growth becomes a way of life, albeit very tenuous in the initial stage. Now, a very thin bridge has been built between the mental aspect of the Monad, the higher mind, and the mental aspect of the personality, the lower mind.

At the first awakening, triggered by the soul via the crown

chakra, a process of alignment of the lower chakras begins, eventually aligning the base chakra to the heart chakra. Until this point, a second center within the solar plexus, which until now has lain dormant, awakens. Soul activity increases its connection with the solar plexus, which is slowly awakened by a dual energy coming from the heart and crown chakras. It is probably around this time that the first initiation takes place. This corresponds to two of the three energies of the soul, spiritual will or atma, and spiritual love or buddhi. The third energy of the soul, mental energy or manas, is related more to the throat chakra as a center of higher creativity, as opposed to the sacral chakra, which is a center of lower creativity. As the throat chakra awakens, it receives two separate energies, one from the soul via the crown chakra and one from the sacral chakra. So, the throat chakra is to the chakras above the diaphragm what the sacral chakra is to the chakras below the diaphragm. The second focus point in the solar plexus is completely awakened prior to the second initiation.

Building the bridge is not something that just takes place during meditation. It is an ongoing process in the daily life of a meditator. The meditator's life becomes a life spent in joy and ecstasy, blissful experience and increasing revelation. The bridge continues to be built by the soul and Monad as the ego loses its grip. Accordingly, the ego's days are numbered as personality experience increasingly provides a vehicle for soul awareness in form. The third initiation completes this process and yet the Monad's Presence increases until soul awareness expands into Monadic awareness. This process finds its peak of awareness at the fourth initiation, an awareness which is not of the individual so much as the divine in human form. Divine awareness is all-encompassing, an awareness of humanity, and of service to the whole. Then, the Monad guides, leads, and includes through its perfect expression on the material plane. Consequently, through his work, his life spiritually lived, and scientifically applied through intention, visualization, and projection, the person has become invocative, and a point of invitation, tension and living energy.

Up to a certain point in our evolution, the work being done on the Antahkarana is done unconsciously. Occasionally, glimpses of this may penetrate consciousness, often as revelations, until further along the path, awareness of the process becomes established. At first, we are not aware of the link between personality and soul, although the soul, from its own level of awareness, is. On the evolutionary cycle, we become increasingly aware of the existence of the soul. The purpose of this stage in the evolutionary process is to transmute consciousness from the ego to the soul. In other words, towards Soul-realization.

There are two aspects to the life of a meditator. A life of spiritual reflection during the day and planned meditations, individual or group. Likewise, there are four stages in the meditation process. In order, these are concentration, alignment, meditation, and contemplation. The aim is to achieve the highest point of focus possible and preserve it. Specifically, it is the use of the mind to contemplate and work with energies that is the goal. Although, for the beginner, it is not usually possible to verify the effects of the building process, as much relies on faith. Indications may appear through a flash of inspiration, a synchronistic experience, or simply an ability to understand the spiritual fundamentals involved.

Therefore, the Antahkarana is built through conscious effort within consciousness itself and not simply doing and saying the right thing. It is the activity of an integrated, dedicated personality. So, it is important to perfect the personality and consciously focus thought intentionally on the mental plane through such processes as meditation. There is little to be gained by simply waiting for something to happen.

It is important to remember all the time that there is a two-way focus. There is a conscious projection of thought into the soul world but, at the same time, there is an increasing ability for the soul to project itself into the personality and an increase in intuition. Once a degree of intuition is attained, a better understanding of the Path is gained. This helps to increase the benefits of meditation and further increase intuition.

The mind needs to be focused through discipline, and an ability is needed to distinguish between intuition and psychic phenomena. Intuition, when received, also needs to be "clothed" in appropriate thoughtforms to be utilized in the physical realm. When intuition is received, it comes from a subtler dimension, where language is not in the form we are used to. Impressions received are filtered by our personality before we receive them. However, this means it is possible to misunderstand the message. Messages are received as symbols, archetypes, synchronistic experiences, and in dreams.

The results of one's efforts in meditation, and the will-to-live as a spiritual being over time, are important determinators in the progress made towards building the Antahkarana. However, a person may not be consciously aware of success in this until later along the Path. The Antahkarana is, therefore, a unified effort of soul and personality to produce a bridge between them, which at the same time evokes a magnetic response from higher spiritual levels, projecting a triple stream of spiritual energy towards the soul and the personality. As soul and personality fusion increase, the creative thread becomes more active, and the person reaches a point where he must now consciously work at building the Antahkarana and fuse the three threads which comprise the Antahkarana. These are life (atma), consciousness (buddhi), and creativity (manas).

The first stage in consciously building the rainbow bridge is to focus energy upon the mental plane at the highest point of which you are capable. In meditation, this is when the mind is focused as steadily as possible. It can be projected outwards to a point such as a candle flame or held steady within the brow or crown chakras. In the initial stages the desired result may simply be the ability to keep one's point of mental focus at one spot but ultimately the need is to focus on the highest possible point to divinity as one can perceive it, e.g., the light, the form of one's guru within the mind or the crown chakra. Experiment with these, but the most suitable for Antahkarana work is a point in the center of the head between the pituitary gland and the pineal gland. Eventually, concentration will shift completely to the pineal gland. Specifically, the pituitary gland is the physical externalization of the brow chakra, while the pineal gland is the physical externalization of the crown chakra. It is important that you use the mind intelligently and consciously. So, this increasing focus will involve an understanding of the difference between the thinker, the mind as the apparatus of thought, and thought itself, including an awareness of thoughtforms and ideas. Much thought will be given by the meditator to spiritual concepts and ideas and an increasing desire to meditate and look within. Then you will see the benefits of visualization exercises, mantras, affirmations, etc.

Meditation requires an ability to use the mind for receptivity to ideas and creativity through thought. Meditation is a two-way process. A link needs to be created between the threefold personality (physical, emotional, and mental bodies) and the soul. In the early stages, the link between them is only rarely recognized consciously, but this increases as the contact between the two is strengthened and eventually becomes the line of least resistance. When this part of the bridge is complete, the energies animating the physical body, the emotional body and the mental body are blended with, and transmuted into, the energies of the soul. These include the spiritual mind with its illumination, the intuitive nature with its spiritual perception, and divine livingness.

Receptivity to intuition, albeit very minimal in the early stages, and the ability to visualize and create ideas and thoughtforms is important. Mind control is an important part of meditation. It is the ability to use the lower mind to focus on and be receptive to the higher mind of the soul, and eventually to the mind of the spiritual triad of the Monad or oversoul. However, for now, we are only concerned with creating the bridge between personality and soul, and consequently building or creating a link between the lower mind and the higher mind. It is the completion of this link that leads to enlightenment as we know it, a person submerged in the bliss of being and without ego. This is the path that creates a soul infused personality. It requires the ability to focus the mind and be receptive to intuition and the ability to distinguish between intuition and psychic ability.

A common misperception is that psychic ability is an indication of spirituality. However, this is not the case. Psychic ability is an ability to be open to the unconscious mind, in particular, the collective unconscious. With spirituality, the personality becomes an instrument of the soul. So, anyone who meditates with the intention of connecting with their soul is building the Antahkarana. This will also show through an improving ability to meditate, lifestyle, and service in the community. Service is a natural quality of the soul, so as one becomes more soul-infused, service comes naturally.

In essence, the Antahkarana is built by a combined effort of the Monad evoking a response from the personality and the personality invoking assistance from the Monad. It is the spiritual will, the will of the Monad, which "informs" the will of the personality, creating a combined approach to building the Antahkarana. You, as the personality, want to build the bridge and create a link with the soul and Monad. Even though you may not realize it, the effort to do so is initiated by and assisted by the Monad. At the personality level, spiritual growth is aided by meditation, invocation, and prayer. A prime example of how this works is the activity of the Kundalini. You may or may not be aware of the Kundalini energy working within you. You have no control over how the Kundalini works. Once the Kundalini is active within the personality, the will of the personality has little relevance. The Kundalini knows what it is doing, and the personality is purely the burning ground. The personality must surrender to the Kundalini and let it do its job. The Kundalini therefore operates at the will of the Monad, not at the will of the personality. It is also important to remember that what we see and experience in our environment reflects what happens within. The Kundalini works to clear impressions, conditionings, issues, etc., which have been stored in your psychological makeup over many lives. To do this, associated events and experiences may appear in your daily life for you to work on and transcend. Often these issues relate to self-worth, love, fear, desires, habits, and all those worldly matters which ultimately keep us from a purely spiritual path and would not serve a soul-infused personality but serve the ego-centric personality. Once you are on the evolutionary cycle out of the illusion of separation, it can be said that all experience is triggered by the Kundalini for transcendence.

Focusing and Containing Energy

So, the first step in constructing the Antahkarana is intention, as in focus. This is not setting an intention as in the usual meaning of the word, but focusing one's awareness at a point in the head and holding this focus. This continued focus gathers energy at the point of focus, following the principle that energy follows thought. Then, continued focus gathers and enhances the energy, while at the same time contains the energy so that it is not dissipated. The better the focus, the better the containment. With practice, focus becomes easier. Do not try to manipulate the energy at this stage. Willfully focus on a point in the middle of your head between the pituitary and pineal glands. Later, the focus will shift purely to the pineal gland. By focusing on one spot, you create a point of tension there.

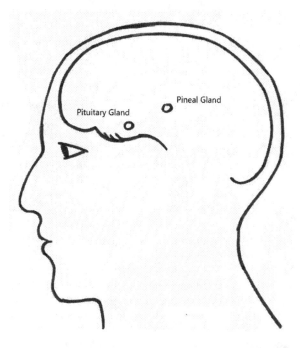

Pineal Gland

Pituitary Gland

Figure 10 Location of Pituitary and Pineal Glands

We've now reached a point where we know how to meditate and create a point of tension in the head. The next step of creative visualization requires perfection to this point. Later, this is followed by "projecting" which is given in the chapter on Advanced Techniques. Increasingly, a connection with the soul is being made, occasional revelations are being received, and not necessarily just in meditation, and slowly you are feeling an alignment with your soul. Even though it is possible for evolution to proceed naturally without these techniques, a conscious understanding and application of a technique of alignment is valuable. An understanding of the seven ray energies which underlie creation will aid in the process as we, as individuals, have a particular ray makeup. This helps with conscious building of the Antahkarana.

Creative Visualization

It is important to remember that we are dealing with energy and it is through the creative imagination, working with energy, that the Antahkarana is constructed. Through the creative process of relating positive and negative energies with each other, in this case the personality is the negative polarity and the soul is the positive polarity, a resultant magnetic force is produced which can then bring together these different expressions of life energy, by building a link between them and revealing the higher to the lower and permitting the higher to experience the lower. This point of magnetic attraction will later attract the creative imagination from the astral body, as well as a Buddhic or intuitive impression from the level of the soul. The creation of this duality is what building the Antahkarana is about.

In terms of the initiations, only those who have completed the first initiation would consciously wish to do this, and the early process itself is a preparation for the second initiation.

During the process, it is important to use the mind to respond to intuition or Buddhic impressions, and through an act of creative imagination gathering and focusing energy while, at the same time, preserving the tension without causing too much strain on the brain cells. At this point of accomplishment, there is a focal point of mental energy, enabling the personality to be aligned and receptive. This also allows the soul to be oriented towards the personality in a state of constant, directed perception.

The resultant magnetic field helps to align personality and soul. Soul awareness of the personality is essential while the Antahkarana is being built. Likewise, the soul's awareness of the personality must exist alongside the intention of the personality. Over time, the use of mental focus will increase the magnetic field in the head until, eventually, in meditation, the mind will immediately move to the focal point with ease. It will be drawn to this point. At such time, there may be an accompanying glow or light which is apparent at the same time. For some people, this may be seen in the brow chakra and may even be accompanied by a sound. Now, sufficient energy has been gathered at the point of focus and it is time to move into creative visualization.

Once the right point of tension has been reached and the reservoir of needed energy has been restrained, then you can use your imagination. Imagination is the personality equivalent of intuition. When the imaginative faculties have been refined so that they respond to intuitive perception, the building of the Antahkarana can proceed more accurately. Remember, the work you do is always accompanied by help from the soul.

Creative imagination is used to affect the energy substance gathered through meditation. It is an active energy able to produce an effect on the mental substance when brought into relationship with the point of tension. "Visualization is the process whereby the creative imagination is rendered active and becomes responsive to and attracted by the point of tension upon the mental plane" (Bailey, 1982b, p.489).

In the early stages, the bridge is a construction between the personality and soul. However, the soul body is itself a temporary construct, so later, as the process continues, the link is being created between the soul infused personality and the Monad. The resources being called forth from the soul are actually effects of a radiation from the Monad. In due time, as this process continues, certain soul qualities will increase in evidence in the person's life, love of the whole, greater wisdom, enhanced bliss, and ecstasy. The person also finds a greater ability to transmute the fruit of experience, which is knowledge, into wisdom.

It is the use of will power that is required for this to take place. The importance of will power is greatly underestimated in the west. However, although some personal will power helps, ultimately it is the Will of the Monad that is required for a person to go much further. The effort we take is more than matched by the soul/Monad reaching down to help us up.

Through creative imagination, one practices using visualization of images in the head between the pituitary gland and pineal gland. Then, when proficient, one focuses on an area around the pineal gland alone. This creates a magnetic field around the gland, and the gathered energy can then be intentionally directed to one or more of the chakras as required. All of this is done as a pictorial process. Using visualization creates a picture form while the energy of thought gives it life and direction. This therefore creates a thoughtform, a link between the emotional/astral body and the mental body. In reality, this is positive, beneficial thoughtform building.

Before the soul is fully infused in the personality, it abides in its own temporary vehicle, the causal body. At the third initiation, the ego, also a temporary construct, is replaced by the soul, and the soul infused personality results. Eventually, by the fourth initiation, the Monad takes over the soul infused personality and the causal body disappears. The triplicity now becomes a duality and is pure Monad in form.

Sutratma and the Antahkarana

Knowledge gained by the personality through past experience is contained in the consciousness thread, while present awareness and the ability to create is found in the creative thread. These combine with the life thread, which is known as the sutratma, to form the Antahkarana. Another name for the life thread is the silver cord. Indeed, the sutratma embodies the will and purpose of any expressing entity and its outer expression. Further, it vivifies and unifies all forms into one functioning whole, whether human, plant, or crystal. In humans, it is a stream of living energy between the Monad and the personality.

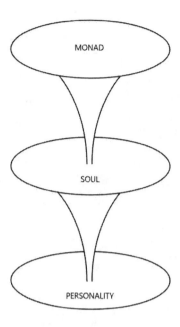

Figure 11 Relationship of Monad, Soul and Personality

The second awakening begins an alignment between the heart chakra and the brow chakra and roughly corresponds to the second initiation. There is, however, a third awakening which takes place before the third initiation and that is at the commencement of the alignment of the brow chakra and the crown chakra. It is during this phase that control of the personality by the ego gradually diminishes until full soul infusion of the personality is achieved at the third initiation, at which time the brow and crown chakras are fully aligned and related.

Using the imagination, the next step is to begin construction of the bridge. With a fine-tuned imagination of the highest order possible, the task is to be as responsive as possible to intuitive perception, received from the Buddhic level. Imagination is an aspect of the astral body, and intuitive perception is an aspect of the soul body. As already mentioned, the construction is not purely a creation of the personality, but a collaboration with the creative aspect of the soul. It is a coming together, a joint exercise and so the necessity to utilize the highest aspect of creative imagination possible from the personality level to be in tune and receptive to Buddhic impressions.

The creative imagination is an active energy which can work with the energy created at the point of tension. Increased tension and a clear process of visualization, leads to a strong and beautiful bridge. The meditator is now working with two energies, a quiescent energy held at the point in the middle of the head and an active, creative, responsive energy utilized in the construction process. So, there is the tension held by the mental body, the Buddhic activity of impression, and the astral activity of imagination.

Once the meditator can consciously know all three processes at the same time, then the work can proceed successfully. The dual Buddhic-astral activities are aligned by a current of force passing through the magnetic force held in the head, organizing the substance there, increasing its potency, ready for the next stage.

Chapter 11

Advanced Techniques

Projecting

It is the will that is required for projection to take place. Although some personal will helps, it is the Will of the Monad that is required for a person to go further. Now comes a difficult part, which is use of the will to project the created substance up towards the soul and higher still to the Monad. There are three aspects to this: continued visualization, use of the will and an appropriate word of power. These are needed to project the created light substance forward. Together, the personality and soul have created a connection. As the third initiation approaches, when soul connection is felt in meditation, it is possible to begin the early projection process. Later, after the third initiation, the personality and soul combined will project a line toward the Monad. A "word of power" is required, which varies from individual to individual and is related to one's soul-personality makeup. Sound underlies creation and forms part of the fabric of existence. The universe, for example, was created by the sound OM and which some meditators can hear vibrating in very deep meditation.

In order to make this projection, the resources of the meditator's soul are needed. These are stored up in "the jewel in the lotus." This is the point in the Egoic lotus of the soul where the Monad is anchored. The qualities to be found here, and which the aspirant needs to use, are those of wisdom rather than knowledge, and love for the whole, plus an increasing power to renounce. At this stage, one is increasingly experiencing a state of bliss and ecstasy which results from an understanding and recognition of the will-to-good. When perfected, the aspirant can evoke the Will, thus linking higher and lower, Monad and personality, and leading to the fourth initiation.

There are three parts to projection:

1. Use of the will according to the soul's ray quality,
2. Awareness that, as personality and soul, the aspirant is consciously building the bridge. Awareness of the point of tension produced and the energies flowing into it from the personality and the soul. Awareness, as far as possible, of the consciousness of the soul ray energy and that it is through this that the Monad expresses itself, and
3. Preparing to use the appropriate ray method to project using the words of power.

The problem is, how can you be consciously aware of your ray energy and how to use it? All I can say is that by the time you have reached this point, many intuitive impressions or revelations will have been received from the Buddhic level of awareness and intuitively you will understand which ray method is most appropriate for you. Alternatively, using a method of communicating with your subconscious can be used, such as kinesiology or conscious dreaming. You may also find that you resonate with one of the ray type processes given for the stages from alignment to soul fusion given in an earlier section. Remember, your personality and soul are likely to be on different rays and it's tricky to determine which is which.

Having determined your soul/personality ray makeup, use the following procedure:

Focus on the now established point of light established in the center of the head and the resultant magnetic field. Then, accepting that this forms a point of contact with the soul, visualize the threefold threads (atma, buddhi and manas) extending toward the soul and further to the Monad and be aware that through this link, intuition will be received. So, with your personal creative effort and that of the soul, through intuition, the connection will be gradually built. If you know your ray makeup, then the bridge can be colored with the two colors representing personality and soul rays as follows:

Ray 1 scarlet,
Ray 2 indigo,
Ray 3 green,
Ray 4 yellow,
Ray 5 orange,
Ray 6 blue-rose, and
Ray 7 violet.

I would point out here that the name "Rainbow Bridge" is called this because it comprises the seven colors of the seven ray energies of which it is made. It is also valuable to point out that the personality ray varies from incarnation to incarnation, so all rays will have been experienced at some time. The soul ray, however, always remains the same. In visualizing soul and personality ray colors, emphasis should be given to the color of the soul ray, which becomes increasingly dominant as soul personality fusion increases.

After visualizing soul connection and the appropriate ray colors, the qualities of the personality and soul rays are synthesized and appropriate words of power for the soul ray are uttered. The combined personality and soul are sending their fused message, through an act of will, to assert through the quality of the soul ray a response from the spiritual triad of the Monad. This is an act of willful invocation, or appeal, evoking a response. However, as we don't know at this stage what ray the Monad is on, we do not consider its ray in this process.

Ray One, working dynamically from a central point of *inspiration*, sends out the command **"I assert the fact."**

Ray Two asserts from a place of *love and wisdom*, **"I see the Greatest Light."**

Ray Three asserts from a place of *active intelligence*, **"Purpose Itself Am I."**

Ray Four asserts from a place of *harmony through conflict*, **"Two Merge with One."**

Ray Five asserts from a place of *concrete knowledge*, **"Three Minds Unite."**

Ray Six asserts from a place of *devotion or idealism*, **"The Highest Light Controls."**

Ray Seven asserts from a place of *ceremonial law or order*, **"The Highest and the Lowest Meet."**

As the Antahkarana is being built, a point is reached where there is a perfect connection between the Monad and the personality. This is when the third initiation takes place. The personality which is infused with soul awareness has a direct link with the Monad. So now, the personality is no longer controlled by the lower mind of the ego, but by the soul. The ego disappears as Soul-realization is attained. By the time of the fourth initiation, there is complete mastery of the personality by the Monad. Then, the love energy of the soul, combined with the higher Will, leads to a loving will, enabling the "Enlightened Master" to serve wisely. The causal body, the vehicle for the soul, disappears. Complete mastery has been achieved of the Monad in form. The man is now Monadic awareness in human form and the soul is no longer needed. The personality still exists, but is now a vehicle for the Monad.

By the fourth initiation, when the Antahkarana is completed and the soul body dissipated, there is finally the real duality of Monad and matter or life and form. Then, the merger between Father and Mother, Monad and personality, Shiva and Shakti, is complete. The divine marriage has taken place in the individual, just as it will later take place in humanity and throughout the whole of creation. The Will of Shiva has aroused his beloved Shakti, the Kundalini, to unite with Him through the human form bringing into awareness all the chakras to operate at their highest vibration with the final merger taking place at the crown chakra.

Now, there is a duality which is aware of its unity, Monad (Spirit) and form (matter). The soul, the consciousness aspect, has been absorbed into both aspects of divine expression. This is Nirvana, which is yet the beginning of the higher Way along which duality is later resolved into unity.

When the Antahkarana is fully complete, the person's individual consciousness can then operate at one of three focuses:

- within humanity through a bodily form, the "mayavirupa," created for Monadic purpose.
- within the Hierarchy using all-inclusive Buddhic awareness, and
- within Shambala, the source of the sutratma.

By the time of the fourth initiation, the Master no longer has a soul. The Master is now effectively the Monad in form, a divine incarnation.

Despite the many threads and stages life passes through, at the end, it is life merging with consciousness. The illusion of separation is never more than just that, and yet by experiencing that which it isn't (illusion) life can more fully be that which it is (Source).

The personality no longer has work to do. It is now a pure instrument of divine will and purpose, affecting and entraining the environment around. One day, the whole of humanity will rejoice as one divine expression on earth.

The blazing light of divine expression utilizes the completed bridge. The individual is no longer separate from the one he knows himself to be, operating as one of the Hierarchy, responsive to impressions from ever higher levels of divine awareness.

Pratyahara (Deep Focus Meditation and Sense Withdrawal)

Sit in a comfortable position for meditation with as few distractions as possible. Then, mentally relax the whole body and be as passive as possible without using mental effort. Next, imagine your body is as still as a mountain and maintain that thought. Do not allow other thoughts to come. Steadfastly maintain the one focus.

With practice, this will become easier, and you will notice your breath rate will decrease. Whereas a normal relaxed breathing rate is around 20 cycles a minute, with practice, this will reduce to under 10 cycles a minute. Eventually, with continued practice, the breath rate will reduce even more. If you can reach a natural rate of around 3 or less cycles a minute, meditation is so deep that there is an automatic withdrawal of your senses. You are still conscious, but awareness of your surroundings disappears. To assist with bringing about a natural slowing of breathing, a sequence can be introduced in the ratio of 1-4-2. One count for the in-breath followed by 4 for suspension and then 2 for the out-breath. If each count is in seconds, then each cycle lasts 7 seconds and thus equivalent to 9 cycles a minute. Over time, this can be increased to 2-8-4, which is equivalent to 4 cycles a minute. Ancient adepts in India were able to apply the practice at a count of 16-64-32. This should come naturally. Do not try to forcefully slow your breathing. As you get more and more absorbed in your meditation, you will observe your breathing naturally slows down.

There is also a thought process you can follow while your breath rate is low to practice sense withdrawal manually. It is as follows.

As you inhale slowly through both nostrils, imagine the very subtle, lightning like Kundalini life force arising from the red triangle in the base chakra. When the inhalation has completed, suspend your breath and imagine that the sense of smell, which is based in the base chakra, has been completely absorbed by the Kundalini. Then, exhale slowly, imagining that you no longer have your sense of smell. There is no timing for this. Just inhale and exhale slowly and fully. For the suspension, hold this for as long as is comfortable.

Next, imagine the Kundalini in the sacral chakra and, using the same breath process, absorb the sense of taste by the Kundalini. Follow the same process to absorb the sense of sight in the solar plexus chakra, the sense of touch in the heart chakra, and the sense of hearing in the throat chakra, respectively. For each of the five chakras, there is one round of inhalation, suspension, and exhalation. So, the entire process comprises five rounds.

Dharana (Deep Concentration with Meditation on a Form)

When deep meditation comes more easily and cycles of breathing naturally slow to below 5 cycles a minute, then it is possible to move to the next level in meditation. Ultimately, the goal is to attain a realization of the inner divinity or supreme consciousness in meditation. Consequently, it helps to visualize "divinity" in a form with which one is comfortable.

Our experience of reality is through a world of duality in which we experience ourselves as separate from others. Although the inner Self is closer in experience to the Oneness of everything, to get to that realization, we need to move through and beyond the world of form. In our spiritual lives, we look to others for inspiration and guidance. These are others who have attained a much higher spiritual realization and have occasionally held out a helping hand to guide us towards the same realization they now experience. Included among these are the great spiritual leaders around whom some of the world's great religions have been formed. There are also sages, saints, avatars, gurus, spiritual Masters, yogis, etc. These spiritual adepts are the closest we can see to divinity in human form.

In dharana meditation, it is necessary to visualize divinity in form. Hinduism has a multitude of divine forms or deities, each with a particular appearance and characteristics, symbolic of the divine qualities they represent. It is often mistakenly believed that Hinduism has many gods, but in reality, these gods represent different aspects of the One God. In Kundalini or chakra yoga, in their deeper understanding, each chakra has deities associated with it, based on an even deeper understanding of the energies associated with that chakra. Unless you have been brought up in the Hindu tradition, it is questionable whether focusing on a Hindu deity in form will provide the same benefit as it would a Hindu. It is important, however, to focus on a divine form with which you can relate. This could be a deity, saint or holy person from your own religion, or an archetype, such as a glorious bright light, full of love, that you can look to. The purpose is to associate your greatest aspirations with that form.

A Hindu, for example, could visualize Brahma, a Buddhist could visualize Buddha or Quan Yin, a Christian could visualize Jesus or the Virgin Mary. In fact, many religions or traditions have a form of the Blessed Mother, representing the consciousness of creation. Whatever, for you, is the highest form of divinity you can visualize is the most appropriate, whether a deity or an archetype, to represent divine qualities. Imagining a vivid form of divinity is valuable, as the form can be focused on to where it is literally brought to life, as if that form is really there. In higher stages of meditation, you will merge with this divinity and realize, ultimately, that it is none other than your own Self.

Dhyana (Meditative Absorption)

The more you can visualize the form of divinity, to see and experience this divinity, then ultimately you can merge with this form and realize that it is none other than your higher Self. Even without a meditation process, as above, biographical accounts of those who have attained Self-realization through the inner

202

workings of the Kundalini show the appearance of a divine form with incredible love and wisdom emanating from it. As a result, this provides inspiration to move closer and closer to the form with ever more wondrous visions. This process continues until eventually all barriers disappear and merger is complete with the subtlest aspects of the divine and Self-realization attained.

Samadhi (Union)

The term samadhi refers to union with the divine. The divine is no longer seen as separate from yourself, instead, now you are the divine. Thus, all barriers, all that which has kept you separate from your true divine nature, all the conditioning which created your third-stage self, all the desires of your animal self, have been transcended. Then, the ego disappears, and you are soul incarnate (third initiation). Later, with total mastery of the world of form, you will become Monad incarnate (fourth and fifth initiations). This is the goal and purpose of human life. Through the experience of many lives in form, and resultant forgetting of your divine nature, you have returned to that which you truly are, and yet somehow more than you have ever been because of the experience.

When a meditator is in samadhi, they are experiencing the bliss of union with the divine. Samadhi has different "forms" representing different levels of union. It is possible to experience samadhi, a glimpse of union, without having experienced permanent union.

Bhutashuddhi Pranayama–Purificatory Breathing

This chakra meditation combines chakra energies and pranayama to utilize internal vital energy or life force for clearing and rebuilding the physical and subtle bodies. In short, this is another technique for increasing Self-awareness. Previously, we saw that diagrammatic representations of each chakra are highly symbolic, and this symbolism provides insight into the energies within the chakra. Care is needed, however, when meditating on each chakra, as an unguided chakra meditation arouses the qualities or energies of that chakra and without care, this can cause randomly pleasant or unpleasant experiences. The purpose of the chakra meditation given here is not to "play" with these energies, but to consciously arouse and purify them in a guided and safe manner. The method used is ancient and known as Bhutashuddhi pranayama, a form of Sahita breathing. This, as well as the power of mantra and concentration, leads to deep, internal purification. The technique of Bhutashuddhi pranayama involves inhalation, breath suspension, and exhalation in the ratio of 16-64-32. The numbers represent the measure applied to the breathing process. These higher numbers are significant when an advanced pranayama is practiced but, according to our ability, we can shorten this to 4-16-8, or 2-8-4, or even 1-4-2, as long as the same proportion is applied. The method does not focus on one individual chakra but links, in sequence, several chakras required for the purification of personal impurities within the subtle body.

Before outlining the techniques used, there are important points to consider. The mantras are known as seed or germ mantras. Each represents a matrika letter associated with the energy of a particular chakra. Thus, correct pronunciation of each mantra is important, so it is good to practice them beforehand, both verbally and semi verbally. Repetition of a mantra is known as japa. The ending of the mantras has a nasal sound which I have identified by "ᵐ" following them. Some texts will show this as a normal "m," others as "n" or even "ng." It is written here in superscript to show that it is the preceding letter that has a nasal sound rather than being a letter itself. For the indu chakra, the "tha" is an aspirated T, as in Thomas. It is not pronounced as a "th" as in "the" or "think." "V" in Sanskrit is pronounced as halfway between a V and a W. Therefore, in English, this is sometimes written with a W.

Mantras for each of the lower four chakras are used, as well as a mantra, to draw energy from the minor indu chakra in the middle of the forehead. Each chakra, with its mantra, quality, color, and purpose in purificatory breathing, is as follows:

For the base chakra, the mantra is La^m, which has the quality of earth, the color yellow, and the purpose of form building.

For the sacral chakra, the mantra is Va^m, which has the quality of water, the color moon white, and the purpose of irradiation and form building.

For the solar plexus chakra, the mantra is Ra^m, which has the quality of fire, the color red, and the purpose of burning and elimination.

For the heart chakra, the mantra is Ya^m, which has the quality of air, the color of smoke, and the purpose of drying.

For the indu chakra, in the middle of the forehead, the mantra is Tha^m, which has the color white and the purpose of rebuilding the body.

Repetition of these mantras in the correct sequence dries, burns, eliminates and renews personal impurities.

A breathing exercise, or pranayama, is used along with repetition of the mantra and follows a particular sequence of inhalation, suspension, and exhalation through each nostril, along with a set time measure for each. This procedure evokes the correct response from the vayu energy (pranic energy or life force) similar to that elicited by the mantra. Breathing causes the vayu energy to become the energy of a seed mantra and radiate the associated color. It requires us to think about the process to enable it to work properly. This follows the theory that energy follows thought. It is easier for beginners to repeat the mantra the correct number of times and visualize the mantra as bathed in the correct color than to perform the difficult breathing exercise. If you wish to practice the breathing technique as well, shorten the inhalation, suspension and exhalation to a time frame that is manageable, ensuring it adheres to the correct time formula.

If you were to follow the original practice given in ancient manuscripts, allowing one second to pass for each repetition of the mantra means one complete round of pranayama will take 112 seconds. Allowing half a second for each repetition will take 56 seconds. Most people cannot hold their breath for this length of time. If you add the fact that there are three consecutive breathing cycles required, it is made even more difficult. So, the time needs to be reduced according to one's ability and comfort level. For this reason, in the beginning a suitable sequence would be 1-4-2, keeping to the same time sequence. As mentioned earlier, the correct time measure is important as, along with the correct use of left or right nostril, it evokes the required quality of vayu energy needed. Over time, this can be increased to 2-8-4, or 4-16-8, or 8-32-16 and perhaps eventually even 16-64-32. Use whatever time sequence you are most comfortable with. There is nothing to be gained by forcing slower breathing. In very advanced meditation, breathing can naturally slow down considerably.

There are three parts to the process. Each part is needed for drying, burning, elimination, and replacing impurities. So, the 16-64-32 sequence is repeated three times, with the alternate nostril sequence changing. The first sequence begins with the left nostril, the second sequence with the right nostril, and the third sequence begins again with the left nostril.

As mentioned, thought is important to the entire process, so concentrating on what you are doing is critical too. Likewise, breathing makes the thought forceful and effective. Thought, breath and mantra are intrinsic to the process of purification. Thoughts are about the sound of the mantra, the color of the mantra, repetition of the mantra, and the desired action of the mantra. Then, along with breathing, the desired effect is attained.

There are three parts to the purificatory process:

Method 1

1. The mantra Ya^m, along with the breathing sequence (inhalation, suspension and exhalation), performs a drying function.
2. The mantra Ra^m, along with the breathing sequence, performs a burning and elimination function.
3. The mantra Tha^m, along with the breathing sequence, performs a rebuilding function.

There is also a technique which divides the third part into a further three parts. Here, the sequence is:

Method 2

1. The mantra Ya^m, along with the breathing sequence, performs a drying function.
2. The mantra Ra^m, along with the breathing sequence, performs a burning and elimination function.
3.
   I. The mantra Tha^m, during inhalation, showers the body with amrita used for rebuilding.
   II. The mantra Va^m, during suspension, irradiates the body with the amrita for rebuilding.
   III. The mantra La^m during exhalation firms the newly created body.

During the process of purification, drying of physical and subtle body impurities is always done by the air germ mantra Ya^m. Burning and removal of the ash is always done by the fire germ manta Ra^m. Then, Tha^m is used to evoke the white-colored amrita from the indu chakra, Va^m irradiates the physical and subtle bodies through the water qualities of the sacral chakra, while La^m helps in building a new form through the earth quality of the base chakra. If method 1 is used, then the mantra Tha^m showers, irradiates and rebuilds through the breathing sequence.

As mentioned earlier, using the Bhutashuddhi pranayama is to remove impurities. There is no mention of what the impurities are other than in the body. I suspect this refers to the physical, emotional and mental bodies. Today, there are many energy therapies aimed at healing. Some focus on any ailments, while others focus on emotional problems. The reasons given why these work vary. I would suggest that all techniques require an intention that healing takes place, similar to the need for thinking through the process given in Bhutashuddhi pranayama. Inevitably, mistakes will be made. As long as the intention is there, the process will still work, even if you are not always aware of the results.

Notes

1. Asserting that all facts pertaining to the Antahkarana, its connecting points, e.g., personality, soul, spiritual triad, Monad, etc., and linkages are true, and this part of projection is completed.
2. Asserting through an effort to see the whole through the greatest light of awareness possible.
3. Asserting that the divine quality of matter and Spirit are essentially one and so identification with Spirit is achieved.
4. Asserting that opposite polarities harmoniously merge into the One they truthfully are.
5. Asserting the three minds, universal mind, higher mind, and lower mind are blended through the Antahkarana.
6. Asserting that the greatest light of consciousness controls all lower lights.
7. Asserting the link between Monad and personality.

Chapter 12

The Way Forward

The path to enlightenment, or Self-awareness, can be a difficult one, particularly in the later stages. It's not so much about what you gain, because in reality you won't gain anything you don't already have. It's just that for now, you have lost sight of who you really are. What you will lose, instead, is your false ego identity, the false "I" that you think you are. However, the ego doesn't give up without a fight, its entire existence is at stake. This chapter is dedicated to the way ahead and the best way to do this is to look at the experience of two people who became Self-realized and how that journey unfolded for them.

B.S. Goel suffered a difficult journey to Self-realization after his Kundalini was awakened, as his ego structure, or cage, as he put it, was so firmly established that he literally thought he was dying and feared he was going insane. Fortunately, as he was going through the process, he documented in great detail what happened, what he saw, and how he felt about it all. Most of this chapter is devoted to Goel's experiences.

Goel was a well-educated Indian. He had an intellectual background and studied political science, history and education. Eventually, he gained a doctorate. Raised in a religious family, he was not particularly religious himself. He had an interest in Marxism, and later, after the initial breakdown, spent a great deal of time undergoing and learning about psychoanalysis, and practiced meditation. At the same time, Goel wrote a book on "Psycho-analysis and Meditation" comparing the two approaches in the search for psychological freedom. Later, he wrote another book called *Third Eye and Kundalini* and it is from that book most of this account is taken. Finally, after his full Realization, he took on the name Shri Siddheshwar Baba and set up an ashram in northern India, near Delhi, which he called Shri Siddheshwar Ashram.

Muktananda followed a different path to that experienced by Goel. He went to live in an ashram with his guru, Nityananda, and eventually underwent an incredible process which took him to enlightenment. Eventually, he set up his own ashram in southern India near Bombay and formulated a spiritual path, which he called Siddha Yoga. There are now Siddha Yoga centers scattered throughout the world.

These two accounts will show you that each person's journey is unique. There are many factors which determine how it will be for each person. It could be easy or extremely difficult. A lot will depend on your meditation and preparation beforehand. Regardless of how your own journey proceeds, some basic understanding of the experience of others is beneficial, as it provides a frame of reference for your own experience.

Both Goel's and Muktananda's experiences recount the "end game," the final stage in the journey to enlightenment. It is not possible to predict when this will happen, but it represents the culmination of a long evolutionary journey and is usually triggered by the grace of a guru. However, the time and intensity of this final stage is very much dependent on one's experiences leading up to this point and the amount of egoic data that needs to be cleared.

Goel's Experiences

As a young adult, Goel practiced yoga and pranayama, but not under the guidance of a qualified teacher. He also studied Marxism. By the age of 29, he was working on a doctoral thesis. At this age, in 1964, he had his first major breakdown. He was standing on the roof of a hostel building discussing religion and Marxism with a friend, when suddenly, a great force rose from the base of his spine up to the crown of his head, at the Brahmarandhra, otherwise known as the nirvana chakra, and he went into a state of ecstasy. However, Goel's Kundalini had been aroused prematurely and not under the guidance of a guru. So, despite a profound spiritual experience, this was only temporary and would lead to incredible suffering once the experience had passed, as it did not form a stable part of his nervous system or personality. He then moved into a phase of paranoid depression.

As a result, Goel went to see several psychiatrists, looking for a cure for his depression. The psychiatrists were not familiar with Goel's experience and diagnosed severe depression, religious delusions, and paranoid trends. Consequently, he underwent psychoanalysis for many years in search of a relief to his condition.

In the early stages of psychoanalysis, Goel came across a Swami who, when told of his interest in yoga and current depression, taught him a technique of meditation that would help. From then on, he continued with psychiatric help and now practiced meditation, too. Together, these formed a valuable contribution to his understanding of how the human mind worked. This also provided a foundation for development of his theory of psychoanalytical meditation.

After almost seven years of meditation, Goel had a dream in which a well-known Indian guru, Bhagwan Sri Sathya Sai Baba, appeared to him and told him it was His will that he was doing meditation and there was a purpose behind this. After that dream, his meditation progressed fast, and he received many other dreams and gained the confidence to no longer receive psychoanalysis. He still, however, performed his own self-psychoanalysis.

Goel's meditation included focusing on a point between the eyebrows, the third eye. Eventually, he noted the emergence of a point of light at that spot, like a small flame, which he called the "jet experience" because of the hissing sound it made. In reality, this is the emergence of consciousness as separate from the ego.

Goel continued to document his experiences as a reference for others to follow.

Goel often referred to two main "nerves," raga and dwesha with their roots in the Brahmarandhra.[1] The Brahmarandhra is a minor chakra which is also known as the nirvana chakra. Rather than nerves, raga and dwesha are really mental formations or currents of energy. Raga is the name given to worldly attachments and dwesha is the name given to worldly aversions. The raga current spirals downwards while the dwesha current spirals upwards. They form at the Brahmarandhra when you take birth, and it is at the Brahmarandhra that they finally dissolve before liberation. In effect, the Brahmarandhra is the "Gateway to God" or the crown chakra, as above the nirvana chakra lies the guru chakra, the seat of the guru and above that is the crown chakra, the Sourcepoint or universal consciousness.

Notably, consciousness often moves between three points: the base chakra, the brow chakra, and the crown chakra with the associated Brahmarandhra to clear many deep-rooted experiences and pains. These can be triggered by external events, as happened with Goel, who had a period of intense mental anguish and suffering triggered by the suicide of a neighbor. External events exaggerate past difficulties in the mind, causing difficult suffering. One feels more sensitive to these issues because of the inner need to relinquish emotional attachments once and for all.

Fortunately, along with the tough experiences come occasional uplifting experiences as your awareness is expanding. This is the peak and process that goes hand in hand with conscious evolution. Consciousness also reminds you that you are evolving into a heightened state of awareness through occasional experiences in meditation. With progress, you realize greater truths and their meanings. Such truths may come in meditation, in dreams, signs, voice messages, and so on. Eventually, the sense mind has to be transcended completely, and this is all part of the process.

By 1972, Goel could receive messages while sitting in meditation and, as a result, on January 1 1973, he began writing his book *Psycho-analysis and Meditation*. Goel noted many positive experiences in meditation, but also some very difficult ones. He recorded these experiences in his book as "50 signals on the path." Number 44 was a very difficult experience in which he experienced intense fear, depression, and insecurity. Even the smallest happenings brought fear such a slight noise or reflection. The first things a newborn baby would have experienced brought on this fear and insecurity. Now these experiences were being brought up again so that corresponding emotions could be experienced and removed. Every single attachment and emotional fear need to be cleared, as the spiritual Self gradually replaces the ego. Number 49 was extremely positive, in which his guru, Sathya Sai Baba, appeared in meditation. Until that point, he had only considered Baba to be a yogi or Saint. This experience confirmed to him without a doubt that Sai Baba was his guru.

By February 1975, the book was almost complete. By the time Goel reached the fiftieth signal in his spiritual journey, he was sure he was near the goal of meditation. He felt bliss and peace for most of the time and thought he had achieved whatever the goal of meditation was. Circumstances were to show this was not the case.

Around March 15 1975, Goel was hurled into a fresh round of experiences, triggered by the suicide of a neighbor in his apartment block. For him, this had triggered a major breakdown. After the neighbour's suicide, Goel found a complete return of intense depression, fear of insecurity and imminent doom. He felt the need to increase his meditation to relieve the pain, but it only brought partial relief. Even the entire process of psychoanalytical meditation he had developed only provided partial relief. In this new phase of intense processing, it was much less effective. This continued for about seven days. He was convinced he was going to die.

Then one night, he was awakened around midnight by Sathya Sai Baba pulling up the blanket under which he was sleeping. Sai Baba asked him to get up and meditate. Surely, he thought, he was hallucinating so tried to go back to sleep. The same thing happened again. Sai Baba told Goel again to get up and meditate, focusing on the midpoint between the eyebrows. So, he got up, meditated, and Sai Baba disappeared. Goel meditated for a few hours and found much relief. Then he slept for three hours. By 9 a.m., the intense depression returned.

Later that day, in desperation, Goel sat down and silently cried out to Sai Baba to save him. He then began meditation and saw a vision in his meditation at the third eye of a thick, blood red vertical line. This provided instant relief for him. He had an intense feeling that behind the red line was Sathya Sai Baba waiting for him. It provided joy and happiness instantly. However, the dark mood returned by the same evening.

Three days later, the red line appeared again, but now it widened into an eye and within the eye was Sathya Sai Baba. He was holding up an egg-shaped Shiva-Linga.[2] Goel felt immense feelings of joy and gratefulness. Five or six hours later, though, the depression returned.

Although Goel would see Sathya Sai Baba in his third eye, he also felt a connection with the Brahmarandhra. It was there that he felt Sathya Sai Baba sat and as long as he consciously focused on that point; he felt no disturbance, but as soon as his consciousness moved elsewhere, the disturbance returned. Unfortunately, keeping his consciousness at that point proved to be very difficult.

On March 27 1975, 11 a.m., after 15 days of intense depression, again praying to Baba, more nerves fell from the Brahmarandhra. The third eye opened, and Baba was there, dressed in red. Goel saw that he himself was also there, dressed in white. Baba said, "I am protecting you." The experience was like a death experience, as he watched the destruction of his ego. He was in a state of ecstasy.

On the morning of March 28, the mood of happiness had mostly disappeared. Yet he could see inside an inward path, which he felt was the sushumna nadi. At the bottom of the sushumna nadi, he saw a dual woman-snake and knew it was the Blessed Mother, the Kundalini. As a result, he was in a state of bliss and happiness.

Again, the next day the depression had returned. Goel continued to shift between stability and depression. When consciousness was associated with the mind, he felt anxiety. When not, there was more realization of his own immortality. All this was controlled from within.

On April 9, while in severe depression, many nerves fell from the Brahmarandhra and a state of confidence returned, which lasted a day or so. However, severe depression eventually returned.

On April 13, in intense depression, and sure his end was nigh, his third eye opened, and he saw Krishna and a large Shiva-Linga. Again, he experienced great ecstasy, happiness, and security. As the days passed, he could see, in his own experiences, the true meaning of the dialogue between Krishna and Arjuna in the Bhagavad Gita. In fact, many spiritual secrets unfolded before his consciousness as he alternated between intense depression and elation.

On April 22, the depression and pain increased and by the next day it was extreme. Goel prayed to Sai Baba and found he entered a dialogue with him. The Kundalini as a ray of light rose from the base of his spine to the Brahmarandhra. Happiness and stability returned. He found he could increasingly see the difference between the ego and the Self.

On May 4, Goel experienced the darkest depression again. Laying before the photo of Sai Baba, the third eye opened, and he saw the Lord Jesus Christ with his head surrounded by white shining pearls of light. Again, he experienced great happiness for a couple of days and then the depression returned. On May 7, he lay before Sai Baba's photo and an inner structure opened, again in bright red. Then an inner communication about his mother's death and cremation took place. It was like a rehearsal, yet beyond Goel's control. Later, the third eye opened again, and an incredibly bright light appeared with five bright white snakes appearing over it as if to protect it. This lasted a few seconds, and Goel was left in ecstasy. He had seen his own immortal soul.

Then May 9, saw the worst experience for the whole of the last 50 days. Goel experienced intense depression and guilt over how he had treated his mother. He would say things such as "Mother, forgive me all the troubles I have caused. Farewell, I will never see you again." It was as if the experience was being orchestrated by his consciousness.

He decided it was time to leave his nephew in Delhi, so he eventually packed his bags. He did not know whether to go to his parents or younger brother. In the end, he got the first bus that came along, which took him to his youngest brother in another city. Not long after this, Goel's mother died.

During one night, just after Goel's mother died, he saw a spiritually significant dream. He saw a golden, crimson disc as large as the sun descending towards him, studded on all sides with shining stars. He saw Sathya Sai Baba on the disk in a deep red gown and with him was the goddess mother Lakshmi in a deep red sari. Somehow, he knew immediately that they were Narayana and Lakshmi. They both blessed him and then the disk ascended into the sky.

On returning to the family home after the cremation, Goel closed his eyes, and his entire brain was full of red aura. Within this he saw the supreme mother, Durga, sitting on a tiger with a Trident in her hand, near to the Brahmarandhra. Likewise, he saw Durga was replacing his mother, who used to sit there.

On the fourth morning after his mother's passing, he went with family members to Haridwar to immerse her ashes into the Ganges River. From there, his brothers took him to Rishikesh. When there, they visited Swami Chidananda and Swami Shivom Tirth, Both Self-realized Masters. They both confirmed that the experiences Goel was going through were genuine.

After returning to Jagadhari, the Kundalini process in Goel increased in ferocity, with immense waves of energy zig zagging up his back. Along with this activity, he could see that his nervous system was being re-generated. Nerves were falling away to be replaced by new ones. He also found he was having many visions, which appeared whenever he closed his eyes.

On occasions, when he related his experiences to various gurus, some seemed to understand and others not. As mentioned earlier, the experiences which one goes through, and the Kundalini process, are unique to the individual in question.[3]

Goel's inner visions continued. These included the feeling that Shiva was breathing through the Brahmarandhra; he saw a beautiful flower at the Brahmarandhra; a flame burning at the Brahmarandhra; and he saw Lord Krishna at the Brahmarandhra. Similarly, Goel's dreams continued, with some related to various goddesses who represent Shakti and the Kundalini and others with a snake representing the Kundalini.

Goel's psychic fluctuations also continued, but to a lesser extent, and by September 1975, he felt his situation was improving. He continued to receive dreams, and his sister had a couple of dreams about him, too. Usually, these were Sai Baba dreams.

The time span between bouts of weeping and depression gradually increased until, by the middle of November, it was time to consider returning to the office after a period of extended leave. Eventually, he went back to normal life and routine, but still with occasional difficulties. Some people at work gradually accepted the truth of Goel's process, although, before, most had been highly skeptical. He also allowed a bhajan (devotional singing) group to meet regularly in his apartment. This became popular.

Occasionally, Goel would get a message about a future happening in the life of his friends. Invariably, this turned out to be true and was a faculty of his still opening third eye.

Goel's Kundalini activity continued, although the suffering had lessened. He found it was difficult to focus for long on anything. So, as his consciousness was expanding, his mind was contracting. Gradually, his mind was dissolving into consciousness. Goel found solace reading about similar experiences had by Swami Muktananda and Pandit Gopi Krishna.

Goel's internal visions also continued. The red aura was mostly there, but occasionally other colors were there too, such as blue and white. Goel referred to colors in meditation. He said the colors he saw referred to the different elements or tattavas, representative of fire, earth, air, water and akasha. The colors for these are respectively crimson red, yellow, green, white, and blue.

Almost daily, Goel would see Shirdi Sai Baba, the previous incarnation of Sathya Sai Baba, sitting at the Brahmarandhra. Shirdi Sai Baba was apparently Goel's guru in his previous life. In this experience, Shirdi Sai Baba appeared to eat and breathe instead of Goel. Now he felt that he and the Kundalini had merged into Shirdi Sai Baba.

Slowly, his experiences showed an increasing merger of his individual consciousness into Supreme consciousness or Shiva. It was the Kundalini that was assisting in this process. He also noticed an electric like humming sound within and also noted many dreams with snakes.

After July 1976, Goel's process appeared to become faster. His eyes became brighter, and objects appeared brighter to him as well. Another noticeable change was that he, as a witness to what was happening, had separated from the ego. To him, it was now the witness "I" that was more real than the mind, or ego, or world around. Goel noted it was like a new mind was being formed based on reality as perceived by the third eye rather than the mind, which was based on reality as perceived by the physical eyes.

Goel's confidence was also increasing while extreme disturbances were decreasing. His internal visions were becoming more attractive and more bewitching. For example, one day, while focusing on the feet of his guru in the red aura of his third eye, the feet transformed into an exquisite flower and an intensely bright sun emerged from within. Then, on November 20 1976, he saw Sathya Sai Baba with five hooded snakes hanging over his head. It became so luminous he couldn't look at it anymore. He also got dreams telling him he was being granted supernatural powers.

On April 4 1977, Goel went to the shrine of Shirdi Sai Baba in the village of Shirdi. Later, on returning to Delhi, he bought and started to read some books on Shirdi Sai Baba. His inner experiences of Shirdi Sai Baba at the Brahmarandhra grew increasingly vivid, and he was more and more able to communicate with him. The Brahmarandhra is the seat of Shiva and Shirdi Sai Baba was considered an incarnation of Shiva. Goel had a dream on April 17, which showed to him that perhaps in his last life he had lived close to Shirdi Sai Baba. Additionally, he felt the dream was telling him that although he was close to Him now; he had not yet merged with him.

He had another dream on April 22, showing that Shirdi Sai Baba would come to him on April 26. Therefore, he organized for Bhajans (devotional singing) to be held on that day to worship Him and placed his photo there, but it appeared nothing happened. Later, one of his friends returned to say that a large quantity of Vibhuti (sacred ash) had appeared on his own photos of Shirdi Sai Baba and Sathya Sai Baba at home. They went to look and were convinced this was what the dream had forecast.

Goel now considered the Kundalini process as being one where the upward movement of prana pushes the nerves until they get burnt or give way, bringing repressed material into conscious awareness and causing the intense difficulties he had been experiencing.

Goel also pointed out that in psychoanalysis one is encouraged to accept, without guilt, all feelings of anger, sex, jealousy, etc. However, even this acceptance becomes part of oneself. Consequently, these formations in the mind also need to be removed by the Kundalini. For a complete merger with the divine, one needs to be free of all formations based on both the third- and second-stage selves in order to become a pure instrument for the divine in form. Goel went as far to say that all his psychoanalysis had added to his tribulations during the Kundalini process and extended his period of suffering.[4]

Goel's visions continued, becoming clearer and sharper than previously, giving him greater clarity and understanding of the continued process of separation from sense impressions, which he said were like a cage imprisoning him. Increasingly, he saw himself as the light and those around him as mere specks floating in the light.

Goel also found that it was becoming easier for him to focus on the third eye in meditation. The red aura was always there but he could now see within the aura the nerve threads, representing deep-rooted mental formations, that were binding his jiva (the "I") and keeping him from moving freely to the Brahmarandhra. In fact, he saw the jiva as strings of light, but bound by dark threads, becoming more deeply entrenched the closer one got to the Brahmarandhra. There was one main string, however, that did travel from the third eye to the Brahmarandhra unencumbered.

By early 1978, Goel was becoming increasingly alienated in the world because of his rejection of other people's advice or opinions. They considered him arrogant and self-righteous. This did not bother him, though, as his sole focus was only to accept guidance from God. He could, however, still feel hurt by other people's comments.

Occasionally, he would think about spiritual concepts which he had difficulty understanding and pray to Sathya Sai Baba for illumination. Answers would come to him as realizations of the meaning, typical of "aha" moments. Being more in tune with truthful concepts through experience allows remaining obstacles to fall away. For example, when he was trying to understand the meaning of equal love for all, he realized the difference between an ego seeing different egos as unequal as opposed to identifying with the One in them. So, rather than equal love, it was rather love for and of the One, the same love, Advaita (non-duality).

Now, when he saw the red aura inside his head, the entire world, here and there, past and present, was all just here and now. All was contained within himself, or as he said, all within the 6 by 9 inches of the mind in his head. Eventually, as this all dissolved, only the "I" of the eternal reality, the light, would remain.

Goel's evolution was progressing fast. In March 1978, Sathya Sai Baba visited Delhi. And when Goel went to see him, he found his concentration spontaneously remained fixed on the third eye for most of the time. He was bathed in a blissful state of divine madness.

After this week, when he returned to his office, his inward vision showed Sai Baba as the original Shiva-Linga, flaming red and covered in dark lines like Baba's curly black hair. The idea occurred to him that the hair represented the dark jungle of his mind.

Another thing Goel noticed was an increase in his willpower. Of course, in reality, the ego has no will power, it only thinks it does. True willpower is a quality of the soul and as the ego diminishes, and soul realization increases, the will also increases.

As the source of light within increased, the light being a deep crimson red, Goel's alignment with this source of light, caused him to see worldly objects, people, animals and so on, all as maya or illusion. Even his own body was seen to be an illusion. He could see that he was the light found in all forms and not bound by any of them, and that eventually this would be a constant realization for him.

The eternal soul was responsible for all that happens, although it was the ego that thought it was the doer. Now, Goel could see this play working out in all that happened to him. He often referred to the "jiva," which is the individual consciousness, and which is the witness to what happens both inside and outside. Therefore, the external environment is brought to the inside via the five senses, along with desires, ideas, notions, and thoughts. Then, to these are attached emotions and feelings. The sum total of these forms the individual mind, which gets attached to the individual consciousness.

Just as the outer world is in constant motion or agitation, so is the inner world or mind. As individual consciousness is attached to the mind, it, too, finds itself in a constant state of agitation. However, individual consciousness can also detach from the mind. When you look inside in meditation, you can observe the agitated mind. As you observe, you increase the ability to "step aside" from feelings, emotions and ideas and become more of a witness to these. This increased detachment is important.

Through regular meditation, attachment to the outer world decreases and identification with the individual consciousness as the "seer" or witness increases. This seer is a part of cosmic or universal consciousness which has been trapped by the individual mind. As identification with the seer becomes stronger, and detachment from the mind increases, the seer eventually realizes its true identity as universal consciousness. However, for Goel, this was not a simple process. As the Kundalini cleared the many formations in his mind, he underwent incredible suffering because the emotions and feelings associated with them were being brought up as part of the clearing process. As these were released, the associated spiritual energy could merge with universal energy and be available for increased spiritual growth. Goel's identification with universal consciousness, as opposed to individual consciousness, increased, and an even greater universal level of awareness grew. This could be seen in his evolving spiritual awareness through visionary experiences in meditation, in dreams, and in his greater wakefulness during the day. This universal consciousness is the universal I, it is Shiva, it is the Self, which is attained in Self-realization. Therefore, the evolving consciousness progresses from egoic mind to individual consciousness to universal consciousness.

On January 8 1979, Goel had an experience during the day. His mind was blank except for a few thoughts on the working of the mind and his office environment. Suddenly, in the inner light which came to him, he saw floating faces of colleagues. They appeared unreal and meaningless. Only the light appeared real. This happened again that night with many images. The whole concept of subject and object, I and you, appeared false. This whole experience created fear and rapture simultaneously. It was the rapture of freedom combined with the fear of being released from a once very familiar cage. The reality or construct on which his mind had been built was gradually giving way to light, peace and bliss from within.

On another trip to Sathya Sai Baba's ashram in Whitefield, Baba blessed the Third Eye and Kundalini book, of which he had, by then, done nine chapters. Sai Baba wrote his blessings on the title page.

Increasingly, Goel was noticing his own behavior to be unlike it used to be. He felt there was some force within himself, making him behave in a certain way. Inwardly, he could see

Sathya Sai Baba constantly with him and journeying with him towards the Brahmarandhra.

One night, on May 25 1979, he closed his eyes, and his concentration immediately went to the point between his eyebrows and Goel saw his whole mind filled with golden light. He became absorbed by it until he felt he was the light. His experiences were showing him the transformation taking place and how much he had changed.

By June 1979, although the difficulties continued, there was much less ferocity in them. The feeling that he was rising toward the Brahmarandhra continued and occasionally more nerves would fall away, and, simultaneously, associated impressions got released. What appeared like a red staff, comprising shining red strings molded together, rising from the base chakra, was closing in on the Brahmarandhra. At one point he saw Sai Baba of Shirdi sitting at the top, as usually happened, but this time Goel was there too, having merged with Him. His inner vision was turned towards the Brahmarandhra, and he even felt he was breathing from there too. Now, breathing was from the Brahmarandhra to the Trikuti, at the third eye, and also from the Trikuti to the Brahmarandhra.

Additional aspects of knowledge also arose. The physical body appeared unreal and later, not just the body, but all human relationships as well. Likewise, this included the associated emotions, expectations, and satisfactions.

By July 1979, he could see that these human relationships, associated faces and structures, and such labels as father, mother, brother, sister, friends, enemies, and so on, were barriers separating individual consciousness from universal consciousness. Modern psychology is based on these relationships and consequently limited and incomplete. These relationships must be transcended for one to merge with God or universal consciousness. Psychoanalysis, however, is based on fixing these relationships rather than transcending them.

An important development took place regarding the red staff in August 1979. Whereas before it had always run from the base chakra towards the Brahmarandhra, it was now seen to run from the Trikuti to the Brahmarandhra.

On August 31, at night, Goel reached yet another milestone. He had become "Om" at the Brahmarandhra. The feeling that came with this was unshakable freedom and liberation from the illusion of maya. From this and earlier experiences, he determined that the inner prana, under the guidance of guru or God, moves in an upward direction towards the Brahmarandhra, clearing psychological formations on the way. Then the prana falls back to the Trikuti again for a rest before continuing again. Goel referred to the Trikuti as the lap of the guru. In the guru's lap, he experienced peace after the cyclic work of clearing or processing.

In September, Goel went through a period where he had pains in his chest which felt like a heart attack. He ignored advice to consult a specialist, leaving his faith in God to take care of him. He was scheduled to go on an office tour and later had planned to visit Sathya Sai Baba in Puttaparthi. At one point, he prayed to Sai Baba and meditated at the Trikuti. Then his attention moved down to the heart chakra where the pain was being experienced, and there he saw Krishna. As a result, Goel determined his chest pains had resulted from Kundalini activity.

Difficulties returned in October 1979, including psychic troubles and negative thoughts. The lights and visions he usually saw disappeared, too. At a low point, he even thought one shouldn't get involved in the spiritual path due to all the Kundalini problems one faces. However, on October 25, he concentrated at the Trikuti, and the thick red light was there again, spreading throughout his head and emanating from the Trikuti. It was shining upward. He himself was sitting at the top of his head in a meditation pose. Instantly, all his pain and suffering disappeared.

Goel soon found, when he closed his eyes, his witnessing mind was observing from the Brahmarandhra, rather than from the Trikuti. On November 20 1979, during a difficult phase, he saw from the Brahmarandhra, that just below there were a multitude of small, four-petaled white flowers in all directions. He was in a state of divine ecstasy at this. In view of this, he wondered if this was the thousand-petaled lotus of the crown chakra.

Through March 1980, Goel continued to notice changes within himself and also had a couple of significant dreams. In particular, he had a dream on March 20, in which the daughter of a spiritual aspirant became associated with Shakti. Later, this turned out to be very significant. The Kundalini was highlighting feelings of infatuation and directing them towards the daughter.

We see that on the evolutionary cycle, desires, and emotions, etc., which previously helped to trap the individual consciousness in form, are now repeated, often painfully and intensely, so they can be worked through and released. Childhood feelings of homosexuality, which had consumed him with guilt and persisted into adulthood, now just disappeared. Goel believed the Kundalini was responsible for clearing these feelings.

By the end of March 1980, Goel thought he was nearing the end of his Kundalini process. He didn't realize, however, that he had only completed the first phase. He was soon to find out that this was what Sathya Sai Baba had referred to in a dream in 1977 when he had said the Kundalini would rise again on completion of the age of 45 (March 24 1980).

On April 15 1980, the second major phase of dissolution began. Prana rushed powerfully into Goel's brain from the Trikuti and disorganized his mind instantly. He wept uncontrollably for an hour. He had not felt this bad for almost three years. Yet again, fear and depression dominated his mood. In fact, he said the hallmarks of this experience were confusion, bewilderment, and blocked emotions. After three days of this, in meditation, he saw Shirdi Sai Baba in his third eye. The communication revealed that he had the deepest mental formations to clear. In addition, it was also communicated to him that he had yet to experience equal love for all. Now, he was completely happy again. This convinced Goel that the guru/God sits at the brow chakra and guides evolution from there.

Things improved for a few days, and then he found Shirdi Sai Baba sitting at the third eye again. Suddenly, it was he himself sitting at this center. The next day, he was again sitting in his own third eye. He was in ecstasy. The next night, however, the darkest depression returned, like the worst he had experienced in the past. Goel had horrible dreams, and he said to himself, "I am dying." Instantly, an answer came from within. "The one who is saying I am dying has to die. I am not this. I am witnessing it." Again, the fear and depression disappeared.

As part of this, Goel underwent a period of infatuation for the young woman mentioned earlier. However, he realized this was part of the Kundalini process. It was, in fact, Shakti that was playing this game with him. The object of one's infatuation is a crucial part of a link between the individual, Shiva, and Shakti as it projected divine qualities onto the object (person). Under normal circumstances, there are three likely outcomes of this. Either the infatuated person gets to possess the object, the infatuated person reaches God in the Brahmarandhra, or the infatuated person experiences a classic nervous breakdown. A breakdown is very common because of the intervention of social reality. Whereas, if the person is under the Kundalini process, they are protected from the breakdown.[5]

At the end of May 1980, Goel was to visit Puttaparthi to see Sathya Sai Baba. The object of his infatuation was also going. On May 27, Goel had a dream with the Goddess Durga emerging out of the nerves near the Brahmarandhra, those responsible for his immense suffering the last couple of months. He also thought this confirmed the authenticity of the object of his infatuation.

On May 29 1980, during intense suffering, Goel closed his

eyes and prayed to his guru. He found the inner path illumined and Shirdi Sai Baba was sitting at both the Brahmarandhra and the Trikuti, with both images connected by a path of light.

Goel's understanding of the Kundalini process continued to grow. He could see that everything is the play of consciousness. All is Shakti. During the involutionary cycle, universal consciousness as Shakti creates a multitude of desires, attachments, and ideas to attract the individual consciousness and increasingly bind the individual into the world of maya (illusion). Then, a point is reached, creating an awakening onto the evolutionary cycle. This changes the direction of Shakti from the downward path to an upward path. On the upward path, the many illusions surrounding individual consciousness are now dissolved until eventual liberation from maya is attained. It is a long, gradual process, but nothing compared to the eons spent on the involutionary cycle. It is by an act of grace of guru/ God that this awakening takes place.

On the evolutionary cycle, it is Shakti which creates all the experiences and difficulties so that the individual can re-experience them and finally transcend them. Different persons are utilized for this process, as with Goel's infatuation. These experiences can sometimes seem to be exaggerated so that deep formations in the mind can be uprooted. Thus, the intense pain often experienced. The result is far superior to what psychoanalysis can offer, as genuine freedom from them is obtained. It is also beneficial for the persons chosen to be instruments in this process and there is usually a strong spiritual connection from previous lives.

Whatever happens to the individual is according to the will of Universal consciousness through Shakti, even if it goes against the norms of society. Take the example of infatuation again, Goel's intense infatuation with the young woman would be wrong under societal norms. However, it was incredibly beneficial for his spiritual growth and fortunately took place in his mind rather than being a physical affair.

The intense period Goel experienced from April 1980 to October 1980 was similar in intensity to the one he had experienced from March 1975 to November 1975. Then, on November 11 1980, Goel had an experience in which he closed his eyes and saw many faces of people. He saw their faces, names and relationships as false. He also saw Shirdi Sai Baba sitting in the Trikuti of each of them. Likewise, the same was true of all the animals, birds and insects he saw, or could imagine. Shirdi Sai Baba was sitting there, too. As a result, he was immensely happy and felt he was moving closer to Advaita or non-duality.

In another experience on December 20 1980, he found that rather than seeing the world through his physical eyes; he saw the world and all the animals and people, etc., as though he was viewing them from the Brahmarandhra. All appeared as One. Again, on January 20 1981, whenever a face appeared in his mind, it immediately dissolved into light. In addition, he noticed difficult emotions became very weak, and he could convert them to light.

By early January 1981, Goel was seldom seeing the red staff nor the thick, deep red color which filled his vision previously. The staff was much thinner and rarely appeared at all. Instead, he now often saw a slit or thin crescent-like opening at the Trikuti, filled with effulgent crimson, intermittently flashing or sparkling light. Goel could also see a sharp point of light hovering near the Brahmarandhra. If it was hovering, he still had formations to clear. He felt that the light represented the Self. The light was being guided by the guru sitting at the Trikuti. Goel somehow knew that if the light could remain stable at the Brahmarandhra, then the guru at the Trikuti would merge with the formless guru at the Brahmarandhra.

On February 19 1981 he had a very significant dream in which the person of his infatuation, as Shakti, disappeared into a crowd of devotees. Then he saw Shirdi Sai Baba and received a message telling him to leave the Shakti and merge with Him. It is the Shakti that guides you on the evolutionary journey ultimately to merge with Shiva (universal consciousness). It is Shakti (with one's individual consciousness) that merges with Shiva and then Shiva and Shakti become one.

In another experience on February 24 1981, while in a state of bliss, Goel saw Shirdi Sai Baba sitting both at the Trikuti and the Brahmarandhra connected by a string of light. Friends and enemies from the past also got changed into Shirdi Sai Baba. Goel knew that eventually, he would see all as one.

In March 1981, he felt no fear of death and often had a desire to leave his body. As a result, Goel likened the feeling to homesickness. On March 30, whatever Goel saw, including objects or thoughts, whether inside or out, was all Shakti. All was Shakti, yet he, as witness, was Shiva. Goel felt ineffable joy at all of this.

On April 7 1981, while talking to some spiritual aspirants after chanting Rama-Nama, Goel entered a strange state. While sitting on a seat, he found himself to be all light with a crown of light on his head. He then found Lord Rama sitting on the seat instead of himself. This showed him that first he was getting closer to the state of Advaita, and secondly that our own ultimate reality represents all forms of God. The same thing happened the next night, too, yet a little stronger. Any idea, any image of a friend or enemy that came to mind, even the entire world, all got turned into light or Rama.

On April 10 1981, Goel had another experience of the energy rising fiercely and clearing more formations. Correspondingly, new insights and understandings were emerging, slowly and automatically. Notably, he gained the following insights. After birth, attachment to the mother and accompanying desires create a major nerve path, known as raga, downwards from the Brahmarandhra. Rejection of these desires by the mother, or other object of attachment, results in another major nerve path, downward from the Brahmarandhra, known as dwesha, forming, and containing the emotional energy of hate, anger, jealousy, etc. These two nerve paths create the illusion of who we are and block our access to God through the Brahmarandhra. Eventually, a point comes in the Kundalini process, when even the most infantile desires and attachments need to be cleared, and this process can be extremely difficult. Goel's experiences with the object of his infatuation, right from April 1980, represented this arduous process. This attachment was still there, but very weak now. When the feelings arose, he would always see Shirdi Sai Baba sitting at the Brahmarandhra, the gateway to God.

Because of the involutionary cycle, the Self has learnt that it is now the body with a multitude of attachments and sense impressions. On the evolutionary cycle, however, through meditation, the Self learns to undo all the previously held attachments, desires, etc., to return to its essential nature, which is light.

On May 18 1981, Goel saw seven golden starry paths leading upwards in his mind and joining near the Brahmarandhra. From that point, a burji, rather like the dome of a mosque, rose upwards and tried to pierce the Brahmarandhra. Goel found himself at the piercing point.

Goel had another experience on May 31, while staying in a valley called Barkot. During the night, he saw a flood of light shining from the Trikuti upwards. Automatically, he said to himself, "I am this light." He soon felt that everything was within himself. His own light was the entire cosmos. In this ecstatic state, everything emerged from him, and back into him, continuously. Goel also experienced objects vanishing from him and emerging back into him in a process of birth and death. The question came to mind whether it would ever become a constant feature for him, and the answer came back, "Yes, it would."

Goel felt increasingly isolated from the world. Human faces and their associated attachments, feelings and emotions no longer affected him, but seemed false. Now, he would peacefully reside in the Trikuti. He felt incredible happiness and gratitude.

Even though Goel's evolution was progressing fast and nearing the end, he still felt feelings of frustration, and particularly felt like a misfit in the office environment. His behavior was more that of a social misfit and he found it difficult to work in the office hierarchy. It was easier for him to discriminate based on truth and untruth rather than the usual opposites found in maya of friend and enemy, mine and thine, high and low, Indian and non-Indian, and so on. Once you have experienced the One, the rules of maya and the laws of an egocentric world seem irrelevant. Others considered him arrogant and full of pride. For him, the behavior of others was irritating.

In late September 1981, Goel had another experience of Oneness or Advaita. While in deep concentration and relaxation, the faces of people who created feelings of love or hate in himself shone in the light of consciousness. They were all found between the Trikuti and Brahmarandhra. To him, these faces were just inert matter. They appeared unreal and meaningless. Instead, he felt he was the One light. The state of bliss and ecstasy lasted for a few hours as he experienced his own eternity.

By September 1982, Goel could see on an inner level that he had moved beyond the mind. He was in touch with Absolute Consciousness, either in its formless state or with form such as Shirdi Sai Baba and Sathya Sai Baba. As he was now always in touch with universal consciousness, or his guru's form, he was no longer repulsed by any forms or attached to any forms within maya. Likewise, he found his guru's form was interchangeable with all the great gurus such as Rama, Krishna, Jesus and other forms of God, but he also found his own form was also interchangeable with them. Goel knew he was nearing the end of his evolutionary journey; he had reached the state of Advaita or non-duality. Now, he saw the One in everything.

By October 1982, this awareness was even stronger. No

barriers at all could separate him from the Lord. Even if any appeared he didn't need to transcend them, they automatically dissolved. He alone was at the Brahmarandhra, where he previously had seen Shirdi Sai Baba and Sathya Sai Baba. If anyone stood before him, he would see straight to their essence, their consciousness. He only saw his own consciousness within the other person. There could be no hatred, only love for the other person.

Goel's vision of Oneness became stronger each day. He saw his own essence within all forms, plants, birds, animals and rocks. In fact, he saw his own essence in all objects, whether animate or inanimate. He saw his own reality behind Shirdi Sai Baba and Sathya Sai Baba.

As Goel settled into Oneness, a strange feeling of love surged within him for all and everything. There was only "I." Until this moment, there had still been feelings of estrangement and alienation towards others and objects, but now this disappeared. There was a warmth towards all. He felt a universal love for everything, which was the natural quality of the Self. This love is God. Goel had returned to the eternal Source from which he came, the home of eternal peace.

Muktananda's Experiences

When Muktananda's guru, Nityananda, conferred Shaktipat (transmission of spiritual energy) on him, he had a blissful awakening. He couldn't believe his good fortune and felt he was truly blessed.

Several days later, Nityananda told him to go to his hut, to stay there, meditate, and gain knowledge. Muktananda didn't know why but did as requested. The next day, when at the hut, he went into a very dark state of mind. Despite several visitors, his confused state of mind continued. He was experiencing strange breathing irregularities and was full of confusion and anguish. He was sure he would die that night from heart failure. The earth and sky were spinning, and he thought he was going mad, and he was extremely fearful. In reality, he was experiencing pronounced Kundalini activity.

That evening, everything appeared to be on fire. The sugar cane field close by was ablaze, people were screaming, and strange human-like creatures up to 50ft high were dancing naked. Then, Muktananda went to sit in a meditation posture in his hut. By now, it seemed the entire universe was on fire, while ghosts and demons surrounded him. He knew what he was seeing was unreal, but still he felt terror. Suddenly, he felt a searing pain in his base chakra, but could not move. It appeared the entire world had been destroyed and only his hut remained.

Next, a white sphere about 4ft in diameter floated into his hut, stopped in front of him and then entered inside him. It penetrated his nadis, and he saw a dazzling light in his forehead. His eyes closed, and it forced his head down to the ground. When his eyes eventually opened, he saw a red light all around. It was shimmering and flickering. He went outside, and all was calm. He went inside the hut and closed his eyes, and the red light was there again. But again, there was nothing when he went outside again. After this, he regularly saw the red light in meditation. The shimmering red light was replaced by a red aura which enveloped him inside and out. Within it flashed millions of tiny rays. When Muktananda watched this red aura, it immediately absorbed him in meditation.

While in meditation, many yogic postures, or kriyas, happened to his body as if some deity had taken over him. In fact, he had been taken over by Shakti, the power of Kundalini, via his guru, Nityananda, who, through his own enlightenment, was one with Shakti.

Muktananda described the red aura as being the color of the gross body and about the same height as a human body. It is through this body with its five senses that we have experience, and through which good and bad deeds are performed, and happiness and pain are experienced. The individual soul gains experience during the waking state because of this body. The Kundalini process purifies the gross body, resulting in a slow dissolution of the ego.

Muktananda referred to meditation at the "red stage" in which he felt the pranic energy moving within and his kriyas continued. Each kriya had a particular cleansing process to perform. He also found types of breathing happened spontaneously to help purify the body and prana.

At one point, he found a huge sex drive arose within him and he kept seeing visions of a naked woman dancing before him. This happened whether his eyes were open or closed. This bothered him immensely, as he had a vow to chastity. Later, he discovered in a book that the kriyas he was having were all because of the blessings of his guru, and the sexual desire was part of changing the direction of movement of sexual fluids to an upward direction for his own spiritual growth. In fact, the naked woman he saw was a personification of the Kundalini. The next day, when he saw the red aura, Mother Kundalini stood there in her supreme, divine beauty. From then on, She, as Shakti, became his guru.

After this, his yoga progressed quickly. He had added enthusiasm now that he knew what was happening to him. When he sat to meditate, a while later, a powerful force took over and the red aura appeared. This time, however, in the middle of the red aura, he saw an oval white shape repeatedly appearing and disappearing. Then it returned to just the red aura again. More and more, the oval white light appeared within the red aura.

The red light or aura comes because of Kundalini awakening, and then everything that is seen takes place within that light. After the awakening, everything that is seen and that happens, comes as a blessing from the divine goddess Chiti (Kundalini).

Later, through his inner eye, and within the red aura, Muktananda saw visions of many faraway places. He saw beautiful yellow, red, and white lights. He also saw the deities and lights of all the chakras. At one point, his body burned and felt like it was on fire. Fortunately, he received a scent from Nityananda, which helped with this.

When he saw a mixed yellow and blue light, he passed into a tandra state of consciousness (a sleep-like meditative state in which visions are had). Then, whenever he saw the white light in meditation, he would enter the subtle body from where he would see a subtle version of the physical world. Later came the black light. He saw the white flame within the red aura and the black light within the white flame. The black light represents the causal body. Occasionally, he saw a dazzling bright sun and some stars within his head.

Muktananda started to see the Blue Pearl, the Self or Sourcepoint. Every day he meditated on the Blue Pearl and heard music and a very subtle sound, the space of consciousness.

Every day, he would always see the red aura, and its brilliance continued to increase. Likewise, the white flame, the black light, and the Blue Pearl each appeared and with ever-increasing brilliance. He also saw what he called the Blue Star. This would appear before him and through this, he would visit many subtle worlds.

Now when he saw the Blue Pearl, it had an aura of gold mingled with saffron. The Blue Pearl came closer, and he realized that whatever was happening to the Blue Pearl was happening to him. One day, the Blue Pearl grew in size to form an enormous egg and took the form of a man. Within it stood a Blue Person made of infinite rays of pure consciousness. Muktananda described him as the "Essence of Muktananda's inner life, the actual form of Nityananda. He was the true form of my Mother, the playful, divine Kundalini. He stood before me, shimmering and resplendent in His divinity." The Blue Person spoke to Muktananda for a while and then the blue egg shrunk back to the Blue Pearl. He realized this was the Blue

Person through whom is granted realization of the ultimate truth. Muktananda was now of the conviction "I am the Self."

One day, Muktananda was meditating on the Blue Pearl in the crown chakra and a sphere of unmanifest light, when suddenly the light was released as bright as millions of suns. The light was so fierce he thought he was dying. He was afraid and lost consciousness. When he eventually regained consciousness, he realized it was as if he had died but was now alive again. He had lost all fear of death or anything else.

No longer did Muktananda identify with the body, instead his awareness was of the Self. He felt "I am Shiva." Meditations continued to deepen, and his experiences of Self became more profound. Still, there was something lacking. Increasingly, he saw his inner Self as the Blue Person. But there was still more to go.

Finally, Muktananda gazed at the Blue Pearl. It expanded and illuminated the entire universe with its radiance. It became infinite light, the divine Light of Chiti from which all forms of life emanate. ParaShiva, Nityananda, Muktananda, all were within the blue light of consciousness, and all merged with it.

From then on, Muktananda still meditated, but with the certainty that he had attained full realization, and always with the radiance of the blue Light of Consciousness. He could see that his own Self pervades everywhere as the universe. He could also see that everything is all just the Play of Consciousness.

Notes

1. There are two nerves found at the Brahmarandhra which are known as raga and dwesha (attachment and aversion) and these are what keep the ego in place and separate it from the soul. If pierced, a classic nervous breakdown takes place. To attain final liberation, these two nerves have to be removed. For this to happen safely, however, the aid of a guru or God is required. These nerves also form the foundation of one's entire personality and the starting point of all nervous paths.

Ultimately, one's whole nervous system must be replaced with a new one.

2. Shiva-Linga is an egg-shaped symbol of the first form which comes from the formless. It represents the Absolute into which the individual soul will merge.

3. Spiritual therapy acknowledges that ultimately, even the mind is not real, whereas normal psychological therapy aims to fix or heal the mind. The various ashrams that are found in the world, particularly in India, often occur in a natural environment and are run by spiritually focused individuals, all of them create a healing environment.

4. In psychoanalysis, the entire process operates through the senses, and new knowledge is added to the nervous system. In the Kundalini process, though, no new knowledge is added to the nervous system from the outside, but it is added from within and connected to the newly forming divine subtle body. Through this, the individual is not subject or object but a witness to the Oneness of all.

5. In the Kundalini process, universal consciousness sets up external realities to match with inner deep-rooted mental formations, so that the person can re-experience past happenings or karmas from this and previous births in order to transcend them.

Supplementary Course

Lesson One—Getting Started

People meditate for many reasons. In this course, I focus on meditation to increase awareness of the soul.

Within the body is a subtle energy system made up of an intricate system of meridians and energy vortices, known as chakras. There are seven main chakras, from the base chakra at the bottom of the spine to the crown chakra at the top of the head. These chakras are connected by a central channel known as the sushumna, through which subtle energy flows.

To ensure the energy flows well, easterners sit in the lotus position with legs crossed. This is the ideal position but is difficult, and usually impossible for westerners. It is, however, important to sit in meditation with a straight back. For this reason, I recommended a firm seat with little back support. You can keep your back straight by lying down, but it is difficult to keep awake. Sit as long as possible. If sitting becomes uncomfortable, then lie down for the rest of the meditation. An hour a day is ideal, however, whatever you can manage is good. If you fall asleep in meditation, it is absence rather than sleep. Absence is an experience of very subtle-dimensional awareness.

As you meditate, keep your head straight or even tilted back a bit. In order to maintain focus, you need to focus on something, for example, your breath. Or you can fix your gaze on a burning candle or close your eyes and focus your attention on the brow chakra, often referred to as the third eye, found a little above and between the eyebrows. Alternatively, you could focus on gentle meditation music, recite affirmations, or chant a mantra. After all, the key is focus, and focus leads to balance. Meditation is a balancing technique and with balance comes a greater inner awareness or Oneness.

For the first meditation, find somewhere comfortable to sit, that you will use regularly, in an environment that supports what you are doing. You may want a mini shrine on which you place objects and pictures that you find uplifting. Also, a candle is a good focal point. Likewise, if you want aromas or incense, use them too. This is your place for meditation. Regular practice in the same place provides a structure and sends a subconscious message that when you sit here, it is to meditate. Eventually, the subconscious association with this "ritual" makes meditation easier. With your back as straight as possible, sit aware of your altar/shrine to get the feeling of your meditation practice. Breathe slow and deep, keeping the in and out breath the same length and maintain a focus to help maintain balance.

Lesson Two—Relaxation Technique

During meditation, it helps to be relaxed. A body scan relaxation technique to enhance physical relaxation is useful. Sitting in your meditation position, start with the toes of one foot and relax them as necessary. After the toes, move to the rest of your foot, repeating the same process, then on to your ankle, your calf, your shin, your knee, and your thigh. Repeat the procedure with your other leg. With practice, you should be able to relax both legs together. Now focus on your hips, your lower abdomen, the area around your navel, moving up to your heart area, lungs, and upper torso. Now, as with your legs, repeat the process with your arms. Start with one arm, your fingers, hand, wrist, forearm, elbow, upper arm, and shoulder. Repeat this for each arm. In the future, both arms can be done together. Continue your scan on your neck and move to your head. Then scan your face, your nose, your eyes, your mouth, your ears, the back of your head and then your head overall, including the top of your head and your crown.

When complete, do a quick scan up and down your whole body to double check that all parts of your body are relaxed. Then return to your breath, ensure the in and out breath are equal and maintain a focus on your breath, remembering that focus increases balance and balance is what you want to achieve in meditation.

As you sit, breathe slow and deep. Thoughts will arise, as thoughts do. Do not stop them, but allow them to drift past without getting caught up in them. As your meditation experience continues, thoughts will become fewer and fewer. There is no harm in being aware of thoughts that arise during meditation. As you reach a peak state in meditation, there may be a subtle shift within as your inner self adjusts to the higher vibratory experience. When this occurs, old patterns make way to accommodate the new. You may experience this as thoughts, emotions, and physical sensations. This is normal. Meditation is not always pleasant; it can be uncomfortable as well. Until all your habits, conditioning and patterns get released, a greater inner or Self-awareness is not possible. Meditation is a gradual clearing. This is like the analogy of a bright light behind a dirty pane of glass. Until the glass is clean, the bright light cannot shine through (enlightenment). The bright light is, however, always waiting to be revealed.

Lesson Three—The Nature of Mind and Emotions

Difficult emotions are stored in different parts of the body. So, when you feel an unpleasant emotion somewhere, try to observe the emotion from a detached perspective. By doing this, you separate from the emotion and gradually the emotion is released. An emotion is often accompanied by a thought. The thought may trigger the emotion, or the emotion may trigger the thought. Together they combine into a "thoughtform." In fact, it is very rare to have an unpleasant emotion without some awareness of the trigger. By observing the emotion in a thoughtform, the energy will dissipate and return to its source as cosmic or spiritual energy. At the same time, you will also have raised yourself to a higher level of awareness.

In a later lesson, I will guide you through the Socratic Process designed to help eliminate unwanted thoughts and emotions. But for now, practice observing these thoughts and emotions from a detached viewpoint.

Lesson Four—The Three Stages of Human Awareness

From birth onwards, you have created an awareness of yourself and who you are. This awareness originates in your genetic code and adapts to your environment to ensure that you are now an acceptable member of society. You unconsciously learnt how to fit in. It is an ongoing process. To be truthful to who you really are, Self, you will need to unlearn much of what you learnt, as you have become a product of this enculturation! You will need to peel away the layers to reveal your Self, or rather, recognize and remember who you really are.

At birth, you were as pure as you can be, an embodiment of your spiritual Self. This was the first stage. You were born with a physical body, a mental body (mind) and an emotional body. Your genetic code gave you instincts so that you could adequately function and survive as a baby. This was the second stage, your animal self. Through interaction with your family and society, you needed to learn how to be acceptable as a human. You developed an ego, your sense of individuality as separate from others, and adapted your ego over time to be the best you can be in your society. This was the third stage. Relative to your Self, it is an artificial self, and has taken you away from the spiritual Self you were born as.

Now, through meditation, you will adapt your sense of who you are to better reflect your spiritual Self. You will perform a backwards journey removing thoughts, emotions and understanding that do not reflect the real you. Contemplate this during the day and be aware of it during meditation. Do nothing, just Be who you are and accept it. Acceptance is a valuable process. It was a lack of acceptance of your animal nature, enculturated in you during childhood, that helped to take you away from your true spiritual Self.

Lesson Five — The Socratic Process

A valuable method to help remove unwanted thoughts and emotions is to use a process of inquiry. As you sit in meditation, observe thoughts that arise, particularly those that are charged with emotion. These thoughtforms are essentially stories that we tell about ourselves. Stories that if we look at them clearly may not be true. For each thought that arises, step aside from the thought and observe it. Then say to yourself, "Is this true?" Really observe the thought, understand it, and from this point of observation ask, "Is this true?" If it is not true or only partly true, ask yourself what you would be without this story.

The ancient Greek philosopher Socrates came up with this method to teach by asking questions. He would get his students to explore answers for themselves. In a debate, he could discredit 99% of what the other person believed. He discredited the other person's stories.

They credited Socrates with saying, "The unexamined life is not worth living," and "All I know is that I know nothing."

So, observe your mind and associated emotions and determine for yourself the truth of what you believe. This ongoing process of inquiry will help lead you to a more truthful understanding of who you are.

Lesson Six — The Present Moment

There is only now. We get lost in thoughts of the past and the future, but if you look closely, you see that these are illusions. You cannot be in the past; it is a memory. You cannot be in the future; it does not exist except in your imagination. You can only ever be in the present moment, the NOW. The more you can be in the Now, the less you dwell on the past or future and the more you are in a truthful awareness. How much time do you spend lost in the past or future? How much time are you in the present moment? It might surprise you to realize that most of the time you are not aware of the truthful reality of Now.

It is a spiritual truth that only Now exists. So, for this meditation, be aware of the present moment. Be aware that you have only ever been in the present moment. Be in the NOW.

Lesson Seven—The Relative Field

Observe the world around you and you will notice a multitude of sights, sounds, smells, tastes, and touch impressions. Within you, there are also many thoughts, feelings, ideas, and so on. You will also notice a sense that you are separate from these. We know this as duality. Your multidimensional being also exists in duality, a multitude of energetic frequencies, and levels of being.

What would a more truthful reality be? Well, the most truthful reality is that there is only One, there is no other. You are that One; we are all that One. Observing a world with a complexity of forms, all separate from you, is duality. It is a realm of polarities, subject and object. Reality differs from this. Perhaps you can now gain an insight into just how far you must have come from an awareness of your true being, a being that only perceives Oneness in everything, and ultimately, is only One.

Don't despair! The experience you are having is because you experience more than the One. The only way you can have any experience at all is by being aware of the other. However, as you increase in awareness of Self, you increase in recognition of the One until, ultimately, you are the One. In fact, you have never been other than the One. That's why in the eastern religions they refer to all as maya. Maya means illusion. We live in a world of illusion. The purpose behind Self-awareness meditation is to see through the illusion and ever more fully be yourself, to be the One.

Somehow, through this experience of being what we are not, not the One, we can more fully experience ourselves as what we are, the One. By some twist of reality, One can more fully Be itself as the One, by experiencing itself as not the One.

Having now totally confused you, I suggest you meditate on it and see what comes to you.

Lesson Eight—The Play of Consciousness

What is the purpose of creation? Why did God create all of this? Or even, is there a God?

The Bible says God created the world in seven days. Charles Darwin says life as we know it has taken millions, maybe billions, of years to evolve to where it is now. Darwin talked about the process of natural selection and adaptive radiation.

But do any of these theories really answer the question? Perhaps we can look at this from a different angle. As humans, we are looking at this question from a human perspective. As discussed in a previous lesson, this perspective is illusory. That we are even asking proves we are experiencing what we are not and that if we could see reality truthfully, then we would have the answer.

In meditation, consider the questions, "Who am I?" and "Why am I here?" If, as you have already been told, the purpose of meditation is to reveal your true Self, then you might ask, "What caused me to be in a situation where I am not aware of my true Self?"

Meditate on who you are in this moment, the different stages you went through from birth to be the person who you are now. Contrast this with the fact that you are meditating with the ultimate purpose of realizing who you really are and meditate on the questions "Why?", and "What is the purpose of all of this?"

Lesson Nine—Maintaining Balance

The key to Self-awareness is balance. To gain more balance and to deepen your meditative experience, there is a simple breathing technique. Instead of breathing normally, observe your breathing and ensure the breathing is deep, and the duration of the in-breath and out-breath are equal.

Thoughts and feelings tend to be more negative than positive, so another way to increase balance is to enhance positive thoughts and feelings to experience greater balance and wholeness.

For this meditation, increase mental balance by repeating positive affirmations to yourself. These should be "here and now" worded and in the first person. For example:

Here and now, in this moment, I am love.
Here and now, in this moment, I am bliss.
Here and now, in this moment, I am peace.
Here and now, in this moment, I am joy.

You may not believe this, but they are the truth for your inner being. Repeating such positive affirmations will help to create balance.

After repeating these affirmations for about 10 minutes, you will notice that you feel more balanced. You may even feel slightly expanded and blissful.

Lesson Ten — Third Eye Focus during Meditation

Relax into your meditation seat and observe and release any physical discomforts and tensions. Watch your breath and ensure it is slow and deep and continue this for a while. As you maintain this pattern of breathing, switch your observation to a point between and just above your eyebrows. This is the location of the brow chakra or third eye. This can be your baseline meditation pattern.

As you meditate, your mind will occasionally roam. Encourage it regularly to return to the midpoint between the eyebrows. Observe, but do not get caught up in these thoughts. Allow them to come and go. It is natural to have thoughts. This is a valuable meditation technique and will get easier over time.

Lesson Eleven—Self-awareness Exercise

The consequence of being brought to a "peak" in meditation is that something needs to give. This usually happens as an energetic clearing. It may be a physical or emotional discomfort, or it may simply be as thoughts. As these sensations and thoughts arise, allow them to pass. Do not get attached to them and get carried away by them. In the light of conscious awareness, these thoughts will naturally dissipate.

After the initial settling exercise, observe your body from a detached, witness perspective and notice any sensations or emotions you can feel and where they are. Be aware that your body is different to how it was as a child, or teenager, or when you were younger than you are now. Your emotions constantly change, and your thoughts are always there. Your body changes over time, but your inner Self remains the same.

Now ask yourself who is watching your body, feelings, and thoughts. Realize this is a detached perspective, and it does not get you caught up in your emotions, feelings, or thoughts. You are a witness to these. This witness you is the real you. Remember, you have a body, but you are not the body. You have feelings and emotions, but you are not these feelings and emotions. You have thoughts, but you are not these thoughts. We know this as witness consciousness and it is a part of the real you, the Self.

Before and after meditation, it can be a good thing to do some aerobic exercise for a few minutes, as this helps to clear unwanted energies.

Lesson Twelve—Self-awareness during the Day

The benefits of meditation increase when there is a focus on Self-awareness during the day as well as during the sitting meditation. Rather than looking at meditation as something that is done for half an hour or an hour a day, the actual goal is to reach a point where the whole day is an act of meditation.

This takes a lot of practice, as years of conditioning and habit formation do not disappear overnight.

Meditation during the day is essentially bringing our consciousness to the Now. Being aware of the Self in the present moment is being aware of who we really are. It is all too easy to be living in the past or future, thinking about what is happening later in the day or what happened in the morning, so that most of the time we are not actually present to what is happening now. Even when we think we are in the Now, the chances are that, in reality, it is still not genuinely Now. What we perceive now results from education, enculturation, conditioning, etc., so it is the now as perceived through the past! For example, you are reading this lesson on Self-awareness. The reason you can read it is that in the past, you learnt to read. It has meaning for you because you have learnt how to receive ideas communicated in the written form, and you understand it based on your previous life experiences. Imagine what this would be like for you if absolutely nothing from the past was to influence what you see and understand in the present moment!

Not only do we need to bring our awareness to the present moment in time, but also to the present moment in place. If we are in the now in time, we may still be somewhere else in space. Our minds may be on that holiday destination, or what the relatives are doing on the other side of the country, or what is happening in the office.

So, what can you do to change this?

First, you can change this by being aware of it. As with anything, by bringing the light of consciousness onto a problem, change can come about.

Second, try to be a "witness" to what you are doing and what is happening around you. Observe, listen, feel, taste and smell what is happening now. When you are washing your hands, take part in it fully. Don't plan what you will say to your boss at work in one hour's time. When you are eating, enjoy the moment, savor the food and be "aware" that you are savoring the food. Not only do you do what you are doing in the present moment, but you also subtly step aside to watch yourself doing what you are doing.

As you go about the day, as often as possible, observe how you respond to people, events, situations, and so on. Are your thoughts positive or negative? Do you see the worst in people or the best in people? Who are you comfortable with and who are you not so comfortable with? Why is this so? As you do this, you will gradually build up a picture of yourself as a person. There is no place for criticism or guilt. There is a reason you are the way you are and, better still, there are things you can do to make changes.

For now, though, it is time to just watch, observe and get a picture of yourself, as you are, now. As you progress with meditation, the you that you are now will become the NOW that is you.

Lesson Thirteen—The Five-Fold Cycle

Even though we hope that meditation will always be a blissful experience, the reality is that we need to clear our habits, conditioning, enculturation, etc., and this happens through an ongoing cyclical process in meditation known as the five-fold cycle.

The five parts of the cycle are: peak experience, evolution, illumination, processing, and integration.

Peak experience

Through meditation, balance increases. When there is balance, there is an expansion in holistic awareness known as peak experience. We may be aware of the peak experience or may not be aware of it.

Evolution

With each peak experience, we are more whole and fulfilled than we have ever been before. This ever-increasing wholeness through each cycle enables us to evolve to be more than we have ever been.

Illumination

With evolution comes illumination, which can be experienced as inspiration, insight, and revelation.

Processing

In order for the new level of experience to substantiate itself, old out-of-date data needs to be replaced and comes to the surface for processing and clearing. When old data is being processed, it may be experienced as thoughts arising or as discomfort at the physical or emotional level. In an earlier lesson, much attention was given to the three stages of human awareness. What needs to be cleared over time, therefore, is the artificial reality we have created within ourselves as a response to our enculturation from an early age as a child. These personality traits were created by us in order to be more acceptable in society. Processing takes place on the mental, emotional, and physical levels of who we are.

On the mental level, we may experience clearing or processing as unconscious, habitual, exaggerated, undirected thoughts, daydreams, dullness, or fogginess. On the emotional level, this may be experienced as moods, anger, fear, jealousy, sadness or exaggerated joy. On the physical level, there can be physical discomforts, specific aches and pains, sensations of heat and cold, involuntary movements, restlessness or reappearance of symptoms from old injuries.

Regardless of the symptoms of processing given, they should be acknowledged as proof that meditation is working and allowed to pass. They are an important part of the meditator's journey.

Integration

Besides processing, the new level of experience gained through illumination also needs to be integrated or assimilated in terms of a greater awareness, and then the whole cycle begins again with the next peak experience.

The five-fold process works on many levels, from unconscious through to major experiences of awakening. Likewise, many cycles may happen at the same time.

Lesson Fourteen—The Rainbow Bridge

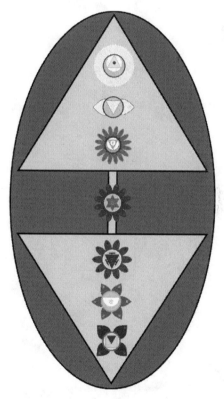

Figure 12 Self-awareness Diagram

If you look at the Self-awareness diagram, you will see upward pointing and downward pointing triangles. The upward pointing triangle represents the soul, with its three aspects of spiritual will, higher mind, and intuition. The downward pointing triangle represents the personality, with its three aspects of physical/etheric body, rational mind, and emotions. These two triangles have a connecting link between them, which symbolically represents the Antahkarana or rainbow bridge. In meditation, we hope to gain more and more connection with the higher triangle.

The rainbow bridge is the connection, or bridge, that we build between the personality and soul and later the personality and Monad. The seven chakras or energy centers of the etheric body go from the base chakra, which represents your basic instinctual nature, and the crown chakra at the top, which is your closest connection to soul. As we become more aware spiritually, the higher chakras become more active. The middle chakra is the heart chakra and is the link between individual and universal consciousness. The vertical shaped eye, which represents the Third Eye or Spiritual Eye, encloses the diagram. The Spiritual Eye is pure intuition and the ability to see from a spiritual perspective. When the Third Eye is open, you may see images within a red aura, representing the lower self of body, mind and emotions.

For this meditation, observe and contemplate the diagram. It is a symbol of who you are on a transpersonal level. Symbols and archetypes are the language of the subconscious mind. Meditating on the symbols may provide you with a deeper understanding of the true purpose of meditation.

Lesson Fifteen—The Mechanics of Balance
In the subtlest dimensions, consciousness is aware of its Oneness and there is a balance between the positive and negative polarities which give rise to diversity in Oneness. Although all is one, there is a perspective of many within the Oneness. As consciousness becomes denser in its experience in the lower physical dimensions, the negative polarity increases in dominance and, consequently, there is imbalance. Imbalance

is necessary for the physical experience we have. It also results in our loss of awareness of Oneness. Awareness is proportional to balance. Therefore, to increase your awareness, you must increase your balance.

Meditation is the foremost balancing technique. However, to experience balance in meditation, it is also necessary to balance the lowest dimensions of our multidimensional being first. Namely, the physical, emotional, and mental dimensions. These three dimensions form your personality. As the default dominant polarity in the lower dimensions is the negative polarity, to create balance requires emphasis of the opposite polarity, the positive.

In the physical dimension, this requires balance in what you eat and regular aerobic exercise. A balanced diet, for example, will consist of an appropriate balance between carbohydrate, protein, and fat.

In the emotional dimension, balance increases by flowing positive, love-based thoughts, particularly whenever negative, fear-based feelings arise. Positive thoughts lead to positive emotions. Because of misconceptions about love, it may be easier to flow feelings of gratitude instead.

In the mental dimension, the mind needs to be directed towards positive thoughts and affirmations, particularly when there is repetitive or negative thinking. There are many meditation techniques which are mostly aimed at focus and reining in the mind, particularly when there is anything other than stillness. Through meditation, there is an increase in consistent holistic awareness.

Through balance, each dimension yields to the next higher dimension. When there is a balance within the personality, it is possible to move beyond the mind into more subtle, unified dimensions.

Just as meditation is the foremost balancing technique, meditation itself can be enhanced by using sound technology to synchronize and balance the brain hemispheres and move the brain's vibrational frequencies to deeper meditative states. Many meditation soundtracks enhance the lower brain wave frequencies associated with relaxation or meditation.

Lesson Sixteen—Gaining Greater Self-awareness during the Day

In a previous lesson, we looked at how to observe yourself throughout the day by bringing awareness to the present moment in time and place. We also looked at how to be a "witness" to what you are doing and what is happening around you and to watch, observe and get a picture of yourself, as you are, now.

Through self-observation, certain traits and characteristics will come to light. There will be ideas, desires, and emotions which you will realize are not serving your aspiration to be more in tune with your higher "Self." It is spiritual energy which has become attached to the ideas, desires, and emotions to form emotional energy.

Fortunately, there are techniques which help to release the spiritual energy from emotional energy, thus clearing the emotion and releasing the spiritual energy for higher purposes. I will outline one particular technique in this lesson.

The Self-awareness formula for greater spiritual awareness:

1. Note the troubling memory which comes to mind. This can be in meditation or in quiet reflection during the day.
2. Visualize all aspects of the event (thoughts, emotions, desires) which are aroused when contemplating it.
3. Go over the event, again and again, as fully as possible, to maximize all ideas and feelings associated with it.
4. Notice how the emotional energy is at the command of the desire or idea associated with the event and not at

your conscious command. Thoroughly observe this until you realize it.

5. Throwing the light of consciousness onto this situation is healing, as you are already one step further detached from the memory than on previous occasions. You realize that your emotional energy is at the command of a memory of an event and not the event itself.

6. Consciously release the memory, repeating to yourself a positive affirmation such as "Here and now, in this moment, I release this memory." The affirmation needs to be focused on the present moment and positive in its wording. The greater your intention for healing, the greater the effect.

The idea is to release energy from the negative emotion so that you can move on to greater spiritual awareness. Sometimes the energy release will be so noticeable that you will suddenly feel uplifted.

Lesson Seventeen — Dream Analysis

There are many books on dream symbolism, and these often approach dreams from the perspective that they contain a message that the unconscious mind is giving to us and that if we find out what the symbolism means, we receive guidance from them. Most of the time, however, dreams will give us a sign of our current state of awareness, and most of the information received is simply a reflection of our day-to-day data. Symbolism plays a part in this. There is no need to interpret every symbol that appears in a dream. With practice, you learn to distinguish those symbols that are relevant.

Dreams are an excellent indicator of where we are on our paths without the interference of the rational mind. For example, you may find that dreams show that you are quite psychic. Yet in the waking state, this may not appear to be the case. Obviously, the rational mind blocks this awareness during the day.

There are seven types of dream as follows and these may overlap:

Spiritual Need
The spiritual need represents our underlying desire to merge back into the permanent Source from which we came. Through our identification with the physical body and the material world, the spiritual need gets converted into attachment, lust, need for objects of love (mother), and so on.

Hunger Need
Having identified with the non-permanent threefold personality of mind, body and emotions, a strong need develops to sustain the body. Through reaction to family and society, various desires and reactions form around this need, including greed, possession, cheating and stealing, etc.

Security Need
A need for security relates to the threefold personality and results in the fears and desires springing from a need to preserve and protect ourselves. These include fear and possession.

Violence Need
This need appears when the previous three needs do not get fulfilled. This leads to a blockage in the flow of psychic energy in the nervous system and a desire to remove the "denier," leading to feelings of inferiority and jealousy, and the ideas of competition and worthlessness.

Ego Data
Ego develops from childhood, which is basically the need to be somebody of value in society. It is a repression of the acceptance of basic desires and reactions in place of a self or "individuality"

which can be acceptable in the world.

Collective Unconscious of Past Lives

There are dreams which do not fit into the five categories mentioned above and which do not seem to fit into present life experiences. Assuming a belief in past lives, these form a category of dreams in which experiences relating to past lives surface. An alternative to the past life theory is that humanity has a collective unconscious database of experiences which can surface during the dream state of any person.

Spiritual

Lastly, there are Psychospiritual or transpersonal dreams in which there is contact with the "Higher Self." Other terms for this include "Spiritual Self," "Transpersonal Self," or Soul. This does not represent a group or cluster, rather than a spiritual connection made during the dream state. These spiritual dreams are distinctive in their character and provide guidance and solace to us, as well as encouragement on the spiritual path.

Finally, an important symbolism in dreams is that of positive or negative polarity, where the positive polarity represents an aspect of ourselves which is more unified or holistic, while the negative polarity represents an aspect of ourselves which is more fragmented and individual in experience. Positive dominance, negative dominance or balance fluctuate regularly. Whether we are male or female, this symbolism is the same. Dreams of male figures represent the positive polarity while dreams of female figures represent the negative polarity. Regardless of the content of the dream, dreams in which female figures are present show a more materialistic focus, while dreams of male characters are more unified and holistic in their focus. If the dream shows harmony between you and the other person, such as in a relationship, whether male or female, then this represents balance. Remember, we are looking at symbolism here. A complete chapter is devoted to understanding dreams.

Lesson Eighteen — Building the Bridge

In a previous lesson, you looked at how to gain greater Self-awareness during the day through observing your traits and characteristics and in particular ideas, desires, and emotions. Once these are revealed, a technique was given for addressing these so that the emotional energy tied up in these formations is released and released for other purposes.

The purpose of meditation is to build a bridge between your personality and your soul. One could even say that the knowledge required to build this bridge is the true purpose of education. Symbolically, the rainbow bridge is the spiritual path one follows when dedicated to pursuing a spiritual life and includes spiritual practices such as meditation and yoga, visualization exercises, mantras and affirmations.

Building the rainbow bridge begins when there is a conscious reorientation to live a spiritual life, and when the "desire" to pursue a spiritual path has become more than simply doing right or wrong.

In building the rainbow bridge, we work with the mind and mental attitudes. As your soul awareness increases, this needs to be expressed through the personality on the physical plane.

In the first stage of building the bridge, a link needs to be created between the threefold personality (physical, emotional, and mental bodies) and the soul. In the early stages, we are barely conscious of this, but it increases as the contact between the two is stronger and eventually becomes the line of least resistance. When this part of the bridge is complete, the energies animating the physical body, the emotional body and the mental body blend with, and transmute into, the energies of the soul. Your regular meditation practice is an integral part of building the rainbow bridge.

Lesson Nineteen—The Divine Within

Throughout this course, I have focused on meditation to gain greater Self-awareness. In an earlier lesson, I looked at the psychology behind our current situation and how we have created an illusory self in response to our enculturation so that we can be acceptable in the world. This is our third-stage self (ego) and is essentially a repression of the second stage, or animal self. Our true identity is, in fact, closer to the first-stage self, the Self within. The purpose of meditation is to recognize our first-stage self, the Self within, and in order to do so, a lot of clearing or processing needs to take place to remove or transcend the limitations we have surrounded ourselves with. The ego wants to enmesh us even deeper in the material world. It has its place and purpose. Most people are subservient to the ego and find they continually seek more and more fulfillment in the world, believing it will bring the happiness they desperately seek. Eventually, there comes a time when this is no longer satisfying. There must be more to life than this! Then an Awakening takes place. It may be profound or it may be so subtle that it is unnoticeable. But once reached, there is no going back to the unconscious way of living in which we have dwelt for so long. The involutionary cycle of ever-increasing densification of consciousness has reached its lowest point, and now the evolutionary cycle of return to our innate divine Self and One consciousness begins. We have learned to be who we are not, and now the recognition of who we are commences and the bliss of Self-realization gradually unfolds.

Latent within each of us lies a dormant spiritual energy called the Kundalini. In fact, different traditions in the world have known this energy by different names, such as chi, qi, and Holy Spirit. Prana is an aspect of the Kundalini and is the life force which keeps us alive. The symbol of this primal spiritual energy is a snake or serpent. At the Awakening, the Kundalini begins to clear the unwanted energies throughout the human body and particularly in the chakras and energy meridians.

Beginning at the base chakra, it works its way up the spine through to the crown chakra at the top of the head. The clearing that takes place because of meditation assists the Kundalini in its process. The more balanced and purer the human body and energy system, the less dramatic the effects of the Kundalini process are likely to be. In all traditions, the Kundalini process is integral to the spiritual journey.

Lesson Twenty—Using Symbolism in Meditation

The unconscious mind, which lies beneath the conscious mind, deals in the language of symbolism. In guided meditation, symbolism is used to trigger associations and to encourage you to experience feelings of well-being and happiness and to help raise your level of awareness so that you receive intuitive impressions. Typical symbols are a meadow, a forest, a lake, a chapel, and a mountain. Perhaps a gentle wind is blowing, music is playing, birds are singing, etc. Such symbols are used to help create the desired environment with symbols which are understood by the unconscious mind. The unconscious mind might also respond with symbols, feelings, thoughts, etc., which provide further insight to help understand a problem, or issue, being experienced by the meditator. Guided meditation can also be more focused, intending to elicit specific results of value to the meditator and the guide.

Being guided to visualize a meadow, for example, may encourage images related to youth, happiness, and health. Climbing a mountain provides a feeling of rising higher, perhaps to a greater level of awareness where issues reveal themselves more clearly. It could represent rising to the higher chakras associated with greater spirituality. At the top of the mountain, there might be a wise old man who will provide words of wisdom.

Symbolism can explore a particular issue or uncover specific knowledge related to the archetype of that symbol. Maybe, in traversing deep into the forest or climbing a mountain, certain obstacles appear. These obstacles can provide valuable insight into what blocks further progress or well-being. The symbol may not immediately be obvious, and it may be necessary to further meditate on the symbol to gain greater insight into its meaning. Mandalas and other less obvious symbols are also used to elicit a response from the unconscious mind.

Meditation symbolism is like dream symbolism. An advantage is that in guided meditation, whether facilitated by a guide or performed alone, it is easier to direct where one wants to explore from a conscious perspective.

Create your own guided meditation using symbolism to take you to a peaceful place. It may be a walk through the countryside to a calm, peaceful lake surrounded by beautiful vegetation, lots of sunshine, a gentle breeze and birdsong. When there, you may decide to jump into a small boat and drift slowly over the lake while listening to waves lapping on the shore or on the side of the boat. Experiment with different symbols and see what the results are for you.

Lesson Twenty-one — The Inner Sanctuary

In meditation, you can use your imagination to create a place you are comfortable to visit in peace and tranquility. The more detail you can imagine of the place, the more real it will be for you. It is a place you will always look forward to visiting as a personal sanctuary or retreat.

Using symbolism, as given in the previous lesson, create an environment that is harmonious and uplifting. Try to include as many of your senses as possible. For example, imagine you are high on the side of a mountain in a small clearing in a forest. From here, you have an incredible view of the countryside below. It is peaceful, there is a light fresh breeze, birds are singing and insects buzz among the many beautiful flowers. As you sit next to a small lake, you take a sip of clean, fresh water.

You see and hear the gentle lapping of the water on the shore next to you. The air is clear, the sun is shining, and there are small wispy clouds floating across the clear blue sky. You love to visit this place. It provides a welcome relief from the busy world below. Behind you, the mountain goes even higher. You are aware of a temple near the top where the wise ones meet. You aspire to go there one day, and, within yourself, you know you will, when the time is right.

Once in a while, one of the wise ones may even come down the hill and stand close by. When this happens, you feel a connection between the two of you, and you may receive a message. The message can come in your meditation, your dreams, or in another way.

In the distance above, you occasionally hear the distant music and voices playing in the temple. It is both soothing and inspiring.

Remember, each time you create this place in your imagination, it will become clearer and more real. This is your Inner Sanctuary and is always there for you.

Lesson Twenty-two—Chakra Meditation

Chakras are an integral part of the subtle energy body and provide the most important connection between your personality, or lower self, and your soul. These vortices of energy control different aspects of your internal energy system from the most physical, found in the base chakra, to the most subtle, found in the crown chakra. When it comes to understanding the chakras, we know very little. Any meditation on the chakras needs to be done with reverence and in the awareness of our limited understanding. A simple, safe, chakra meditation is given here.

Base Chakra

Imagine you are sitting on a rock. This rock formed a long time ago when the earth was still cooling from its original molten state and contains crystals with beauty and precision. As your bare feet rest on the solid rock, you feel connected to the earth below.

Sacral Chakra

You are sitting next to a lake of clear, cool, fresh water. The water is still. It creates a sense of wonder in you about what lays deep within. You can see small fish swimming among the plants just below the surface and you imagine it was like this long before humans appeared on the Earth. You notice birds and insects around you. The birdsong is enchanting. You also notice a pair of rabbits hopping around and a deer grazing in the distance.

Solar Plexus Chakra

You ponder on the fact that the world is now dominated by humans. We, too, are animals, but we have our own unique characteristics. Each of us is an individual, aware of our own identity, separate from others and the world around. We have learnt to utilize the rocks, plants and animals for our own purposes. Our crowning glory was the discovery of how to create and use fire. As you contemplate your own uniqueness and Self-awareness, observe your hopes and wishes and realize you have your own unique personality.

You want to experience more and more of the world around you and search for happiness. You know it is important to relate to other people, and you have learned appropriate ways to behave.

Heart Chakra

You are learning to feel with the heart and not just think with the head. You have experienced life in the material world and have your own ideas and beliefs about it and even about what will happen after you die. Now that you, personally, have gained mastery over the material world, there is a stirring inside, a distant voice calling you back, a recognition that this is not all you are. There is something more than this. You are aware of a connection, a link, with a more subtle aspect of who you are. It has a language and reality not of the world. It is time to return to an awareness of who you really are, along with all the experience you have gained from this material journey. It is familiar, yet at the same time unknown.

You are on the threshold of this expanded awareness. Perhaps you are now sitting in your previously created Inner Sanctuary. You look up at the temple in the clouds above. It is alluring. Now is the time to make the journey there. There is also a feeling that when you get there, you will find it is your home. It is a home you never really left, except in forgetting it, in order that you could have this limited experience of duality, where all is separate from yourself, and so different from the Oneness that you really are.

Throat Chakra

As you ascend higher, you are aware that you need to create yourself anew. A new reality dawns. The path is steep and narrow and there are many obstacles on the way. You have to travel light and need little baggage. The comforts you have in the world below will not serve you anymore. Only the bare necessities are needed now, and even these will be discarded when you reach the top.

Brow Chakra

You slowly become aware of new insights. The old rule books don't seem to apply anymore. Increasingly, you are guided by your intuition. There are flashes of inspiration, and all the while, the goal, the temple, beckons. The Master awaits you there. It's not that easy. Your old habits and conditioning die hard. Perhaps, you think, the old ways weren't so bad. At least they were familiar. Every so often, an inspiration or message prompts you to continue. Deep down inside, you know you can't go back.

Crown Chakra

As you reach the temple, it is magnificent, and the views are stunning. The entire world below looks beautiful. This world served you well and you are grateful for having been there. The search is over, and you realize what you were looking for was the one who was looking all the time. But now, because of your sojourn in the material world, the temple is truly appreciated for what it is. Even though it is where you originally came from, it couldn't be appreciated as much as it is now. It was all worth it. As you look for the Master in the temple, you realize that you yourself are indeed the Master. You laugh. A feeling of love surges within you, a love for everything around you and within. You are that love.

Glossary

Spiritual and Sanskrit Terminology	Meaning
Advaita	Nondualism
Ajna	The guru's order
Ajna (brow) chakra	Subtle energy vortex located between the eyebrows. Seat of the guru
Alta Major	Subtle energy vortex of energy located at the base of the skull
Anahata	Subtle energy vortex located in the heart region
Antahkarana	Central energy channel, bridge between the brain/mind and the transcendental self
Archetypes	Universal symbols
Atma	Soul or transpersonal self
Bhagavad Gita	Divine song. Sacred Hindu scripture
Bhakti yoga	Devotional yoga
Bhramarandhra	Subtle energy vortex located at the top of the head. Nirvana chakra
Bliss	Everything from baseline contentment through to radical, opiated, intoxicating blissBlue
Pearl	The Sourcepoint. Abode of the spiritual Self
Causal	Level of the soul body
Causal body	Sheath enclosing the soul
Chakra	Subtle vortex of energy within the body

Cosmic Consciousness	Universal Consciousness. Shiva in Hindu mythology
Cosmic Energy	Universal Energy. Shakti in Hindu mythology
Diaphragm	The primary muscle for respiration located just below the lungs and heart
EEG	Electro-encephalogram. Brainwave monitor
Ego	The individual "I" separate from all others
Egocentric	Centered on the ego
Enlightenment	Full of light or universal awareness
Evocation	A calling forth. Cause to appear
Guru	An enlightened spiritual teacher#
Guru chakra	Subtle energy vortex located just above the crown of the head
Hatha yoga	Yoga based on physical postures
Hierarchy	Ascended beings
Indu chakra	Subtle energy vortex located in the middle of the forehead
Initiate	Someone who has had an initiation or expansion of consciousness
Integrative Peak	When peak and processing happen at the same time
Invocation	A calling upon or appeal to
Jiva	Individual consciousness
Jnana yoga	Yoga of knowledge
Karma	Law of cause and effect
Karma yoga	Union through selfless action
Kriya	Involuntary movement caused by the Kundalini

Kundalini	The transformative energy within, the Shakti within
Mandala	A geometric pattern of symbols
Manipura chakra	Subtle energy vortex located in the solar plexus region
Mantra yoga	Chanting mantras
Matrika	Divine mother concealed in a mantra
Maya	Illusion
Meridians	Energy channels within the body
Monad	Transcendental self. The Spirit
Muladhara chakra	Subtle energy vortex located at the base of the spine
Nadi	Subtle channels which carry life force
Nirvana chakra	Subtle energy vortex located t the top of the head. Also known as the Brahmarandhra
Nirvikalpa	A samadhi in which there is no thought or form
Noumenal	Not observable through the senses
Pericarp	The ovary wall of a fruit
Prana	Life giving force
Royal Road	Journey between the brow and crown chakras
Sahaja	Spontaneous or naturally born
Sahasrara chakra	Subtle energy vortex located above the crown of the head
Sahita breathing	A form of breath retention
Samadhi	A state of meditation in which individual and universal unite
Sangha	Community of like-minded spiritual people
Satori	A sudden spiritual awakening

Savikalpa	A samadhi in which there is thought or form
Self	The Monad or Spirit. In a more general sense, it can also include the soul
Self-awareness	Conscious of the Self, Spirit or Monad within
Self-realization	Attaining awareness of the Self
Seven Rays	Seven qualities or energies underlying manifestation
Shakti	Cosmic or universal energy. The created universe
Shiva	Universal Consciousness. The creator
Shiva-Linga	Oval-shaped form of Shiva
Soul	Transpersonal self
Sourceful	Of Source or self
Sourcepoint	Abode of the spiritual Self
Spirit	A spark of Universal Consciousness. The Monad
Spiritual Emergence	Spiritual awakening
Spiritual Emergency	Crisis caused by spiritual awakening
Spiritual triad	Sheath enclosing the Monad
Superego	Socially acceptable component of the ego
Supra-causal	State of consciousness representative of the Self
Svadhisthana	Subtle energy vortex located in the navel region
Third Eye	The spiritual eye of consciousness
Thoughtform	A subtle energetic combination of thought and emotion
Transcendental	Realm of the Self

Transcendental Self	The self, Spirit or Monad
Trans-egocentric	Higher than the ego
Transitory Psychosis	Brief psychotic disorder
Transpersonal	Of the Soul
Transpersonal integration	Soul-personality integration
Transpersonal intuition	Utilized in the technique of building the antahkarana
Transpersonal self	The soul
Trikuti	Confluence of three energy meridians at the brow chakra
Vayu	Wind. An energetic force moving in a specific direction
Vibhuti	Sacred ash
Vishudda chakra	Subtle energy vortex located in the throat region
Wakefulness	Ability to be present and witness to what's happening
Yoga	A practice leading to union with the divine

Bibliography

Abraham, K. (1987) Introduction to the Seven Rays. New Jersey: Lampus Press.

Assagioli, R. (1965) Psychosynthesis: A Manual of Principles and Techniques. London: The Aquarian Press.

Assagioli, R. (1993) Transpersonal Development: The Dimension beyond Psychosynthesis. London: Thorsons.

Assagioli, R. (2000) Psychosynthesis: A Collection of Basic Writings. Amherst: Massachusetts. 01002 USA: The Synthesis Center.

Babcock, W. (1983) Jung, Hesse, Harold: A Spiritual Psychology. New York: The Harold Institute.

Bailey, A. (1950) Glamour, A World Problem. New York: Lucis Publishing Company.

Bailey, A. (1982a) Esoteric Astrology. New York: Lucis Publishing Company.

Bailey, A. (1982b) The Rays and the Initiations. New York: Lucis Publishing Company.

Bailey, A. (1987) Education in the New Age. New York: Lucis Publishing Company.

Bailey, A. (1988) Esoteric Psychology II. New York: Lucis Publishing Company.

Bailey, A. (1989a) A Treatise on Cosmic Fire. New York: Lucis Publishing Company.

Bailey, A. (1989b) From Bethlehem to Calvary. New York: Lucis Publishing Company.

Bailey, A. (1989c) Discipleship in the New Age I. New York: Lucis Publishing Company.

Bailey, A. (1991) Esoteric Psychology I. New York: Lucis Publishing Company.

Bailey, A. (1992) Initiation, Human and Solar+. New York: Lucis Publishing Company.

Bailey, A. (1993) Esoteric Healing. New York: Lucis Publishing Company.

Bailey, A. (1994) Discipleship in the New Age II. New York: Lucis Publishing Company.

Britannica CD. Version 97. Encyclopaedia Britannica, Inc., 1997

Coon, D. (1989) Introduction to Psychology. (Fifth Edition). St Paul: West Publishing Co.

Egan, G. (1994) The Skilled Helper. (5th Edition). Monterey, California: Brooks/Cole Publishing.

Ferrucci, P. (1982) What We May Be. New York: Jeremy P. Tarcher/Putnam.

Fordham, F. (1963) An Introduction to Jung's Psychology. Mitcham, Victoria: Penguin Books.

Foundation for Inner Peace. (1996) Supplements to A Course in Miracles, Psychotherapy: Purpose, Process and Practice., Ringwood, Victoria, Australia. Viking Penguin, Penguin Books.

Goel, B.S. (1989) Third eye and Kundalini: (An experiential account of journey from dust to divinity). (Second Reprint). Third Eye Foundation of India, Shri Siddheshwar Ashram, Bhagaan: – 131033, Haryana, India.

Goel, B.S. (1992) Psycho-Analysis and Meditation: Certain Related Essays. (First Reprint). Third Eye Foundation of India, Shri Siddheshwar Ashram, Bhagaan: – 131033, Haryana, India.

Goel, B.S. (1993) Psycho-Analysis and Meditation. (Second Reprint). Third Eye Foundation of India, Shri Siddheshwar Ashram, Bhagaan: – 131033, Haryana, India.

Goswami, S.S. (1980) Layayoga: The Definitive Guide to the Chakras and Kundalini. Boston: Routledge & Kegan Paul.

Graham, H. (1986) The Human Face of Psychology: Humanistic Psychology in its Historical, Social and Cultural Contexts. Milton Keynes: Open University Press.

Greenwell, B. (1995). Energies of Transformation: A Guide to the Kundalini Process (Second Edition). Saratoga: Shakti River Press.

Grof, S. & Grof, C. (1989) Spiritual Emergency: When Personal Transformation Becomes a Crisis New York: G.P. Putnam's Sons.

Grof, S. & Grof, C. (1995) The Stormy Search for the Self: Understanding and Living with Spiritual Emergency. London: Thorsons.

Grof, S. with Bennett, H.Z. (1993) The Holotropic Mind: The Three Levels of Human Consciousness and How They Shape Our Lives. New York: Harper Collins.

Ivey, A.E., Ivey, M.B. & Simek-Downing, L. (1987) Counselling and Psychotherapy. (2nd Edition) Boston: Allyn & Bacon.

Ivey, A.E., Ivey, M.B. & Simek-Downing, L. (1997) Counselling and Psychotherapy: A Multicultural Perspective. (4th Edition). Needham Heights: Allyn & Bacon.

Jayakar, P. (1988) J. Krishnamurti: A Biography. New Delhi: Penguin.

Kieffer, G. (1979) Evolution and the Gnostic Tree of Life New York: The Kundalini Research Foundation, Ltd. [Handout]. Available from the Kundalini Research Foundation, Ltd. PO Box 2248, Darien, CT., 06820, USA.

Krishna, G. (1972) Sex, Politics and the Laws of Evolution. [Essay taken from The biological basis of religion and genius]. New York: Harper & Row. [Handout]. Available from the Kundalini Research Foundation, Ltd. PO Box 2248, Darien, CT., 06820, USA.

Krishna, G. (1973, October 6) Beyond the Higher States of Consciousness. [Extract from forthcoming book "Higher consciousness" New York: Julian Press.] The New York Times. [Handout]. Available from the Kundalini Research Foundation, Ltd. PO Box 2248, Darien, CT., 06820, USA.

Krishna, G. (1974) Why Kundalini Brings Higher Consciousness. [Extract from Book "Higher Consciousness" New York: Julian

Press.]. [Handout]. Available from the Kundalini Research Foundation, Ltd. PO Box 2248, Darien, CT., 06820, USA.

Krishna, G. (1993) Living with Kundalini: The Autobiography of Gopi Krishna. Massachusetts: Shamballa Publications. Inc.

Krishna, G. (1997, July) About consciousness research and how we can help save the world. USA: The Golden Thread Enterprises. [Handout]. Available from the Kundalini Research Foundation, Ltd. PO Box 2248, Darien, CT., 06820, USA.

Krishna, G. (1997, October) Creation vs. Evolution: new light on an old controversy. USA: The Golden Thread Enterprises. [Handout]. Available from the Kundalini Research Foundation, Ltd. PO Box 2248, Darien, CT., 06820, USA.

Kundalini Research Foundation, Ltd. (1978) The Transcendental Experience. [Handout]. Available from the Kundalini Research Foundation, Ltd. PO Box 2248, Darien, CT., 06820, USA.

Maslow, A.H. (1971) The Farther Reaches of Human Nature. Ringwood, Australia: Penguin Arkana.

Mookerjee, A. (1991) Kundalini: The Arousal of the Inner Energy. Rochester, Vermont: Destiny Books.

Myers, D.G. (1987) Psychology. (Third Reprint). New York: Worth Publishers Inc.

Parkhurst, J. (1977) The Individuation Process. Glen Forrest, Western Australia: Open Mind Publications.

Redfield, J. & Adrienne, C. (1995) The Celestine Prophecy: An Experiential Guide. Sydney: Bantam Books.

Robbins, M. (1996) Tapestry of the Gods Volume I. (Third Edition). Mariposa, California: The University of the Seven Rays Publishing House.

Robbins, M. (1996) Tapestry of the Gods Volume II. (Third Edition). Mariposa, California: The University of the Seven Rays Publishing House.

Singer, J. (1972) Boundaries of the Soul: The Practice of Jung's

Psychology London: Victor Gollancz Ltd.

Swami Muktananda. (1983) Kundalini: The Secret of Life. (Second Reprint). New York: SYDA Foundation.

Swami Muktananda. (1994) Play of consciousness: A Spiritual Autobiography. (Fourth Edition). New York: SYDA Foundation.

Swami Satyananda Saraswati. (1996) Kundalini Tantra. (Second Edition). Munger, Bihar, India: Bihar School of Yoga.

Swami Sivananda Radha, (1992). Kundalini Yoga. (First Indian Edition). Delhi: Motilal Banarsidass Publishers Private Ltd.

Synchronicity Foundation, (2002). The Synchronicity Experience. Nellysford: Synchronicity Foundation International.

The Gospel According to John, the Bible containing the Old and New Testaments. Revised Standard Version (1952). W.M. Collins Sons & Co. Ltd. For the British & Foreign Bible Society.

The transcendental experience. (no date). [Handout]. Available from the Kundalini Research Foundation, Ltd. PO Box 2248, Darien, CT., 06820, USA.

Van Der Leeuw, J.J. (1927) The Fire of Creation. (Second Edition) Adyar, Madras: Theosophical Publishing House.

White, J. (1977, August) Sex and Sublime Awareness. Human Behaviour. [Handout]. Available from the Kundalini Research Foundation, Ltd. PO Box 2248, Darien, CT., 06820, USA.

Whitmore, D. (1998) Psychosynthesis Counselling in Action. (Fifth Reprint). SAGE Publications, London, UK.

Wilber, K. (1996) Up from Eden: A Transpersonal View of Human Evolution. (First Quest Edition) Wheaton, Illinois: Quest Books.

Yogananda, P. (1987) Autobiography of a Yogi. (Eleventh Edition). Los Angeles, Self-Realization Fellowship.

Index

MANTRA
BOOKS

EASTERN RELIGION & PHILOSOPHY

We publish books on Eastern religions and philosophies. Books
that aim to inform and explore the various traditions that began in
the East and have migrated West.
If you have enjoyed this book, why not tell other readers by
posting a review on your preferred book site.

The Less Dust the More Trust
Participating in The Shamatha Project, Meditation and Science
Adeline van Waning, MD PhD
The inside-story of a woman participating in frontline meditation
research, exploring the interfaces of mind-practice, science and
psychology.
Paperback: 978-1-78099-948-7 ebook: 978-1-78279-657-2

I Know How To Live, I Know How To Die
The Teachings of Dadi Janki: A warm, radical, and life-affirming
view of who we are, where we come from, and what time is calling
us to do
Neville Hodgkinson
Life and death are explored in the context of frontier science and
deep soul awareness.
Paperback: 978-1-78535-013-9 ebook: 978-1-78535-014-6

Living Jainism
An Ethical Science
Aidan Rankin, Kanti V. Mardia
A radical new perspective on science rooted in intuitive awareness
and deductive reasoning.
Paperback: 978-1-78099-912-8 ebook: 978-1-78099-911-1

Ordinary Women, Extraordinary Wisdom
The Feminine Face of Awakening
Rita Marie Robinson
A collection of intimate conversations with female spiritual
teachers who live like ordinary women, but are engaged with their
true natures.
Paperback: 978-1-84694-068-2 ebook: 978-1-78099-908-1

The Way of Nothing
Nothing in the Way
Paramananda Ishaya
A fresh and light-hearted exploration of the amazing reality of
nothingness.
Paperback: 978-1-78279-307-6 ebook: 978-1-78099-840-4

Readers of ebooks can buy or view any of these bestsellers by
clicking on the live link in the title. Most titles are published in
paperback and as an ebook. Paperbacks are available in traditional
bookshops. Both print and ebook formats are available online.

Find more titles and sign up to our readers' newsletter at
http://www.johnhuntpublishing.com/mind-body-spirit.
Follow us on Facebook at https://www.facebook.com/OBooks
and Twitter at https://twitter.com/obooks.